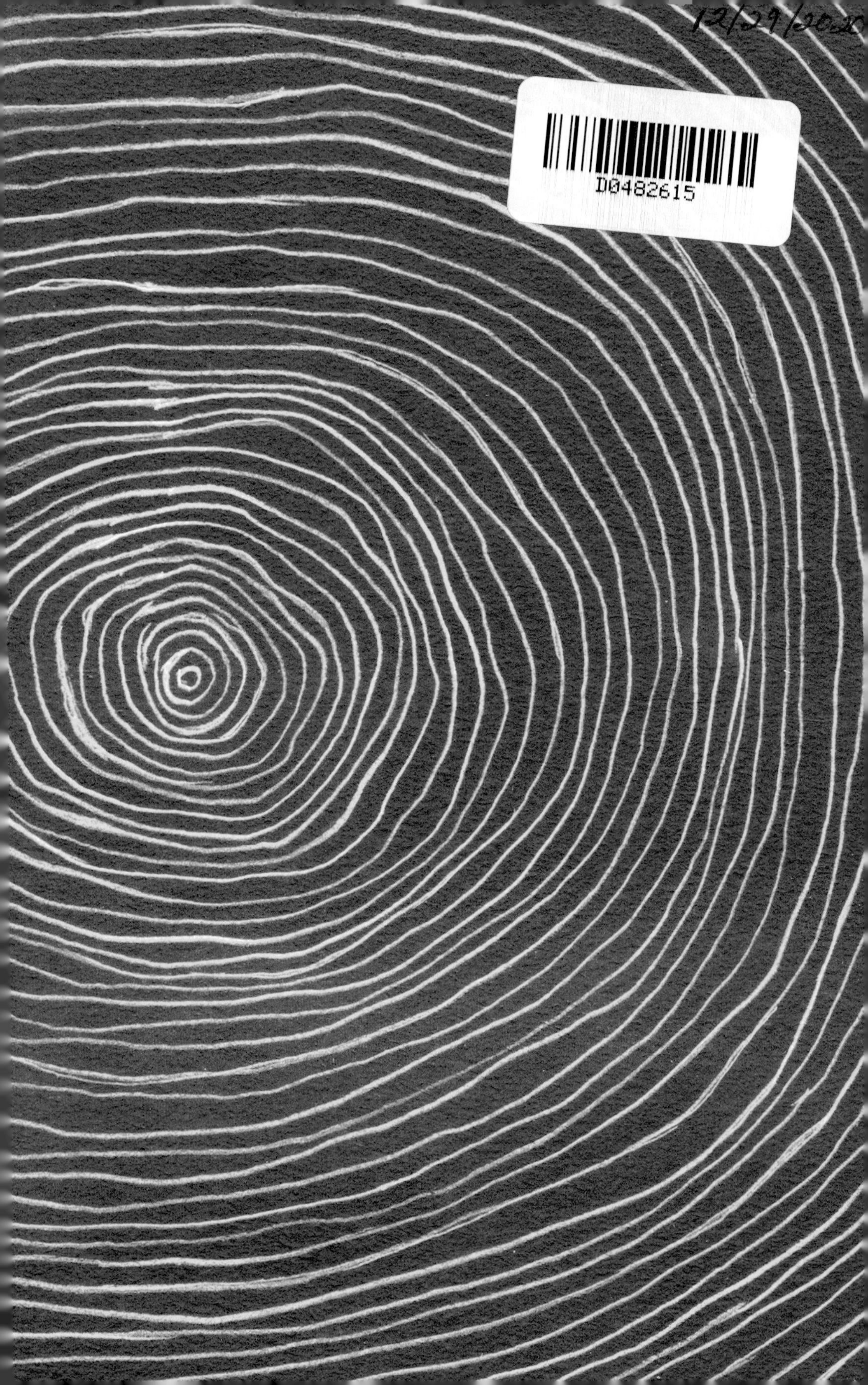

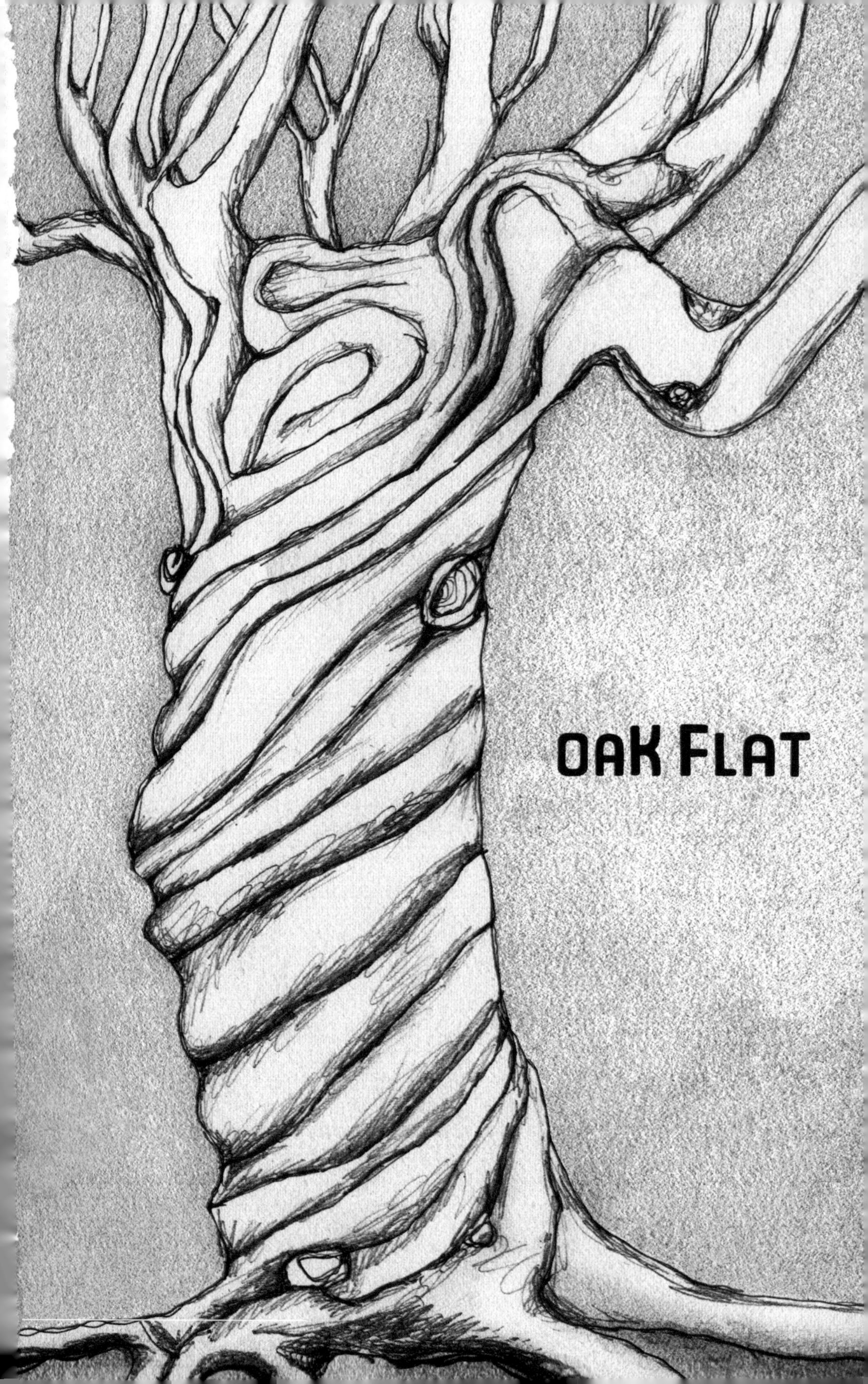
OAK FLAT

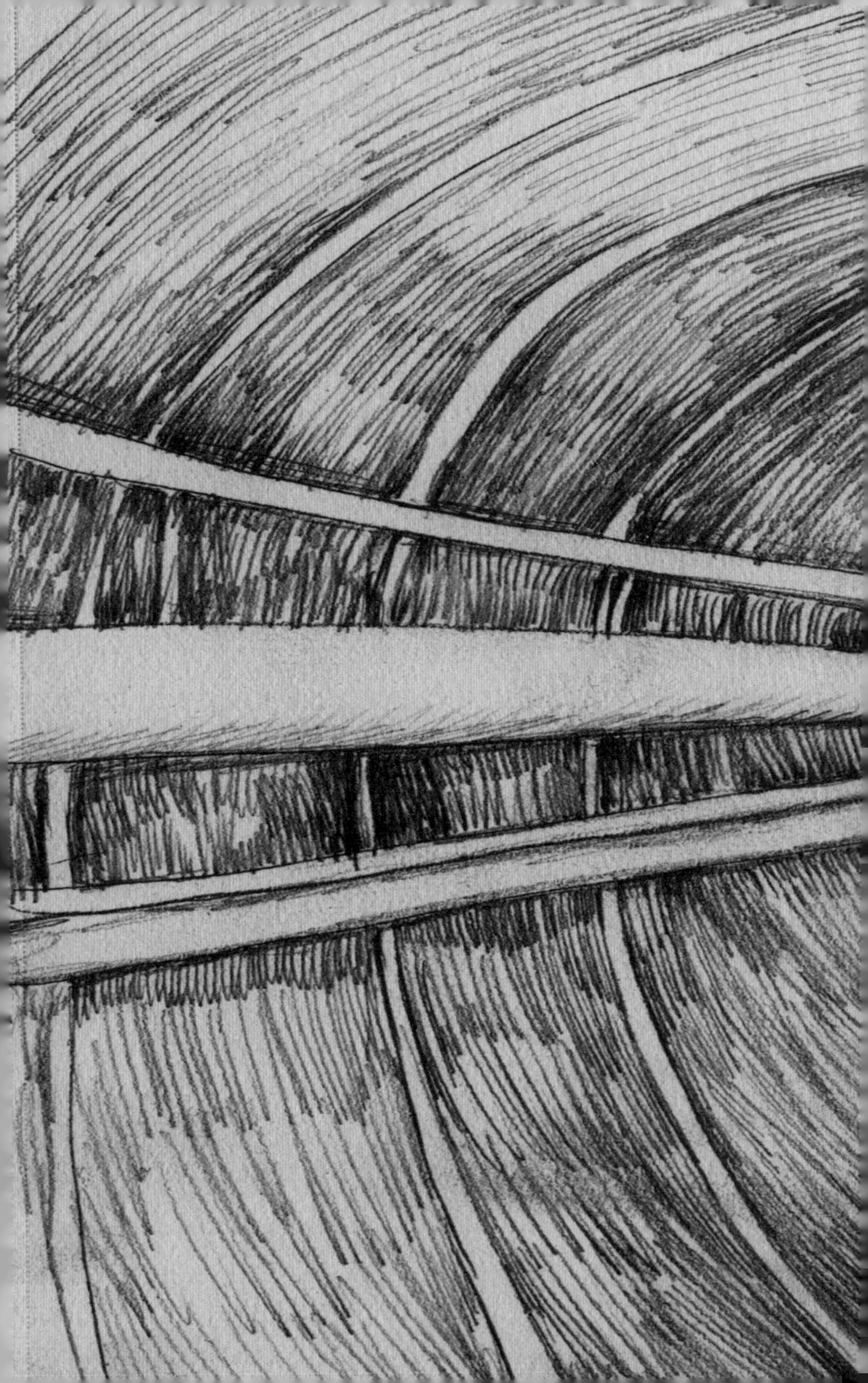

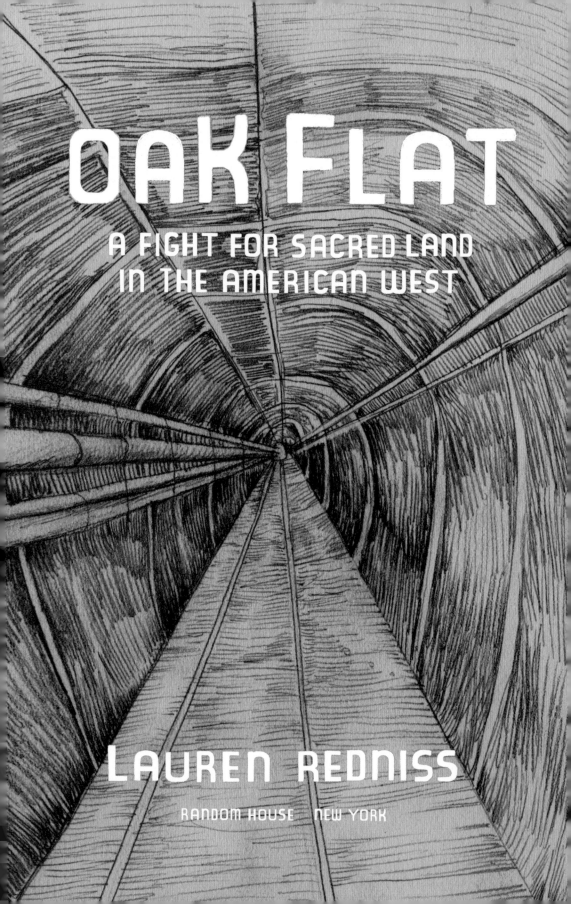

OAK FLAT

A FIGHT FOR SACRED LAND
IN THE AMERICAN WEST

LAUREN REDNISS

RANDOM HOUSE   NEW YORK

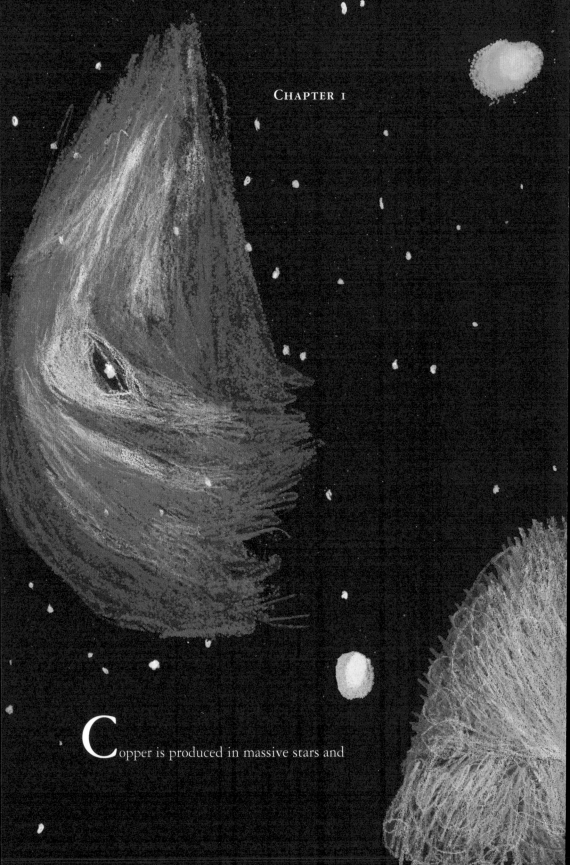

CHAPTER 1

Copper is produced in massive stars and

flung

out into

space as

those stars

explode.

We look into the night sky; the heavens appear still and quiet. But as you gaze upward, you are a distant witness to cataclysmic violence.

Each glittering star is a cauldron of nuclear fusion reactions many light years away. The light we see is the release of energy as the star fuses hydrogen into helium. When a star runs out of hydrogen to fuse, it surrenders to gravity and begins to contract. The star's core becomes hotter and denser. This heat and pressure spur further nuclear reactions, forming elements of increasingly higher mass. As a large star burns through all the energy it can generate from fusion, its core tightens into a blazingly hot fist of iron.

The star implodes, then rebounds outward, forming a supernova, an explosion bright enough to outshine entire galaxies. The star is dying, collapsing in on itself at velocities of up to 70,000 kilometers per second and spewing dense clouds of hot gas into space at a third of the speed of light, driving a shock wave dozens of light years across. A supernova has the power to forge metallic elements, and as it explodes, it expels these elements into space. In these dense molecular clouds, new stars and planets form.

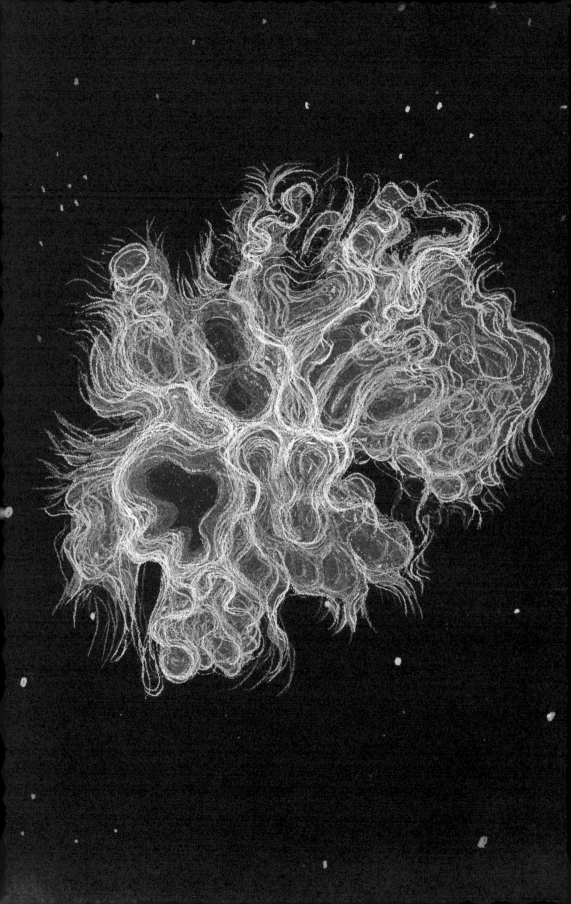

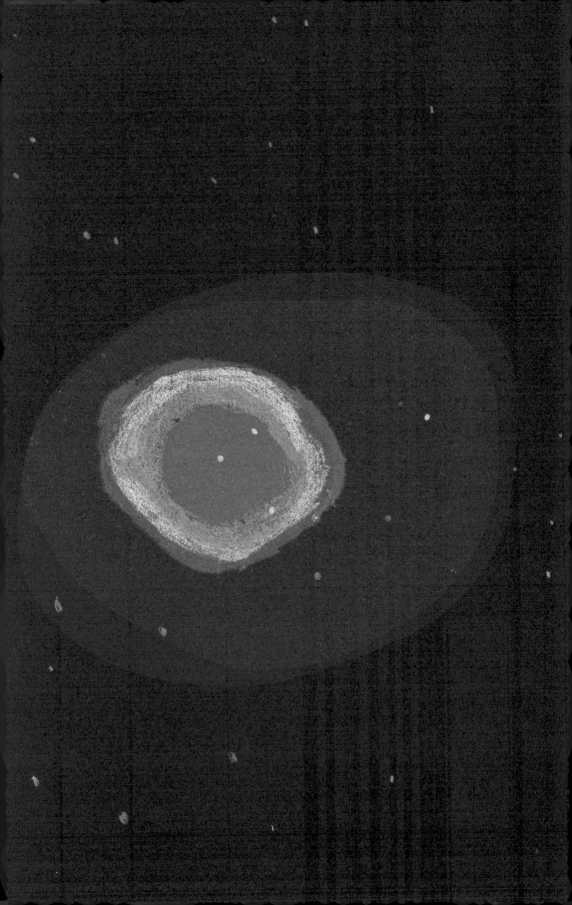

Some four and a half billion years ago, one of those new stars was our Sun. As cosmic debris orbited the nascent Sun, particles began clumping together, becoming asteroids, planetesimals, and, finally, over millions of years, planets, including Planet Earth.

Young Earth was a seething ball of molten rock and metal. Comets, meteors, and asteroids crashed into the new planet. Eventually, Earth's surface began to cool and solidify. Water vapor and ice became oceans. Continents collided, were torn asunder, slid past each other, were re-formed. Molten rock known as magma churned under Earth's surface. Magma that spews from Earth in a volcanic eruption is called lava. Magma can also crystallize underground over hundreds of thousands or even millions of years. Most magmas cool into common granites, but a small percentage concentrates metals to form an ore deposit.

Ore deposits contain coveted minerals, including gold, silver, iron, and copper. Humans have mined these materials for millennia. Today we use mined metals in construction and manufacturing, in medical devices and in agriculture, in power generation and telecommunications. In the twenty-first century, the ore close to Earth's surface has mostly been harvested, so we dig ever deeper to access what remains.

In 1995, a body of copper ore was discovered in southeastern Arizona, on the edge of the mining region known as the Copper Corridor. About 3,000 people live in the nearby town of Superior. The San Carlos Apache Indian Reservation is 15 miles to the east.

The land above the ore was federal land, an area of the Tonto National Forest known as Oak Flat.

The copper deposit was huge, one of the world's largest untapped reserves. Whoever mined it stood to reap enormous profit—many billions of dollars—but because the ore was located within a national forest, legislation was required to transfer the land from federal ownership into private hands.

In 2014, two of the world's largest mining conglomerates, BHP Billiton and Rio Tinto, formed a subsidiary called Resolution Copper. Resolution Copper began lobbying the U.S. Congress to pass a law that would allow the company to gain possession of the land and access the ore. The company claimed that a mine at Oak Flat would be able to produce 25 percent of the United States's annual copper demand.

Environmentalists balked: a mine would cause irreparable damage. Some residents of Superior supported the proposed mine, optimistic about the jobs it could create. Others objected. They had lived through mining's boom-bust cycle before and were wary. Native Americans protested. Oak Flat, the San Carlos Apache believe, is sacred land.

Arizona's Copper Corridor is wild desert country, with undulating mountains and riparian canyons. The landscape is also studded with man-made canyons—vast open pit mines.

There is the Asarco Ray Copper Mine in Kearny, a short drive from Superior, and the Freeport-McMoRan Copper & Gold Mine,

18 miles northeast in the town of Miami. There are the three chasms of the Morenci mine to the east, and the defunct Lavender Pit, to the south in Bisbee. If you stand at the edge of these mines, you could imagine you have arrived at the ruins of an ancient civilization. You are alone in a colossal abandoned amphitheater. An open pit mine is as monumental as the Pyramids of Giza or Mexico's Teotihuacan. Spiraling ledges descend into the depths of the mine canyon. Canyon walls shimmer in shades of green, blue, pink, red: malachite, azurite, oxidizing iron.

An open pit mine is an enormous gash in the earth, an eyesore so spectacular it becomes sublime.

The proposed Resolution Copper mine would be different. It would not be an open pit. The company plans to extract the ore using a method known as block caving, which removes the ore from underneath.

Mineshafts would
be more than a mile deep,
the deepest in North America.

Temperatures
at the deepest levels would reach
180 degrees
Fahrenheit.

As Resolution's block caving operation causes progressive layers of

earth to fall inward, eventually the ground surface itself would give way,

leaving a crater in the landscape. This is known as subsidence.

The company predicts that the subsidence crater would be

up to two miles wide and a thousand feet deep.

If the mine proceeds as planned,

Oak Flat will collapse

into the

void.

The contested copper under Oak Flat was created by stars that were born and died billions of years ago. The copper is older than Earth itself.

A mine here would operate for about 40 years.

Within Oak Flat's series of remote desert mesas,

natural springs flow.

There are clusters of old-growth oak trees and

outcroppings of volcanic rock.

Bears and javelina roam.

At night, with little light pollution to dim them,

stars shimmer overhead.

CHAPTER 2

"When I went to Washington, D.C., I wore my buckskin.

We walked into this elevator, and a guy passed me,

and he was like, 'Wow, your costume's beautiful.'

I was like, 'This is not a costume.'"

NAELYN PIKE WAS 14 in November 2013. She wore braces and dark hair past her waist. Her buckskin, a long fringed dress made from deer hide, was sewn with tin jingles. "In D.C., when you walk into the Capitol, you have to get scanned for metal and stuff. I was like, 'I am so going to get detected.'"

It was a Wednesday. Naelyn had skipped school and traveled from Arizona with a small group, including her mother and grandfather, to attend congressional hearings on the proposed mine at Oak Flat.

NAELYN PIKE: "It was the first time I flew on an airplane. I was so nervous, because I'm afraid of heights. We went up, and my stomach dropped. I was like, *Just let me land.* But it was fun and we got free drinks or whatever. Everything was new. I'd never been in a taxi."

From the taxi window, Naelyn could see the Lincoln Memorial, the Washington Memorial, rows of government buildings. She arrived at the Capitol in the early afternoon. At the building's entrance, as she had predicted, the jingles on her dress set off the metal detector.

NAELYN PIKE: "The security guards were like, 'Oh my gosh.' But I couldn't take my dress off. So they kind of patted me and said, 'Just go.'"

"People were staring. Everyone was like, 'What are you?'"

"Like, 'I'm Apache.'"

FOR GENERATIONS, Apaches have gathered at Oak Flat. Oak Flat is the site of religious ceremonies, including a coming-of-age rite for girls. The Sunrise Dance is a four-day ritual central to Apache community and culture during which a girl who has recently begun menstruating reenacts the Apache creation myth. In the past, Oak Flat was also an Apache burial ground. In the summer, Apaches harvest medicinal plants and collect acorns to grind into flour for bread, soup, and dumplings. Close by is a cliff, nearly 5,000 feet in elevation, known as Apache Leap, where Apache warriors are said to have jumped to their death to avoid capture.

NAELYN PIKE: "My great-grandmother and her family came from Oak Flat. The same ground that I touch is where my ancestors touched a thousand years ago."

Soon after the discovery of copper in 1995, the newly formed Resolution Copper Mining LLC began its effort to acquire the land. Despite the support of a number of Arizona politicians, the company encountered resistance. Between 2004 and 2011, ten versions of a land transfer bill were introduced in Congress. In the House, Arizona representatives Paul Gosar (Republican) and Ann Kirkpatrick (Democrat) pushed a version of the land exchange forward, and in the Senate, corresponding legislation had the backing of Republicans John McCain and Jeff Flake, a former lobbyist for Rio Tinto. In each proposal, Resolution Copper agreed to trade various parcels of land scattered around Arizona to the government in exchange for the land with the copper ore. Each of these bills was either voted down or never made it out of committee. Still, proponents did not give up. An eleventh bill, the Southeast Arizona Land Exchange and Conservation Act of 2013, was introduced in both the House and the Senate in February of that year. In a statement, Senator McCain said the Resolution Copper mine "presents an enormous opportunity to revitalize one of the most economically depressed areas of Arizona."

Resolution Copper estimated that the mine would create 3,700 jobs and pump $61 billion into the economy. The company's project director, Andrew Taplin, told the *Arizona Daily Star*, "If you can imagine five Super Bowls . . . every year for 60 years, that's the level of economic boost and economic activity this mine is going to generate."

JOHN McCAIN: "Hope is on the horizon for this hard-hit community."

◆ ◆ ◆

NAELYN PIKE HAD COME TO WASHINGTON, D.C., that fall afternoon in 2013 with a group led by Terry Rambler, the San Carlos Apache tribal chairman. Rambler was scheduled to testify against the Resolution Copper mine before the Senate subcommittee on Public Lands, Forests, and Mining. Naelyn Pike, Terry Rambler, and the others were escorted through the network of underground tunnels that ring the Capitol, emerging in the Dirksen Senate Office Building, a seven-story, 750,000-square-foot block of white marble. They rode the elevator to the third floor and took their seats in one of Dirksen's committee rooms. Walnut-paneled walls gleamed in warm light cast by bronze sconces. At the front of the room, a semicircular table and 17 leather chairs faced a long conference table.

The Southeast Arizona Land Exchange and Conservation Act was one of several pieces of legislation on the day's agenda. Senators began to filter in: the chairman of the subcommittee, Joe Manchin III, Democrat from West Virginia, Arizona Republican Jeff Flake, Wyoming Republican John Barrasso, Oregon Democrat Ron Wyden, New Mexico Democrat Martin Heinrich, Colorado Democrats Mark Udall and Michael Bennet, California Democrat Barbara Boxer. John McCain was unable to attend. He sent regrets and a prepared statement. Senator Manchin made opening remarks. "Some of these bills are noncontroversial, and a few of them are very controversial." The bill designed to trade Oak Flat to Resolution Copper fell into the latter category.

Senator Flake spoke in favor of the legislation, acknowledging the controversy. "Given the large areas of reservation land and Indian trust lands as well as federal lands and the proximity of these parcels of non-Indian communities, there are bound to be disagreements."

The San Carlos Apache Tribe had prepared a sheaf of documents that made environmental, economic, and cultural arguments against the mine. There was an easel to display maps and photographs. Chairman Rambler submitted into the record a list of Native tribes allied in opposition to the land exchange. He also invoked prominent environmental organizations that were siding with the Apache, including the National Resources Defense Council, the National Wildlife Federation, and the Sierra Club.

In a written statement, Rambler described Oak Flat as "a place filled with power." Apache elders, he wrote, teach that Oak Flat is the home of the *Gaan,* the mountain spirits. To mine this land was an assault on Apache religion. If the mine were to go forward, Rambler wrote, "our spiritual existence will be threatened."

An hour and forty minutes into the hearing, Rambler addressed the committee.

TERRY RAMBLER: "Just as Mount Sinai is a holy place to Christians, Oak Flat is the equivalent for us. . . . There are no human actions or steps that could make this place whole again or restore it once lost."

Toward the end of his remarks, Rambler said, "I'd like to ask Naelyn Pike to stand."

Naelyn rose and faced the senators. Rambler drew the committee's attention to photographs of Naelyn taken the previous year, at her coming-of-age dance. In the photos, Naelyn is dressed as she was at the hearing, in a beaded buckskin dress. She is in a field, her face tilted toward the sun, eyes closed. An iridescent abalone shell rests in the center of her forehead. Family and friends surround her under the boughs of a tipi frame. In one photo, the camera captures the figure of an Apache mountain spirit dancer as he passes in front of Naelyn. His arms are outstretched, face cloaked in a black hood, wooden headdress spiking into the air. His body is painted white with black zigzagging lines.

Rambler asked to have Naelyn's written account of her Sunrise Dance entered into the Congressional Record.

NAELYN PIKE: "My name, Naelyn, means 'Apache woman.'

"My great-grandmother and her people fought to keep Oak Flat and Apache Leap. My great-grandmother and my ancestors lived along the ridge of Oak Flat and along the river which runs down from the north. My younger sister, Nizhoni, will be having her Sunrise Ceremony at Oak Flat in October. Oak Flat was brought to her in a dream. Now I am preparing for her ceremony. We pray that this holy place will not be destroyed by this time, so my great-grandmother can see her great-granddaughter be blessed into womanhood where our ancestors once called home. . . .

Why would you want to mine and destroy Oak Flat and Apache Leap? Will there really be that many jobs? For a long period of time? Can you not see the life it gives? Are you blinded by your greed? Please make me understand why you could do such horrid things to these holy precious lands."

Chairman Rambler concluded his remarks and thanked the committee in both English and Apache.

The House of Representatives scheduled a November vote for the land exchange. But it turned out that the annual White House Tribal National Conference, a gathering of Native leaders from across the United States, had been planned for the same day, which made for awkward timing. The vote was canceled. By the end of the year, the bill had been shelved. Another defeat. It seemed as though no law supporting a mine at Oak Flat could pass.

But Congress has workarounds for divisive legislation. Tacking a contested measure onto a larger legislative package sidesteps debate and avoids the risk that it will be voted down. In December 2014, proponents added the land exchange as a so-called midnight rider to the National Defense Authorization Act of 2015, a comprehensive bill that authorized some $600 billion in government spending, including the entire budget for the Pentagon.

TERRY RAMBLER: "The Land Exchange was included in Section 3003 on page 1,103 of a 1,700-page bill that was unveiled after 11 p.m. the evening before it came up for consideration."

In nearly a decade of efforts, supporters had failed to pass freestanding legislation authorizing a land transfer, but when it was slipped at the last minute into a military spending bill, Congress approved the measure. Two weeks later, on December 19, President Barack Obama signed it into law.

◆ ◆ ◆

WENDSLER NOSIE IS NAELYN PIKE'S GRANDFATHER. Nosie served as the San Carlos's tribal chairman for four years and sat for 16 years on the Tribal Council. When the land exchange passed, Nosie founded the Apache Stronghold, an alliance of Apaches and others determined to stop the Resolution Copper mine from becoming operational. Building the mine's infrastructure would take time, a decade or more. That time represented opportunity. Public opinion could be swayed, lawsuits filed, repeal legislation introduced. Nosie decided to set up camp at Oak Flat.

The Apache Stronghold put out a call to "People from all Nations."

"Light the fires and join the occupation."

On a February morning in 2015, two months after the passage of the land exchange, more than 100 people began a two-day, 45-mile walk from the San Carlos Apache Reservation to Oak Flat. Marchers carried tents and food. They hauled materials to build wickiups, traditional Apache dwellings. The group set out on reservation roads, heading west onto AZ 170, west again along US 70. They carried handmade signs ("Water Is Life," "Protect Oak Flat") and curved staffs wrapped with fur and hung with eagle feathers. Naelyn's sign showed a painted hummingbird. In Apache folklore, the hummingbird is a messenger, the reincarnation of a young warrior killed defending his people from a ferocious bear. When the marchers crossed the reservation boundary, they conducted a prayer ceremony. Naelyn told a reporter, "Once we cross this line, we're in the fight."

The group camped overnight in a parking lot in Globe, Arizona. The next morning they set out to complete the remaining 20 miles to Oak Flat. They walked on highways, hugging the shoulder of the road. A relay of young runners closed the distance as they approached Oak Flat. Naelyn, wearing black leggings, a black T-shirt, and an orange reflective safety vest, was given the honor of running the final leg of the journey. She carried two ceremonial staffs, which she held over her head and shook as she crossed the final stretch of pavement.

Entering Oak Flat, she wept.

NAELYN PIKE:

"We're not going to leave Oak Flat.
If they want to take this away they're
going to have to force us out."

WENDSLER NOSIE: "A groundswell is building."

TERRY RAMBLER: "We are committed to shining light on the
land exchange and the proposed mine
until we have no breath."

Resolution Copper says it hopes the mine will positively impact the San Carlos Apache. The company has enlisted Apache spokespeople and has begun awarding a Native American college scholarship. Resolution has pledged to hire "as many Native Americans as possible."

WENDSLER NOSIE: "But we don't want to be miners. We want to be educators. We want to be doctors and attorneys. This mine degrades southeastern Arizona, like all we know is to mine and carry a lunch bucket."

There are 15,000 members of the San Carlos Apache Tribe. About 10,000 live on the 1.8 million acre San Carlos Reservation. According to tribal officials, there is 70 percent unemployment in San Carlos. The median income is $25,000. Approximately 45 percent of tribal members live below the poverty line, including 59 percent of children under 12. One in two children in San Carlos tests positive for drugs or alcohol at birth. In 2015, the life expectancy of a Native American in Arizona was 60, 16 years shorter than non-Natives in the state.

Resolution Copper has invested more than a billion dollars in the proposed mine and expects to sink some $7 billion more into the project before any minerals are pulled from the ground. The company estimates it will extract $144 billion worth of copper over the life of the mine. Resolution's parent companies, BHP and Rio Tinto, run mining operations in Chile, Papua New Guinea, Indonesia, Zimbabwe, Madagascar, Namibia, South Africa, Australia, Canada, Peru, Mexico, Colombia, Brazil. In 2018, BHP employed some 62,000 people and reported profits from operations of $16 billion. Rio Tinto employed 47,000 people and took in $18 billion in profits from operations.

WENDSLER NOSIE:

"Once we started

fighting this

fight, I realized,

man, we're

going against

a giant.

"It's war."

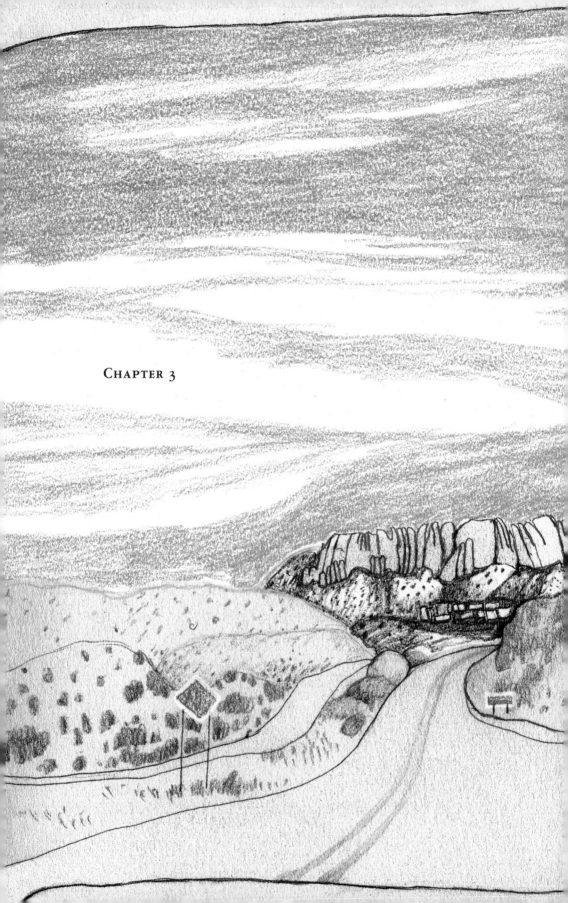

CHAPTER 3

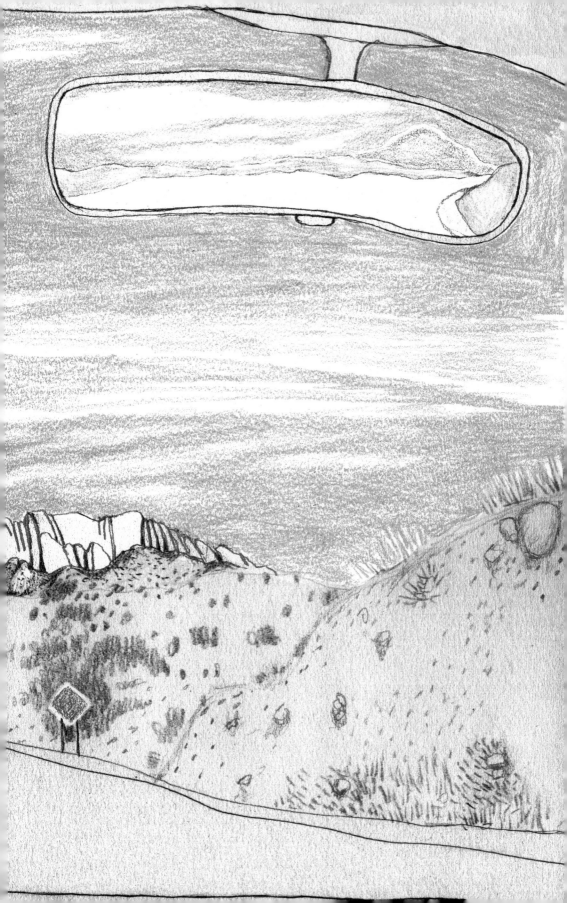

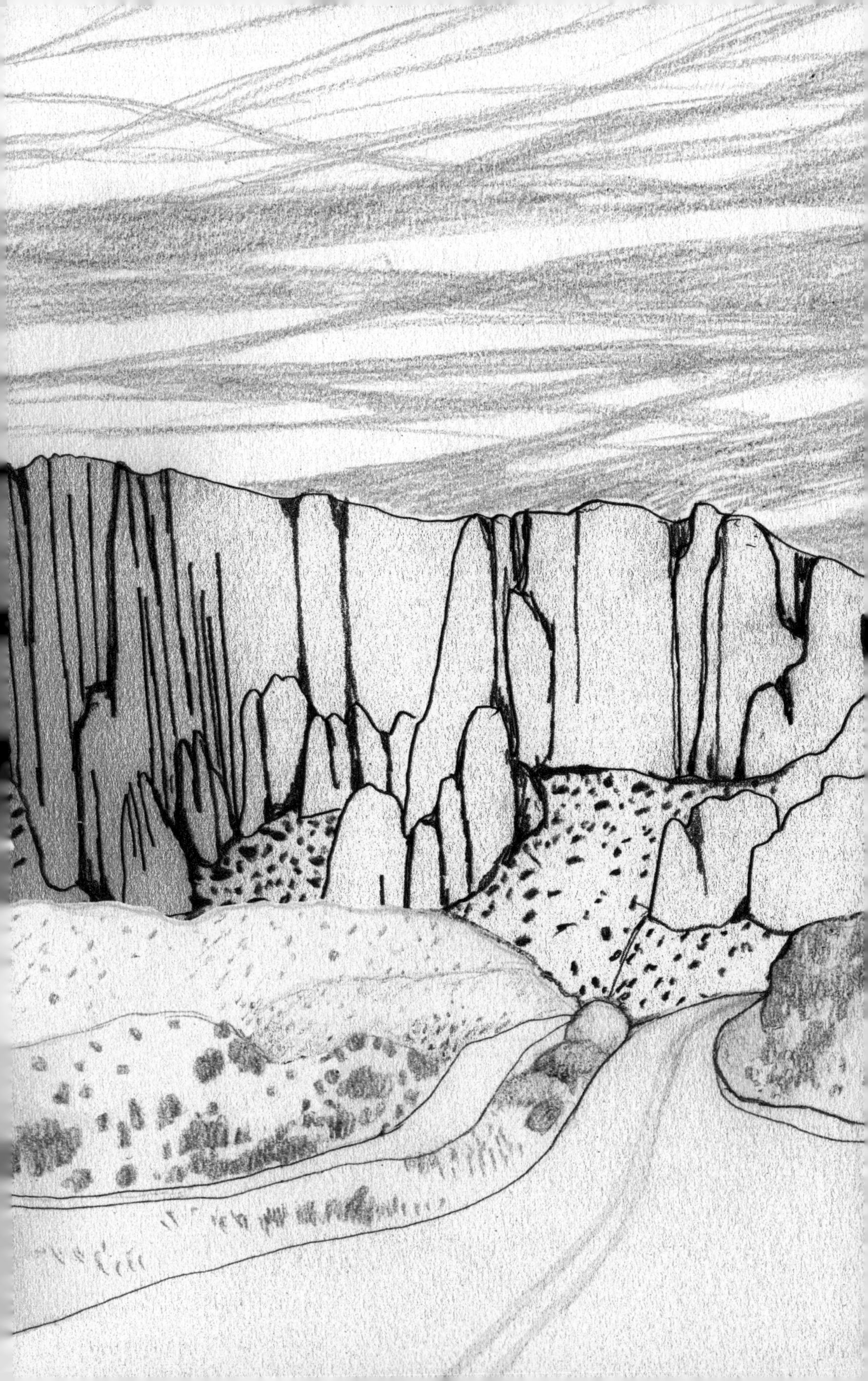

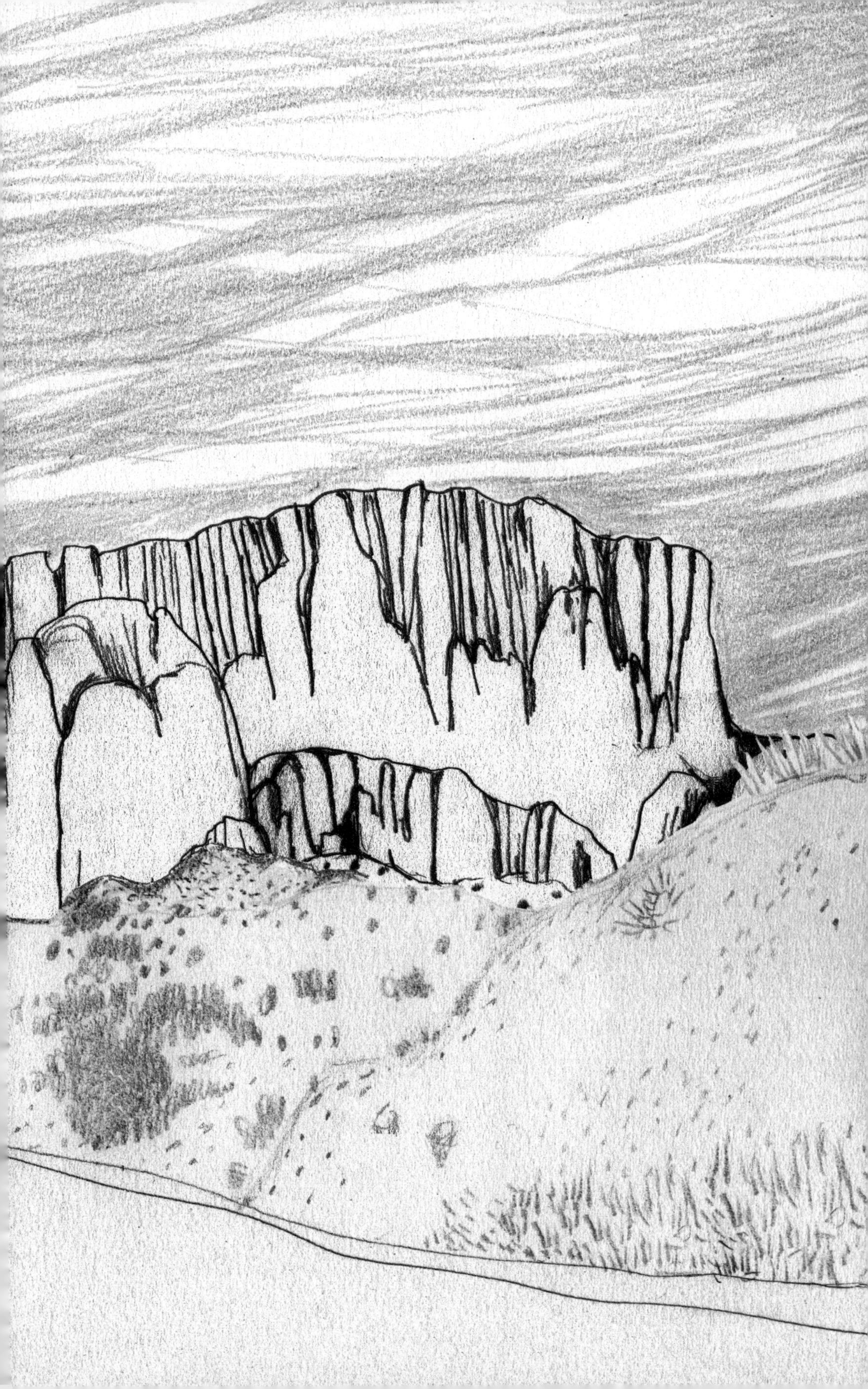

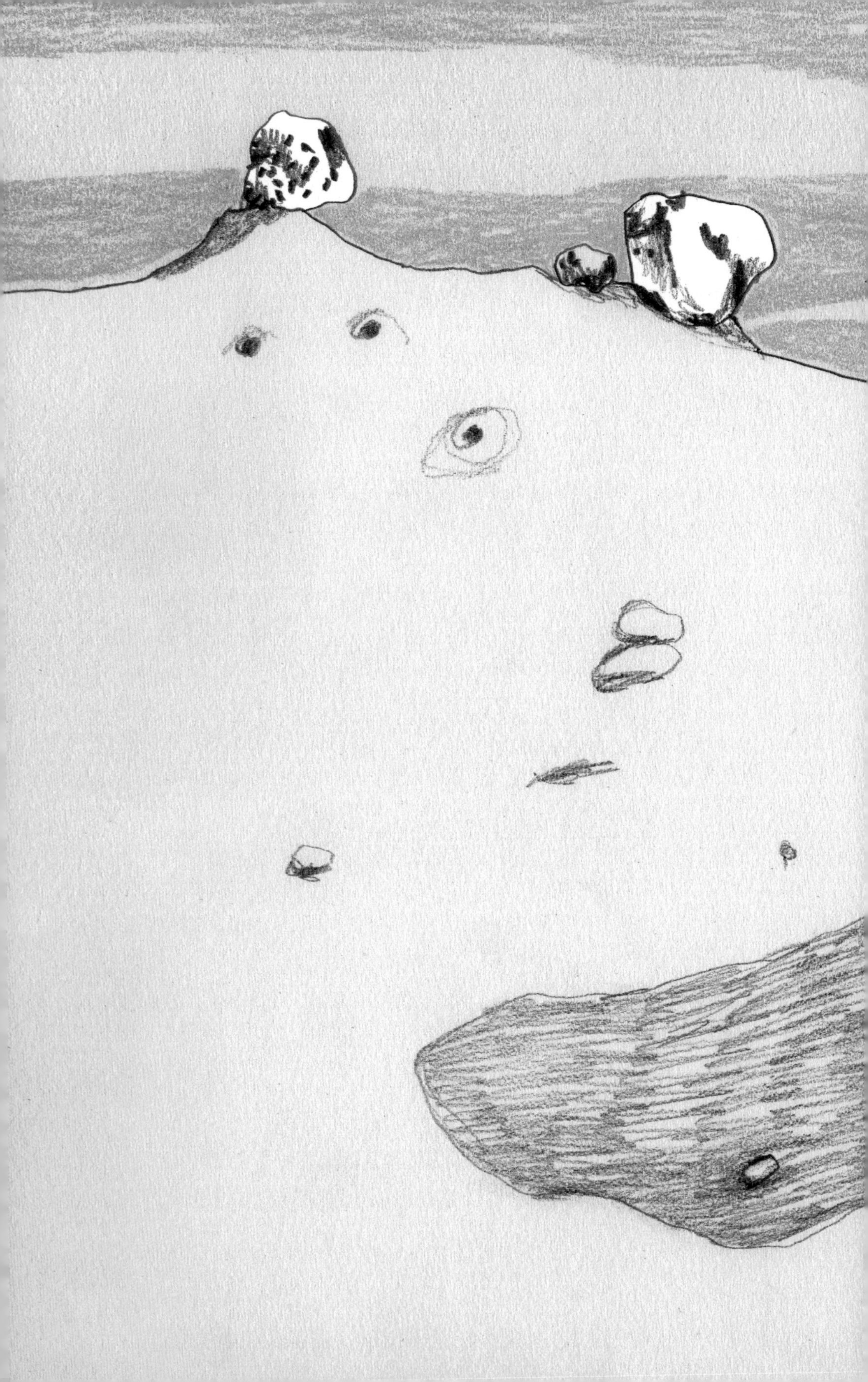

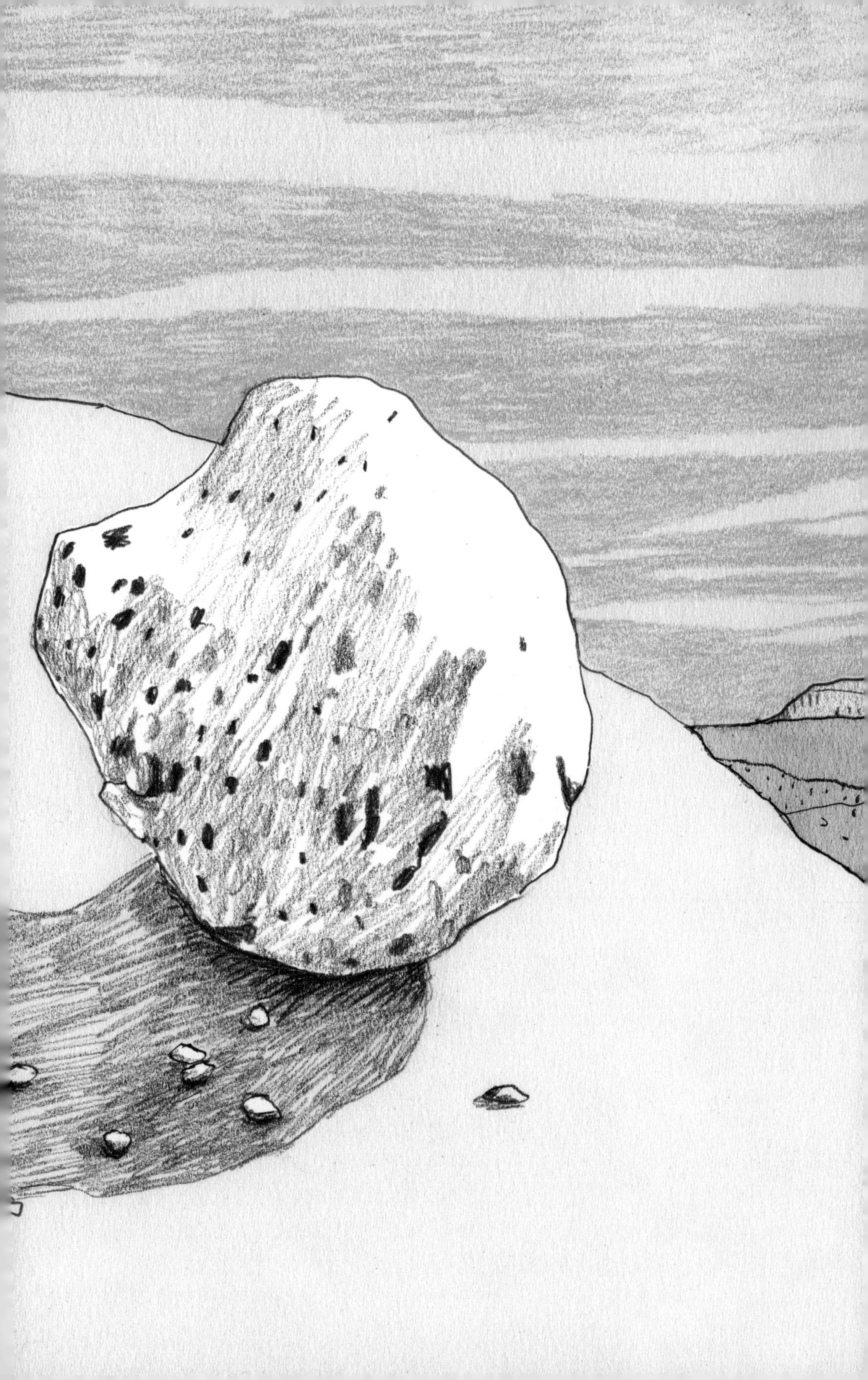

Driving into Superior, Arizona, on US Route 60 East, you face Apache Leap, the cliffs that drop like a stone curtain behind the town. Route 60 winds past Superior's Main Street, through the mountains, and into the Queen Creek Tunnel. You burst out of the tunnel to face brilliant sunlight. The road snakes along the edge of a steep chasm that rock climbers know as Atlantis. The ground levels and, about two miles up on the right, there's a turnoff. You wind downhill through a field to a clearing.

It's mid-July. In Phoenix, the temperature is 113 degrees. It's cooler here at Oak Flat. There is a breeze. A trailer is parked under the branches of a tall oak tree. Attached to the trailer is an open-sided maroon tent, about 15 feet square. Under the tent, a long table is covered with patterned fabric, an assortment of condiments, and a propane tank. Nearby, half a dozen people sit talking. A fire is burning. Two wickiups stand in the clearing. A painting depicting a leaping fox, teeth bared, is propped against a tree. A third wickiup is draped with several large tarps and a "Support the Save Oak Flat Act" banner, secured with twine.

WENDSLER NOSIE: "This is our sweat lodge. This encampment is the hosting area, there is cooking for everyone. People put up their tents."

Nosie's parents' first language was Apache, but like most children of his generation, he was given an Anglo name. "Wendsler" was his parents' interpretation of the word "Winslow," the name of a local town.

WENDSLER NOSIE: "If you look at Arizona, a lot of it is desert. At Oak Flat, you could be born and live your entire life. You have everything. Water. Animals. Medicine plants."

The Tonto National Forest, where Oak Flat sits, was named for the Tonto Apache who were pushed out of the area and onto the Camp Verde

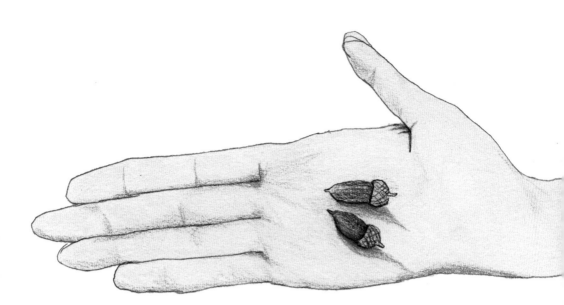

Reservation in 1871. When that reservation was dissolved in the winter of 1875, the Tonto were forced onto the San Carlos Reservation.

When there is an event or a ceremony at Oak Flat, a crowd gathers. There is cooking, drumming, dancing, and praying. Standing Rock Sioux chairman David Archambault II visited the Oak Flat occupation in 2016 while his tribe waged its own battle to stop the construction of the Dakota Access Pipeline. That same year, Miss Native America, Ashley Nailihn Susan, came to the site and made frybread. Non-Natives also show up. Activists, environmentalists, New Age seekers, politicians. Jane Sanders, the wife of Senator Bernie Sanders, made a speech at the Oak Flat encampment during the 2016 presidential campaign.

Naelyn Pike is often here. She comes with her mother, Vanessa Nosie, and her younger sisters, Nizhoni and Baasé-O. They build campfires and prepare meals. They swim in Oak Flat's natural pools and skateboard on the dirt roads.

NAELYN PIKE: "Everyone is usually around a fire. We have an open area for the children who want to play—play football, play tag."

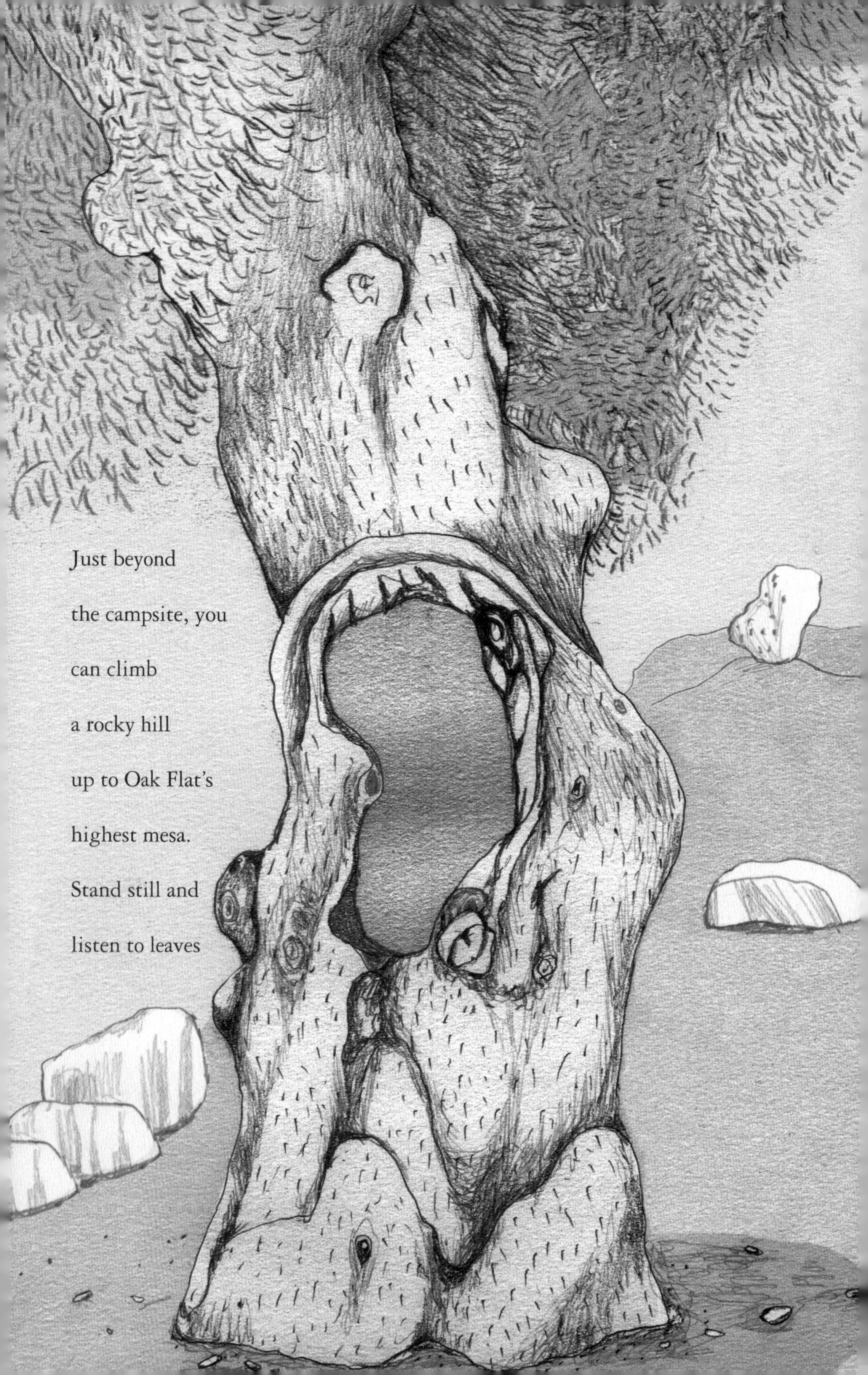

Just beyond
the campsite, you
can climb
a rocky hill
up to Oak Flat's
highest mesa.
Stand still and
listen to leaves

rustle in the wind. Watch
a storm build in the distance.
Climb down a canyon and
walk through a dry riverbed.
Run your palm along
the smooth underside
of a boulder that
cantilevers
over the ravine.

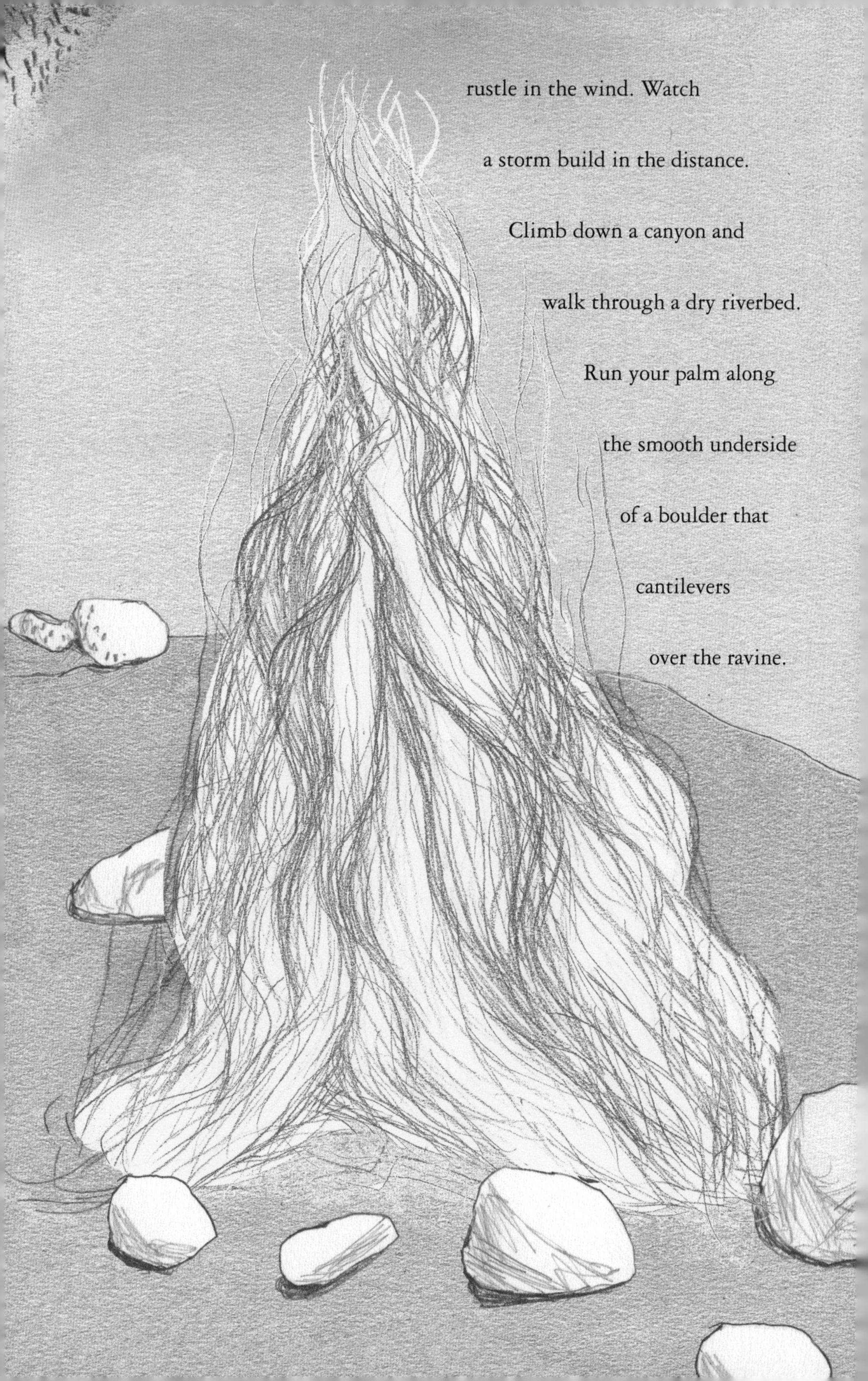

Mamie Eisenhower picnicked at Oak Flat in the early 1950s. She was delighted by the place and reportedly urged her husband to safeguard it. In 1955, President Dwight Eisenhower issued Public Land Order 1229, creating the 760-acre "Oak Flat Withdrawal Area" and protecting it from "all forms of appropriation," including mining. Some proponents of the Resolution Copper mine claim that the Mamie Eisenhower story is apocryphal. Others say that the 1955 order was not a declaration of the cultural importance of the site, but simply a bureaucratic measure to protect the government's investment in infrastructure—picnic tables, horseshoe pits, outhouses—in a public recreation area.

Surrounding the Oak Flat encampment are groves of old-growth Emory oak trees with thick, twisting trunks. There are juniper trees, agave plants, yucca, red-berried skunkbrush, green sprangletop, hairy grama grass, Arizona hedgehog cactus. Bobcats, foxes, and mountain lions wander through the site. Bears leave gobs of dung at the base of lichen-encrusted boulders. At least one ocelot, a threatened species that looks like a house cat in a leopard costume, has been spotted in the vicinity. Prickly pear cacti sprout scarlet fruits shaped like hand grenades.

There are petroglyphs on some of Oak Flat's volcanic rock walls. Stone ruins lie unmarked not far from the highway. In addition to evidence of shelters and cooking fires, the area has yielded broken pottery, arrowheads, and stone tools. In August and September, you will come across Apache women harvesting the long, thin acorns of the Emory oak. According to Dr. John R. Welch, Simon Fraser University professor of archaeology and former historic preservation officer for the White Mountain Apache Tribe, Oak Flat holds "the best set of Apache archaeological sites ever documented, period, full stop."

NAELYN PIKE: "My great-grandmother and her grandmother, this is where they lived freely."

The drone of lusty male cicadas rises and recedes.

"Apache" is an umbrella term for a number of linguistically and culturally related peoples. The ancestral homelands of Apache groups extended south from what is now southern Colorado and Utah into Mexico; Apache lands stretched west from modern-day Oklahoma into Texas, New Mexico, and Arizona. Europeans began encroaching on Apache territory in the late 1500s. Conflict between settlers and Apaches escalated in the nineteenth century, culminating in nearly four decades of the so-called Apache Wars. It had become clear that the lands of the Southwest were mineral rich. Natives fighting to defend their homelands stood in the way of economic development. Apaches were vilified in the press as subhuman and homicidal.

In 1859, a letter published in *The New York Times* described Apache physiognomy and character in grotesque terms:

> Fingers long and pointed, like claws; eyes keen and wild . . .
> He eats anything a wolf will eat, from roots to carrion. He goes
> about by stealth, seeking dark and hidden routes, and never
> pounces on his prey except [when] he has all the advantage.

According to Major General George Crook, who led the military's campaign against the Apache from 1871 to 1886, "We have before us the tiger of the human species . . . the Apaches of Arizona."

On October 12, 1862, Brigadier General James Carleton issued an order to Colonel Kit Carson:

> All Indian men of that tribe are to be killed whenever and
> wherever you can find them.

In September of the following year, Carleton wrote to his superiors in Washington, D.C.:

> If I can but have troops to whip away the Apaches, so that
> prospecting parties can explore the country and not be in fear

all the time of being murdered, you will, without the shadow of a doubt, find that our country has mines of the precious metals, unsurpassed in richness, number, and extent by any in the world. Rich copper, in quantity enough to supply the world, is found at the head of the Gila [River]. Some of this copper abounds in gold.

In his letter Carleton included a copper specimen and two lumps of gold, one of which he suggested be given to the president. "Please give the largest piece of gold to Mr. Lincoln," Carleton wrote. "It will gratify him to know that Providence is blessing our country."

Decades of conflict took the lives of countless Natives, as well as many settlers and soldiers. By the end of the nineteenth century, the Apache had lost some six million acres of their traditional homeland.

At the entrance to the Apache Gold Casino, an LED sign flashes upcoming entertainment listings. Karaoke, Boxing, Apache Laffs Comedy Night. Great-tailed grackles, black songbirds with yellow eyes, flit among the cars and RVs in the parking lot. Near the casino's front door, a nine-foot statue, an Apache man cast in bronze, presides over the scene. He wears a breechcloth and high moccasins. If his face looks familiar, it is because the model for the sculpture was Wes Studi, the Cherokee actor who appeared in the movies *Dances with Wolves, The Last of the Mohicans,* and *Geronimo: An American Legend.* What at first seem to be weapons in the figure's hands turn out to be a pole and a hoop. He is an athlete, a game player.

The casino sits at the edge of the San Carlos Reservation. Inside, the air is smoky and dim. Barry White plays on the sound system. Then Weezer. Slot machines ding, buzz, and simulate the sound of smashing glass. The gift shop sells straw hats and rhinestoned flip-flops, nail polish and soda. Enlarged black-and-white photos hang in the hallway. There is a picture of an Apache woman, head bowed, face in shadow, holding a child in a cradleboard. There is a photo of Geronimo, whose hand reaches for the pistol tucked into his waistband. The roulette and blackjack tables are empty, draped in heavy drop cloths. Retired couples and scattered loners gaze intently at screens, pulling levers and punching buttons. According to casino promotional materials, "At the Apache Gold Casino Resort, the magic of the 'Apache Gold Legend' lives on. Untold riches lie in this desert oasis, awaiting discovery."

Wendsler Nosie rolls down his truck window and orders a chai latte from the casino drive-through. He exits the parking lot and turns east. Desert hills roll out in all directions.

WENDSLER NOSIE: "You just entered Apache country."

As a teenager, Wendsler Nosie attended high school in Globe, Arizona, the town closest to the San Carlos Reservation. Globe was once inside reservation boundaries, but the United States seized the area by executive order in 1876 after silver was discovered.

WENDSLER NOSIE: "In 1974, in the town of Globe, they still had signs, 'Dogs and Indians Keep Out.' We still had to order outside of restaurants. We really didn't start eating in restaurants until the 1980s."

Nosie was a high school sports star. He had always been athletic.

WENDSLER NOSIE: "When my voice was changing, my mom had me get out early in the morning and go run. She'd tell me, 'Go get this. Go get that. You gotta run. Your body's changing.' Running was the antidote for the aches and pains of adolescence. My mom had mostly sons. She said, 'If I didn't make you do these things physically, then you would be like a wild horse.' She was teaching us self-control."

At Globe High, Nosie ran track and played basketball and football. In 1977, he became Globe's first Indian quarterback. During one game, Nosie confounded his teammates, messing around with the play's call signals and incurring multiple offside penalties.

WENDSLER NOSIE: "'Ready! Now! Set!' So everybody goes up and then goes down. So I go: 'Ready! Now! Set!' Everybody goes up, they go down. I stood there. The whistle blew. The referee threw the flag. Five yards— moved us back five yards. We huddle. 'All right, same play! Ready! Now! Set!' We do the same thing. *Bhrrrt!* They throw the flag again. Five yards. The coach called time out. 'Nosie! Get over here!' I go over. 'What's wrong?' 'Coach,' I said, 'I never thought I would see the day where I control ten white boys.' He laughed. 'Go run the play!'"

Members of Globe High School's sports teams were required to wear their hair short. Nosie's hair was long.

WENDSLER NOSIE: "When you dance in the Apache way, you need your hair long."

Since Nosie refused to cut his hair, he was excluded from team photos. Later, he objected to the way American history was taught and organized a walkout of 600 students. At graduation, the principal handed Nosie a diploma but wouldn't shake his hand.

◆ ◆ ◆

THE SAN CARLOS RESERVATION is one of the world's main sources for peridot, the semiprecious green gem. Jojoba plants are indigenous to the area. You may catch sight of quail, wild boar, or the lizard known as a Gila monster. Red-shouldered hawks drift overhead. In February, the landscape is stippled with golden-orange poppies.

A sparse network of roads laces the reservation together. A cluster of aging municipal buildings includes the San Carlos Apache Tribe Planning and Economic Development office, the Bureau of Indian Affairs, a hospital, an EPA office, the fire department, a post office, a library, an elementary school, a high school. There is a cemetery for Apache veterans who served in the United States Armed Forces. The Boys & Girls Club is a converted bowling alley with an outdoor lot where kids skateboard. The windows of the Technology Building are boarded over in plywood. There are churches: Mormon, Pentecostal, Baptist, Roman Catholic.

In the 1940s, Ace Daklugie, son of the renowned Apache chief Juh, recorded an oral history.

> San Carlos! That was the worst place in all the great
> territory stolen from the Apaches. . . . The heat was terrible.
> The insects were terrible. The water was terrible. What
> there was in the sluggish river was brackish and warm.

WENDSLER NOSIE IN HIGH SCHOOL

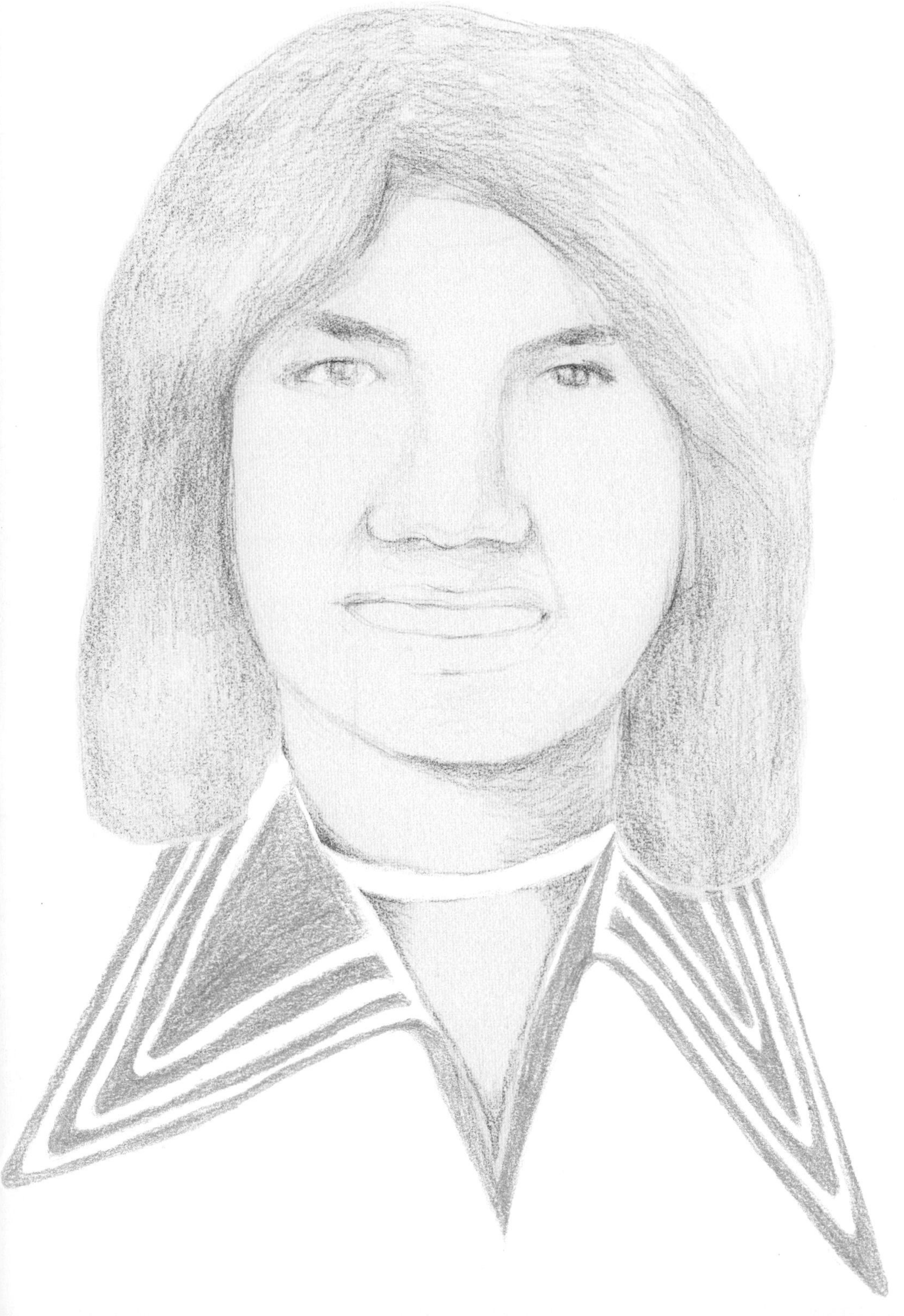

Pools alongside the channel afforded places for insects to hatch. They served, as I know now, as breeding places for clouds of mosquitoes. Insects and rattlesnakes seemed to thrive there. . . . At times it was so hot that I am sure a thermometer would have registered well above 120 degrees. At San Carlos, for the first time within the memory of my people, the Apaches experienced the shaking sickness. Our Medicine Men knew of herbs that would reduce bodily temperature but had nothing effective against the strange and weakening attacks that caused people to alternately suffer from heat and cold. At times the attacks caused people with high temperatures to feel cold and to shake uncontrollably while covered with blankets. And this sickness sometimes lasted for weeks unless the patient died.

U.S. soldiers stationed at San Carlos also found the place difficult. One officer posted there in the early 1880s wrote:

> San Carlos won unanimously our designation "Hell's Forty Acres." . . . Scrawny, dejected lines of scattered cottonwoods, shrunken, almost leafless, marked the course of the streams. Rain was so infrequent that it took on the semblance of a phenomenon when it came at all. Almost continuously dry, hot, dust and gravel-laden winds swept the plain, denuding it of almost every vestige of vegetation.

Conditions in San Carlos were so merciless that the army strictly limited periods of deployment. But Natives were prohibited from leaving. Congress's 1876 appropriations act for Indian Department expenses stipulated that "Indians shall not be allowed to leave their proper reservations." The legislation was enforced unevenly across the United States, according to the discretion of the agent in charge of a particular reservation. In San Carlos, enforcement was rigorous. According to historian Donald L. Fixico, "When [the Apache] left their reservation without permission, they were routinely hunted down and killed." The U.S. military posted marksmen at high elevations around San Carlos.

WENDSLER NOSIE: "You can go to the top of these mountains, you can still find military posts. Those were the snipers."

All Apache males over the age of 14 were required to wear identification tags. Confinement on the reservation disrupted traditional subsistence patterns. In San Carlos, there was virtually nothing to eat. Each week, the Apaches had to line up at the government's reservation headquarters to receive rations, and to be counted. This often meant hours waiting in the beating sun. The elderly and the unwell who were unable to withstand the heat received nothing that week. Today the tribe's official website states: "The San Carlos Apache Reservation was established on November 9, 1871. It is the world's first concentration camp still existing to this day."

At night, the near absence of artificial light in much of San Carlos means that you are enveloped by undifferentiated darkness. The dark erases any indication of the horizon and nearly every feature of the landscape, natural or man-made. You make your way through the blackness, a scattering of stars and the band of the Milky Way overhead. In the distance an occasional lit window appears to float in midair.

Wendsler's parents, Elvera Ward and Paul Nosie, met here in the 1940s, when Elvera was in her late teens.

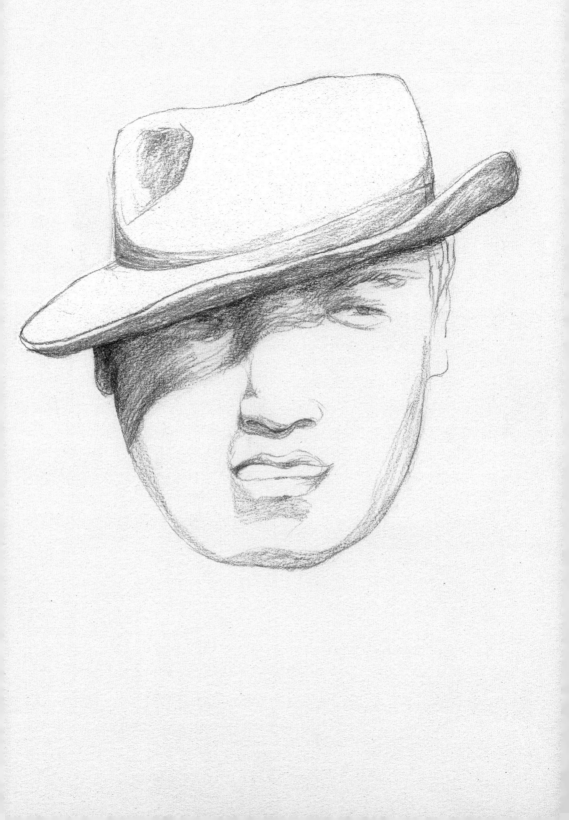

PAUL NOSIE

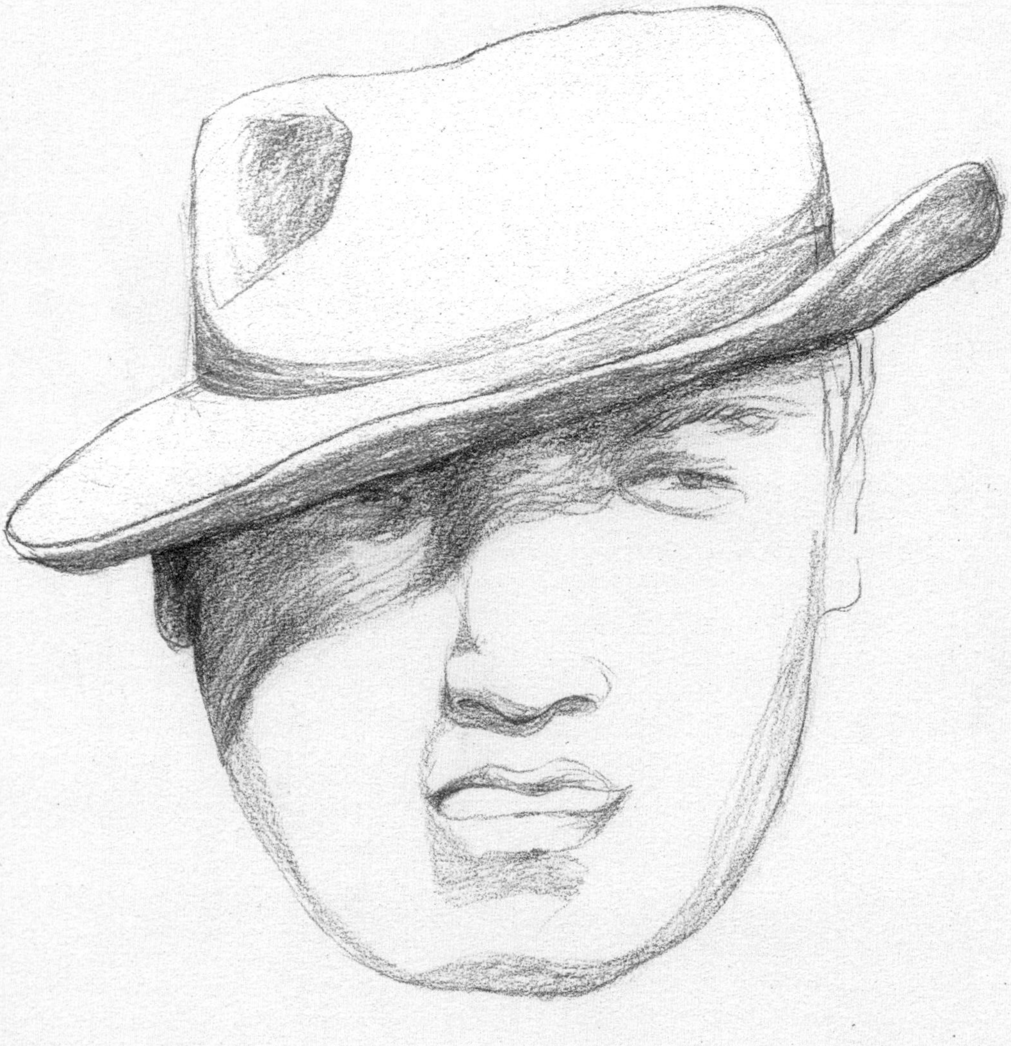

ELVERA WARD NOSIE

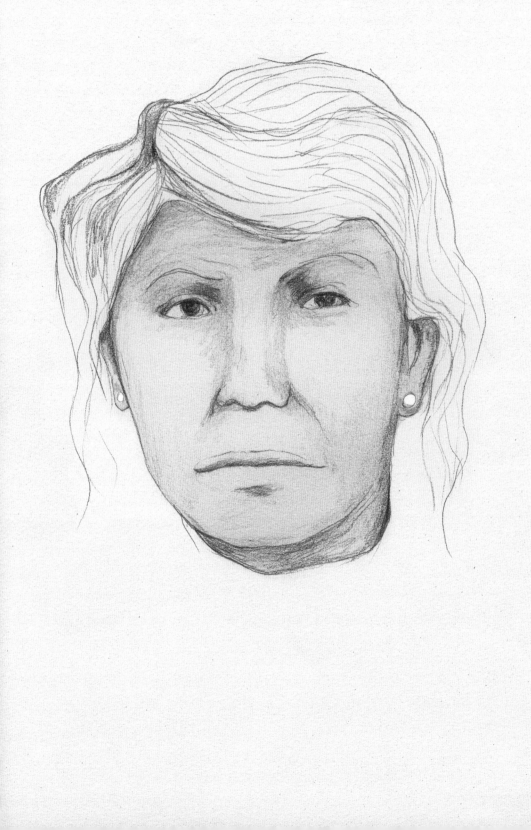

WENDSLER NOSIE: "My mother was walking with her girlfriends on the railroad tracks. My dad came along on a horse."

There's a photo of Paul Nosie when he looks to be in his mid-twenties. His face is broad and handsome with smooth cheeks. He squints into the sun, fedora askew over one eye, his body pressed into the heavy canopy of an oak tree. Paul and Elvera married and had seven children. Wendsler was the youngest, born in 1959. Paul Nosie worked at an asbestos mine in Seneca, at the northern edge of San Carlos. It was his job to install dynamite, light a fuse, and run out of the mine as the explosion occurred.

The Nosies' home was a tar-paper shack near the railroad tracks. Nine people lived in one room. In 1964, the Nosies were one of ten San Carlos families chosen to register for a joint Bureau of Indian Affairs and federal Public Housing Administration program called Mutual Help. The program was designed to address the pervasive lack of housing on reservations across the United States. The Housing Administration provided materials; future homeowners supplied land and labor. In the Southwest, families enrolled in the program assisted each other in constructing concrete block homes just under 1,000 square feet in size. The floor plans were, according to an Interior Department press release, "designed to blend well with the landscape on any reservation."

Elvera assumed most of the work on their Mutual Help house while Paul was away, working at the mine in Seneca. In an article about the program, the *Arizona Daily Star* reported, "Mrs. Nosie drove a pickup, shoveled gravel and leveled the patio porch, filling in the foundations, so the cement porch could be poured." She planned to grow fruit trees in the yard, she told the paper. In a photo of Elvera Nosie at her new house, she is dressed in a striped shirt-dress, her arm delicately touching the building's facade. It appears a front door has yet to be installed, and a shadow falls into the empty interior.

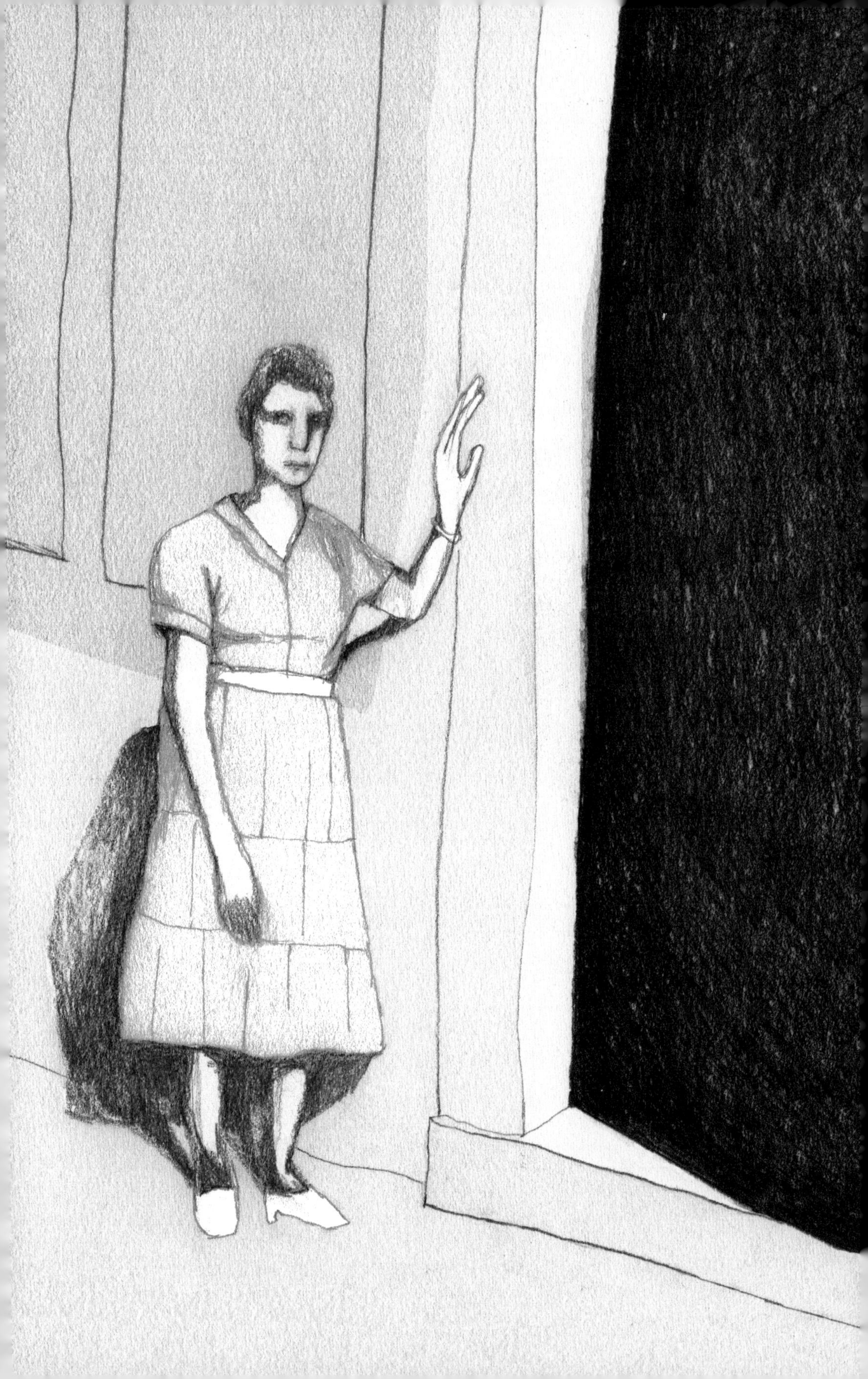

It is very difficult to get a mortgage on an Indian reservation. (The U.S. Treasury Department's "Guide to Mortgage Lending in Indian Country" describes the obstacles as "not insurmountable.") The San Carlos Apache Tribe is legally recognized as a sovereign nation, but there is no bank here. The San Carlos Reservation's 1.86 million acres are categorized as "trust land." This means the tribe retains "beneficial interest"—tribal members can live here and use the reservation land—but the federal government holds legal title. The ambiguous status of trust land has historically made banks reluctant to grant loans, since the land is considered ineligible for use as collateral.

WENDSLER NOSIE: "It's like building it on a military base. You can't get a loan, and on top of that, you can't even sell it.

"The banks will only fund what they can roll out. If you don't pay, they can roll out your car, they can roll out your trailer, but anything that is stuck to the ground, they're not going to support."

Most people in San Carlos still build their own houses. When Wendsler and his wife, Theresa, needed a home for their seven children, they went to Home Depot.

WENDSLER NOSIE: "We brought in the supplies. We read instructions. We hardly made any mistakes, even with the floor. The measurements to lay those tiles, I thought it would be easy. It's not easy! Everything is not as square as you would think. It's a good thing my wife is into math."

In the Nosies' driveway, there are half a dozen trucks and SUVs, a pickup filled with barbed wire, and a wheelchair. In the spring, the oleander bushes bloom, fuschia and white.

THERESA NOSIE: "They're the only flowers the gophers won't eat."

In the yard there is a jungle gym and a "Save Oak Flat" sign jabbed into the grass. In back, the porch and a wooden gazebo are piled with tools and equipment. There are trailers out of which the Nosies operate a barbecue catering business and a tribal weekly, *The Apache Messenger* ("The Independent Voice of the Apache People"), founded by Wendsler and Theresa in 2011. It comes out, more often than not, on Wednesdays. Scotch-taped to the front door is a placard that reads, "Wendsler Nosie Tribal Chairman," with a drawing of Nosie in profile. Nosie completed his term as tribal chairman in 2010. During his years on the Tribal Council, he represented Peridot, the most populous of San Carlos's four districts.

There is a wicker chair on the front porch, and sometimes you find a tribal member there, waiting to ask Nosie for a favor, like help with an electric bill. In one corner of the living room hangs a large Oakland Raiders banner. Wendsler is a lifelong fan. The opposite corner is dedicated to the Arizona Cardinals, Theresa's team. Ceramic vases and Apache mountain spirit dancer figurines balance on a thin ledge high on the wall. There are leather couches and linoleum floors. Bookshelves hold graduation pictures, sports trophies, and archived editions of *The Apache Messenger*. Mail and other papers are tucked between spindles on the ascending treads of the staircase: a makeshift filing system. In the bathroom, a white cup holds 14 colorful toothbrushes. There are large framed photographs of the Nosie daughters and granddaughters celebrating their Sunrise Ceremonies. Children weave from room to room, watching television and goofing around.

Theresa Nosie is in the kitchen making acorn soup. Theresa grew up in Cameron, Arizona, on the Navajo reservation.

THERESA NOSIE: "My mother is Anglo—Irish, I think. She owned a trading post in Flagstaff. My dad had an account there.

He would buy groceries for his family

back on the Rez every week. Then

his brother got shot over in

a town called Eden.

That town doesn't

exist anymore.

My dad didn't

have a car,

so he asked her

if she could take

him to the funeral.

That's how they

got together."

The Nosies consider themselves to be at war with the United States. Yet Theresa has worked for the Internal Revenue Service for more than 30 years. She specializes in Indian tribal government tax compliance. Wendsler and Theresa first met at a "cultural day" held by the IRS.

WENDSLER NOSIE: "My niece invited me down to do a presentation. Theresa was the coordinator."

In 2007, while tribal chairman, Wendsler Nosie went to D.C. to testify before the House Subcommittee on Housing and Community Opportunity. "We are decades behind the surrounding areas in our ability to provide decent, safe, and sanitary home ownership opportunities for our tribal members," Nosie told the committee. Forty-three years after his mother built her Mutual Help house, the program had not fulfilled its promise. Nosie described the housing crisis in San Carlos. His presentation included a series of photographs from around the reservation that showed rudimentary structures in states of disrepair: bare plywood walls listing or splitting open, rotting eaves, ill-fitting tarps thrown over leaking roofs. Many homes lacked plumbing, telephone service, or electricity.

"Before I came to Washington," Nosie told the Committee, "I asked my mother, 'What can I say? What should I say?' She said, 'You know, the intent was good [with the Mutual Help houses] . . . but it seems like they idled off and have gone backward, because now many of our people need homes.'

"She asked me to ask you:

'What happened?'"

♦ ♦ ♦

JUST BEFORE AN APACHE GIRL'S SUNRISE DANCE, the girl constructs a traditional dome-shaped wickiup. The wickiup frame is assembled from local materials and oriented with its opening toward the rising sun. By building her wickiup, a girl proves she is a competent homemaker, able to provide shelter for her family. The wickiup is her home throughout the days of the ceremony. Today, when the Sunrise Dance is over, the wickiup is dismantled. In pre-reservation times, the wickiup that a girl built for her dance could become her actual home.

THERESA NOSIE: "If it was back in the day, she would be living in the house she built. The house lasted for a while and then they'd move, depending on the food availability and the safety of the area."

WENDSLER NOSIE: "We didn't originate from the reservation. We were never a desert people. We were a mountain people. We were marched in, or brought by covered wagon, and told, *This is your home now. This is where you have to raise your family.* For people who lived in the pine trees, who were accustomed to that kind of life, you come here, you don't know what's edible. There's nothing like what you find at Oak Flat, the foods, the medicine plants. And it gets up to 115, 117 degrees right here. I think everybody scratched their head and said, *Why do we live here?*"

Copper is strong and flexible. It can be manipulated into nearly any shape and drawn thin into filaments. Copper conducts electricity and heat. It is recyclable and resists corrosion.

A smartphone uses about 15 grams of copper. High-speed Internet connections depend on copper cable. Home heating systems and air conditioners depend on copper. Copper is antimicrobial. Surgeons use copper-plated scalpels that conduct heat and cauterize wounds. Some IUDs are made with copper. It has been reported that certain National Security Agency buildings have exteriors clad in copper to form an electromagnetic shield. Weapons systems rely on copper. Vehicles—trains, subways, airplanes—rely on copper.

Clean technologies generally require more copper than traditional technologies. Wind and solar use about four times more copper than conventional energy to generate one megawatt of power. The average conventional car requires up to 55 pounds of copper; an electric car uses triple that. Usage of copper has climbed dramatically in recent years. In 2017, the International Copper Study Group reported a global market for copper of 26 million tons. In the coming decades, we will need to dramatically increase usage of solar and wind power to keep global temperatures down. Mitigating planetary warming will almost certainly cause a further surge in demand for copper.

Worldwide, there is a vibrant trade in stolen copper. When commodity prices rise, so does the number of copper thefts. Small-time operators take utility wire, gutters, and funerary urns to scrap metal dealers who don't ask questions. Organized crime rings loot electrical substations, cell towers, railroads, water wells, and construction sites for copper, with implications for "the flow of electricity, telecommunications, transportation, water supply, heating, and security and emergency services," according to an unclassified FBI report. Between 2001 and 2008, the price of copper rose by more than 500 percent. China was on a building spree. Demand was up from other developing nations as well.

When the subprime mortgage crisis hit the United States, copper thieves used publicly available lists of foreclosed homes to systematically raid vacant houses and strip them of copper. On occasion, thieves snatched copper gas-line pipes.

With the gas left running

as the thieves fled,

some of these homes

later exploded.

CHAPTER 6

On Main Street in Superior, Arizona,

on a Thursday afternoon in August,

you can hear the hum of a solitary air conditioner.

Cicadas buzz, birds chirp.

It's very hot.

If you park your car and return to it later, every

object inside will be nearly untouchable.

A book left on the seat is cooked

like a slab of meat on a grill.

The sidewalks are empty, the buildings mostly

boarded up. The 300-foot smokestack of the defunct

Magma Copper smelter stands on a hill overlooking town.

The exterior of the *Superior Sun* newspaper office is

hand-painted with Gothic lettering and stylized palm

trees. A sign hangs on the door:

"Closed until further notice."

Among the few operating storefronts on Main Street is the cheery Sun Flour Mart, a café and secondhand shop offering "Quality Products, Old-Fashioned Prices." Across the street, Copper Triangle Mining Services sells mining equipment, used books, stuffed animals, and the highly polished obsidian nuggets mined locally and marketed as Apache Tears. The stones are said to "help release negative emotions" and bring good luck.

Resolution Copper's headquarters in Superior sits at 402 West Main Street. The office is modest, with cubicles and a pressed tin ceiling. A 3-D topographical map of the area and the proposed mine occupies most of one wall.

Main Street climbs uphill until it dead-ends into the pink stucco arches of the Pinal County Administrative Building. Cypress trees jut into the sky; behind them, the Apache Leap cliffs loom. The setting is cinematic. Superior appears in *The Gauntlet* with Clint Eastwood and *How the West Was Won* with Gregory Peck and Henry Fonda. In Oliver Stone's 1997 Wild West noir *U Turn,* Sean Penn's car breaks down in Superior, where he gets sucked into a deadly love triangle with Jennifer Lopez and Nick Nolte.

Your cell phone vibrates: *Dust storm warning until 4 p.m.* You look up and see a man with pale blue eyes and a cowboy hat on a wooden bench in front of the Superior Chamber of Commerce. Next to him sits a tiny woman with white hair. She leans back and laughs. You don't live around here, and when you walk by, you are conspicuous.

"Where you from?"

"Have a seat."

The blue-eyed man is Michael McKee. Everyone in Superior knows that on Thursdays, Mike works at the Chamber, and people come by to reminisce, catch up on community news, and gossip. The woman by his side, Patricia Brown, is his aunt. The two are close.

MICHAEL McKEE:

"The only people in town we don't know is if they moved here yesterday."

PATRICIA BROWN:

"But then, we're starting to know them."

In the summer of 2018, uncertainty still hung over the proposed Resolution Copper mine. But the company could be felt in nearly every aspect of Superior's civic life. Resolution has invested millions of dollars in the town. Resolution funds community festivals, summer swim days, photo contests, and parental education at the First Pregnancy Care Center. The company supports academics, athletics, and a nature club in local schools. Resolution also contributes to the budgets of Superior's fire department, police department, and other emergency services. When Superior buys a new ambulance, the town invoices Resolution Copper.

A blue Dodge Ram pickup pulls up to the curb and a man in his eighties with a plaid shirt and a slight limp gets out of the driver's side. Jackie Gorham. A woman with short grey hair, wearing a turquoise cross on a chain, shuts the passenger-side door. Jackie's wife, Evelyn. Jackie Gorham is Patricia Brown's older brother and Mike McKee's uncle. Jackie and Evelyn step onto the sidewalk. A few minutes later, Deb McKee, Mike's wife, arrives.

The family has deep roots in Superior. Patricia and Jackie's maternal grandfather was George Westfall, a miner and a prospector, and later a judge, born in Galena, Illinois, in 1850. As a young man Westfall made his way to California, and, in 1874, drove a 16-mule team across the desert from Los Angeles to Mineral Park, Arizona. He followed the Klondike gold rush to Alaska, with little luck.

JACKIE GORHAM: "It was too late when he got there."

JACKIE GORHAM

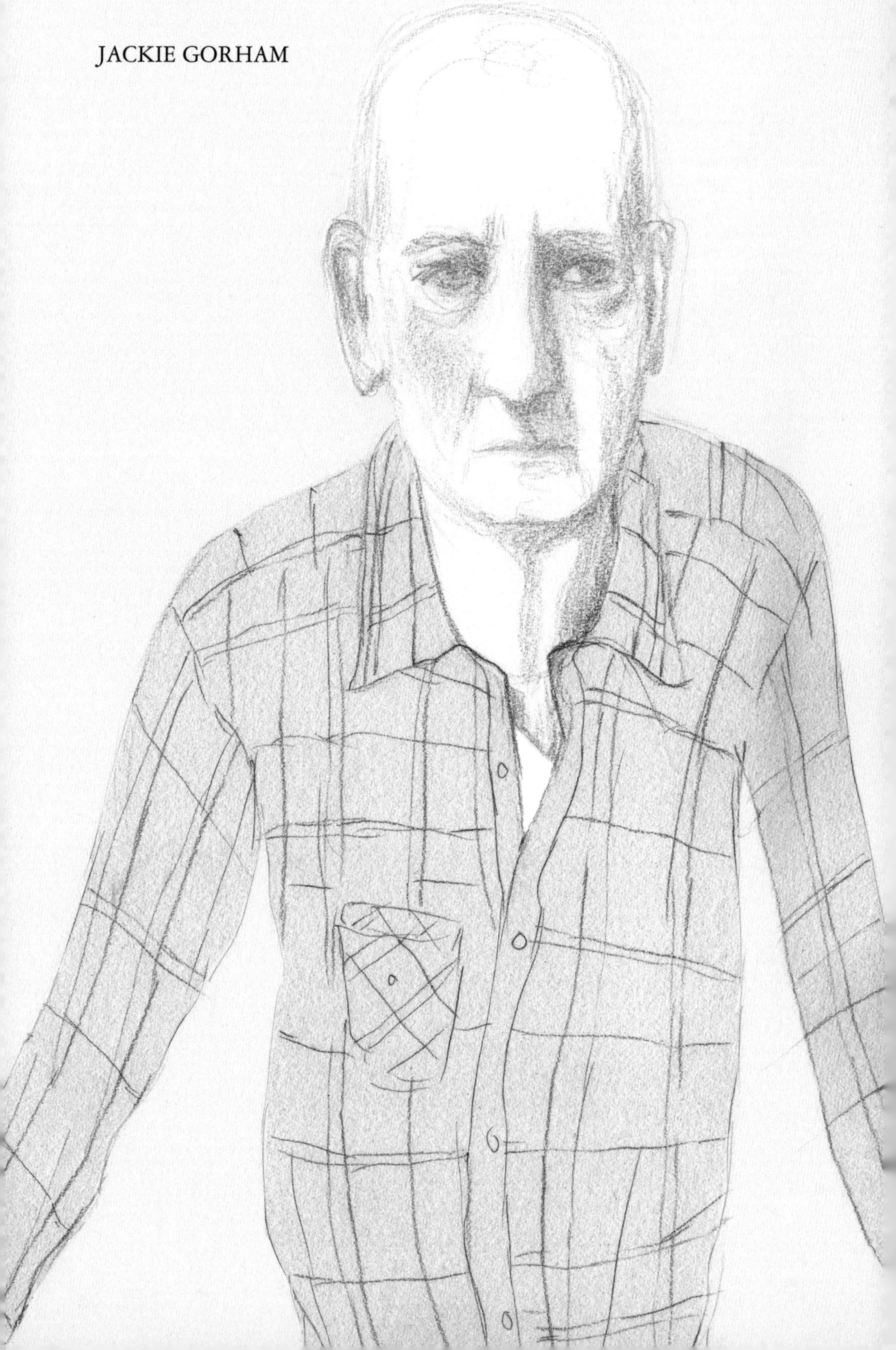

Westfall returned to the Arizona Territory, became manager of a copper mine in Casa Grande, moved on to the Reymert mine nine miles from Superior, and, through the government's Homestead Act, acquired 160 acres of land, where he raised chickens and hogs and grew alfalfa. While working at the Reymert coke ovens, he met a Mexican woman named Maria Concepcion Yepiz.

MARIA AND GEORGE WESTFALL

Maria was 25, George was 40. He spoke no Spanish, she spoke no English. They married in 1890 and had seven children. The second was a little girl with dark eyes and dark hair named Mollie. A little brother, Frank, was bitten by a rattlesnake at age nine.

JACKIE GORHAM: "They couldn't do anything but just sit there and watch him die."

Patricia and Jackie's paternal grandfather, Peter Gorham, was also a miner. He and his wife, Ann, had come separately from Ireland. Ann's ship was called the *Odyssey*. Peter sailed on the SS *Kangaroo*.

JACKIE GORHAM: "He came on the *Kangaroo* to New York. That was the same ship that they used to haul the Irish to Australia, the convicts and the Catholics and everything."

Peter made his way to Pennsylvania where he worked in a coal mine. He and Ann raised five children, including a son named Patrick.

PETER GORHAM   ANN GORHAM

PATRICIA BROWN: "Something happened in the mine—a cave-in? I don't know—but Peter Gorham got killed in that mine. The company pulled him up and threw his body on the doorstep."

For Peter's son Patrick, it was a turning point.

PATRICIA BROWN: "Daddy said, 'That's it.'"

JACKIE GORHAM: "He decided he did not want that life, so he packed up and went west."

But mining was hard to escape. A gold-mining job brought Patrick Gorham first to Lead, near Deadwood, South Dakota, and then around 1900 to Bisbee, Arizona, where he worked at the Copper Queen mine before becoming a guard at the state prison in the town of Florence. Later, he worked as a bodyguard for Arizona's first governor, George W. P. Hunt. When Gorham was 42, he met Mollie Westfall, 21, who had a job at the Florence post office. They married in 1917 and

MOLLIE WESTFALL GORHAM

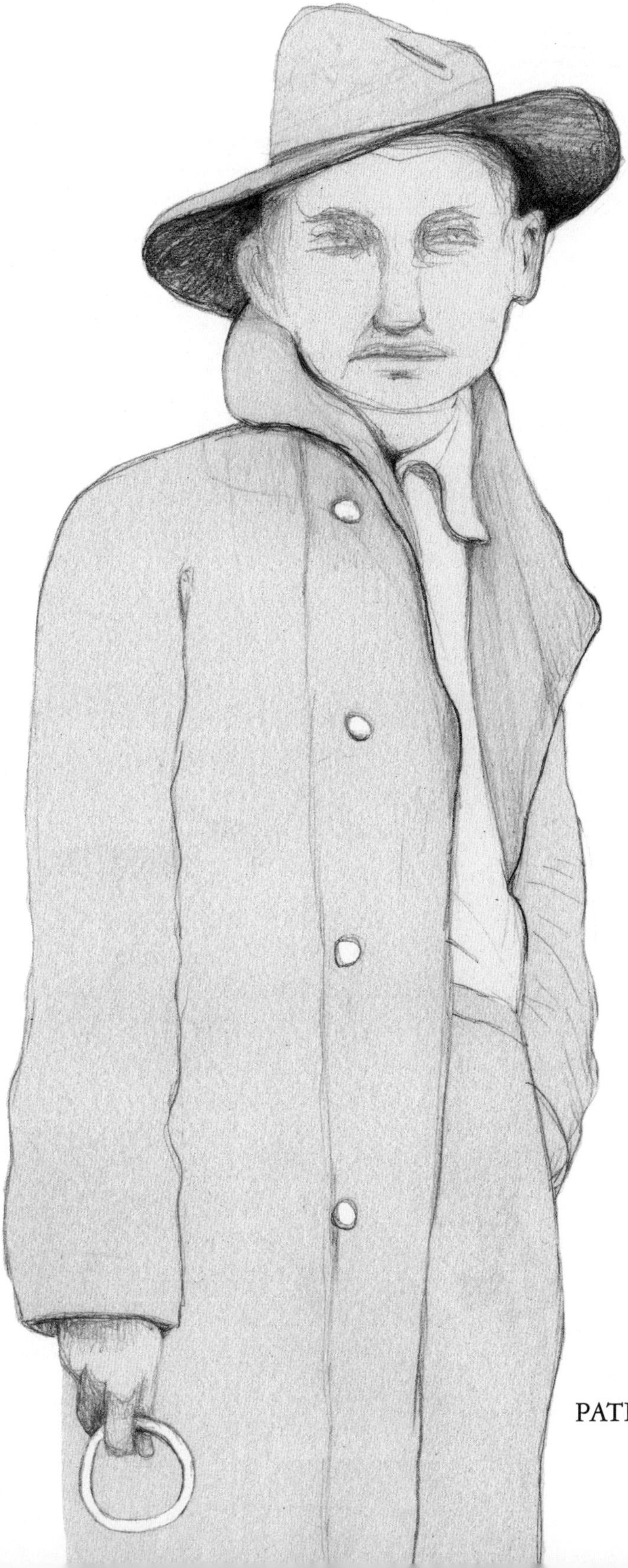

PATRICK GORHAM

by 1939 had 11 children: Mary, Patrick, Peter, Barbara, James, Thomas, Loretta, John, Daniel, Phillip, and Patricia. Most of the kids had nicknames. Phillip was Pinky, Patrick Jr. was Patsy. John was called Jackie.

JACKIE GORHAM: "Pinky died at two of diphtheria. Patsy was killed in France in the Battle of Saint Lô."

Loretta's nickname was Bebe, Patricia was Tinka. Tommy was Rattlesnake.

PATRICIA BROWN: "When we all ate at a dinner table, we could not talk. Dinner was to eat. Our dad was at one end, my mom at the other, and all of us around. It was silent."

JACKIE GORHAM: "Daddy showed us how to box, and he let us box on the porch. He'd say, 'The winner gets the teeth!' and he'd push his false teeth out with his tongue."

PATRICIA BROWN: "He just had to look at us and we walked a straight line. Mama was the one that carried the stick."

MICHAEL McKEE: "She was mean, but she was the type of woman that didn't waste anything. When I was a kid, she'd tell me, 'Go get that turkey out of the coop.' I'd get it, and we'd hang it up and we'd kill it. We'd have boiling water, and we'd pluck it and gut it. Same thing when we had to kill a cow. She ate the brains, the tongue, the eyeballs, the milk glands, the stomach, I mean, she ate everything. If she didn't want you to know what she was talking about, she'd talk in Spanish."

PATRICIA BROWN: "She cooked cactus with green chili or scrambled eggs. Anytime we'd have leftover tongue, she would grind it and make cockles. Michael and his sisters would come over and say, 'What is it, Grandma?'

"'It's meat.'

"'Okay. We'll eat it.'"

◆ ◆ ◆

IN 1873, A SOLDIER working on the construction of a road just north of Oak Flat discovered black lumps of silver. The area was part of the traditional homelands of various Native tribes, including the Hohokam, the Salado, the Yavapai, and the Apache. Fortune-seekers staked claims and two mines were built, the Silver King and the Silver Queen. By the turn of the century, the value of silver had plummeted, the mineral veins were nearly exhausted, and the silver mines closed. Prospectors in the area turned to copper. A Michigan firm called the Lake Superior & Arizona Mining Company invested, and the tent communities where silver miners had lived—Pinal, Hastings—were dismantled. By 1902, the place had a new name: Superior. The Magma Copper Company was established in 1910. Between 1912 and 1996, the Magma mine yielded 1.3 million tons of copper. The town of Superior grew up around the mine. Businesses were established, children born and raised. Superior existed to support the Magma Copper Mine, and the mine sustained the community.

Superior was often violent.

MICHAEL McKEE: "There used to be 22 bars in this town."

PATRICIA BROWN: "There was the 'Bucket o' Blood.' You know why they called it Bucket o' Blood? Because in the morning, before they opened up, they'd have buckets of water and clean the blood from the night before off the sidewalks. Fights."

Which bar was the wildest?

MICHAEL McKEE: "All of them."

In 1918, Superior was looking for a sheriff and Patrick Gorham was offered the job. Patrick, Mollie, and seven-month-old Mary arrived in town on November 11.

JACKIE GORHAM: "When they came into Superior, miners were in the streets shouting and shooting their weapons into the air."

Mollie thought that her family was being welcomed with great fanfare. In fact, the town was celebrating the signing of the Armistice by Germany and the Allied powers. World War I was over.

The work of a sheriff in Arizona in 1918 was improvisational. Vigilante justice was common. When Patrick Gorham became Superior's sheriff, Arizona had been a state for just six years. There was no other elected official in town. Gorham made up the law and he enforced it.

PATRICIA BROWN: "There was no mayor, no police department. He ran the show here."

MICHAEL McKEE: "It was the rip-roaring days. If you didn't say, 'Yes sir, no sir' to him, he'd knock the crap out of you."

PATRICIA BROWN: "One time, some gamblers, professionals, about five of them, came up here from Phoenix and tried to take over the gambling in bars—all the bars had gambling, because the miners liked to gamble. Daddy rounded them up and took them out here to Gonzales Pass. You gotta remember, the road was dirt. He took them up there, took off their shoes, tied their hands behind their backs, pushed them out of the car, and said, 'Get to Phoenix and don't come back.'"

Another time, a man known as Star Daley was arrested for murdering a traveling salesman and raping his wife. Locals were incensed about the crime. As Daley was being moved from one jail to another, some 50 men, masked in white handkerchiefs, intercepted the convoy, snatched the prisoner, and brought him back to the scene of the crime to administer their own punishment. The *Arizona Daily Star* reported that Daley himself "showed a member of the mob how to make a noose" and only lost his composure when the group "recited the Lord's prayer in unison for him." After the lynching, someone called Patrick Gorham. Gorham arrived and cut the dead man down from the telephone pole where he hung. But then reporters appeared and asked that Daley be strung up again, so they could get a photograph.

JACKIE GORHAM: "Pat hung him back up. Everyone posed for pictures."

THE HANGING OF STAR DALEY

Jackie Gorham maintains the family photos and papers.

JACKIE GORHAM: "This here is my dad's time book, okay? If you look at the thing, all these charges are women, fined for 'Vagrancy.' The fines were ten cents. They were whores, working the street. Then the fines stop suddenly, because the mining company told him to leave them alone. They were keeping the miners happy."

PATRICIA BROWN: "If the miners got in trouble, Daddy would throw the guys in jail, but he'd get them out in time to go to work so they didn't lose a shift. The county paid Daddy, and the mining company paid him, too, to make sure that there were no problems. And he was getting money from the Belmont Hotel. That used to get my mom so mad."

DEB McKEE: "Because the Belmont was the house of ill repute."

The building that for decades housed the Belmont Hotel stands at 271 West Main Street. Posed in an empty lot next door are boulders, pockmarked with circular cavities. This is where Superior's annual Apache Leap Festival miners' drilling competition is held. Competition entrants are each given a jackleg drill and assigned a square in grids drawn on the boulders.

JACKIE GORHAM: "Whoever drills deepest in one minute wins."

The former Belmont Hotel is a narrow three-story structure. Wiry grasses grow around the walls and poke out in tufts through the cracks in the back door.

PATRICIA BROWN: "My dad made things safe for the girls. The madam was Bessie O'Brien. Bessie O'Brien used to buy all my clothes. I had a beautiful white fur coat with a muff and little hat from her."

JACKIE GORHAM: "First time I went up there, I was 14."

MICHAEL McKEE: "Jackie was a frequent visitor."

PATRICIA BROWN: "He said it cost three dollars."

JACKIE GORHAM: "Then they raised it up to five dollars.

"I was in high school. The girls were ordinary people, making a living. Just like the miners, going underground."

PATRICIA BROWN: "They were beautiful women."

JACKIE GORHAM:

"One morning I was having breakfast. Mama was sitting there. She said, 'You were up in the Belmont.' And I said, 'How did you know?' She says, 'I know.'

It didn't dawn on me till later. She could smell the perfume on me."

BELMONT HOTEL, SUPERIOR, ARIZONA

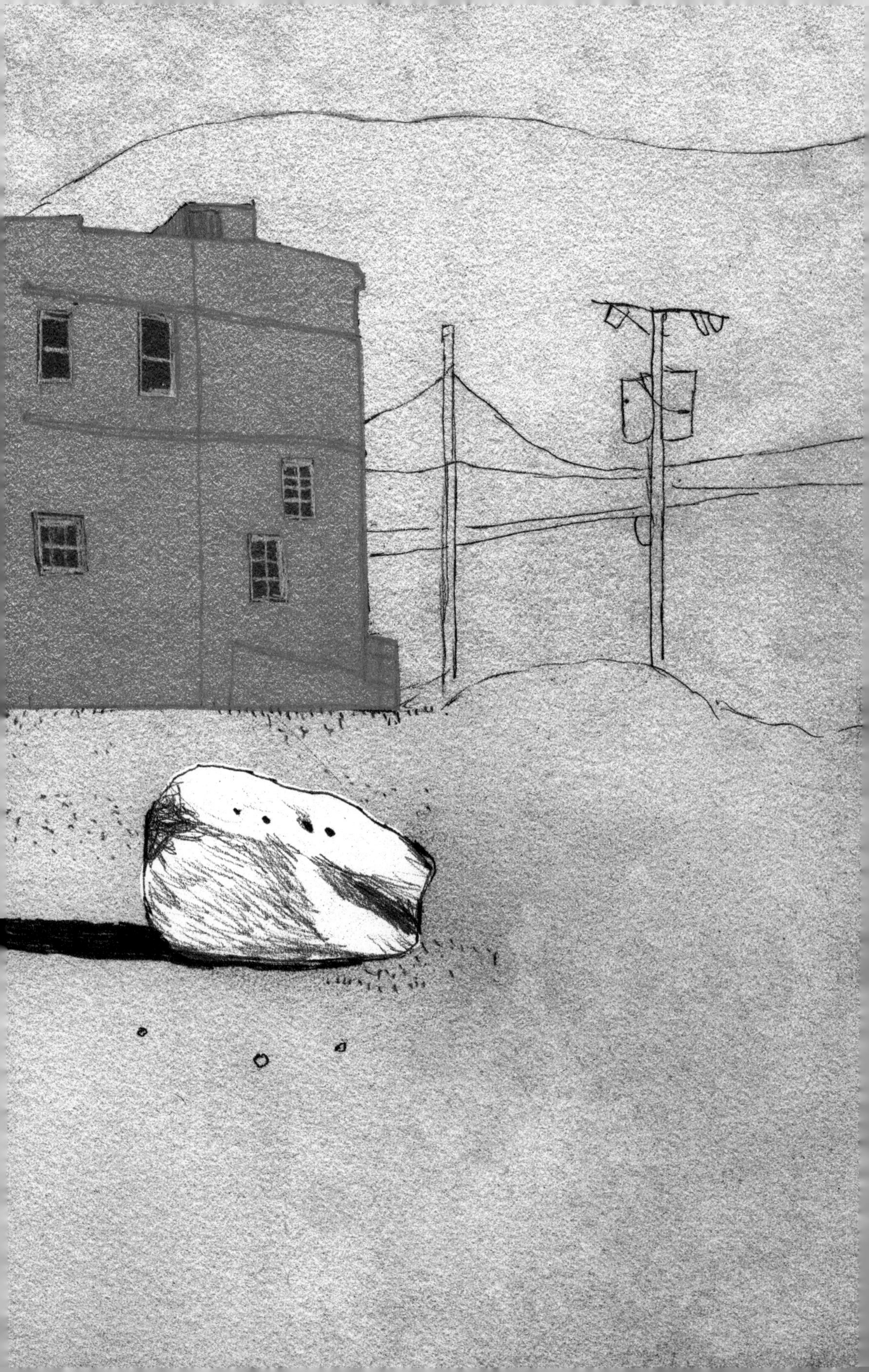

JACKIE GORHAM: "The girls didn't talk to you on the street. That was forbidden. I never questioned them about what brought them to Superior. For some reason you didn't do that. Every Thursday before payday—payday was Friday—they were taken to Dr. Boozer's and checked for venereal disease."

MICHAEL McKEE: "They'd walk from the hotel down there, all in a line, straight up Main Street to the doctor."

JACKIE GORHAM: "Then they'd go in the drugstore and eat a hamburger. If you were in there, they would not acknowledge you. They would look straight ahead. They'd get through eating and march right back to the hotel."

MICHAEL McKEE: "Dr. Boozer had his little office on the side over there. He used to say something in Spanish, something about an enema. He did abortions and he got sent up for it."

PATRICIA BROWN: "There were steps in the back of the Belmont, and we lived right across. We could sit at our kitchen window and see men go up the back stairs."

MICHAEL McKEE: "We'd always see these guys go to the back door and knock. They'd give this lady some money, go in, and they'd come out smiling. When we were kids, this friend of mine, Albo Guzman, and I went and stole Coke bottles, and we got 75 cents, and we knocked on the door. The lady came out and we handed her the 75 cents. She grabbed us by the head and—*pow*—smashed us together. My friend goes, 'I'm sure glad I didn't get a dollar's worth.'"

JACKIE GORHAM: "All the mining communities had a brothel."

Mila Besich-Lira is mayor of Superior.

MILA BESICH-LIRA: "I worked in the Belmont later, when they turned it into an office building. Before, there were no windows on the downstairs part.

"When they made it an office building, they put in windows, and my window was by the handicap ramp on the side. This little old lady came and she starts pounding on the window, 'You let me in. You let me in. I know he's in there. You make him come out.' We went and opened the side door. She's like, 'I know you have my husband in here. You need to let him out.' We showed her around, and we were like, 'Ma'am, it's an office building now.'"

PATRICIA BROWN: "I think the Belmont closed in the late '50s."

MILA BESICH-LIRA: "We could fix our budget problem, if we could just bring it back."

◆ ◆ ◆

ARIZONA'S STATE SEAL depicts one human figure above a vast landscape: a miner, holding a pickaxe and a shovel. He looks a little disheveled and holds his tools awkwardly. A red sun burns on the horizon. Above the drawing of the miner and the sun is the Latin phrase *DITAT DEUS*, "God enriches."

But Arizona's mining towns are poor.

The towns close to Superior—Kearny, Winkelman, Hayden—are tiny enclaves full of abandoned buildings and "For Rent" signs. Kearny was created as a company town when the nearby Asarco Ray mine's open pit expanded in the 1950s. Kearny's wide main street, Alden Road, dead-ends in a cliff with a sprawling view of undeveloped desert below. Fewer than 400 people live in Winkelman, a quarter of them below the poverty line.

The movie theater in Hayden hasn't screened a film since 1979. For years, people in town complained about "clouds of blue smoke" coming from the Hayden smelter, a refining facility for copper ore from the Asarco Ray mine. In 2007, an Environmental Protection Agency investigation found the Hayden smelter was emitting illegal levels of lead and arsenic. In 2015, the EPA and the Justice Department announced a $150 million settlement with Asarco requiring the company to install pollution control technology. The area was later declared a Superfund site.

In Superior, residents remember pools of "blood red" water collecting on the hillside near the Magma mine smelter. The smell of sulfur permeated streets and backyards. Arsenic dust wafted over Superior and settled into the soil. Arsenic and lead accumulated in piles of mine waste, known as tailings. Fourteen million tons of tailings sat untreated for decades, until Resolution Copper arrived and began a multimillion-dollar cleanup effort. David Lira, a cousin of Mayor Besich-Lira, worked for Magma for 48 years. His daughters attended the Harding elementary school, located just below the Magma smelter. Cheryl Lira-Castro is David's daughter, the middle child of three Lira sisters.

CHERYL LIRA-CASTRO: "That was before the days when they had the EPA. I can still taste that sulfur. You'd be out in the playground for recess or P.E. and they're like, 'Go inside.'"

MICHAEL McKEE: "When we walked to school as kids, you'd cough and your eyes would burn because of the sulfur. But we grew up with it. We knew how to handle it. We didn't play that hard when it was real thick and heavy.

"We went to an environmental meeting recently, and this one kid got up and said, 'Arsenic causes cancer.' I told him, 'No, it doesn't. It kills you, stupid!'"

Mike McKee worked for 24 years as a mechanic "in the pit" of the Ray mine. In 2002, he was diagnosed with multiple myeloma.

MICHAEL McKEE: "It's kind of like leukemia. It's in the blood and in the bones. Mine is caused by petroleum products, welding, painting, gasoline, oil—everything I did."

McKee holds no grudge against the mining company.

MICHAEL McKEE: "Everything in the world causes cancer. At the mine, you were making 21 dollars an hour. Good money. Plus the insurance. You can't beat the insurance. We've lived a good life with our retirement and especially the insurance. I don't regret it one bit."

JACKIE GORHAM: "We all worked for the mine."

PATRICIA BROWN: "I did. My daughter did."

JACKIE GORHAM: "I worked in the smelter. Tommy worked in the smelter. Patsy worked in the smelter. Pete worked in the smelter. Danny worked in the smelter. I think it takes a certain person to enjoy working in the smelter. You're breathing this nasty gas all day long. I was a welder, and then I ran the crew. It would be so gassy sometimes that your eyes would just burn."

EVELYN GORHAM: "The heat is unbelievable."

JACKIE GORHAM: "I would never tell Evelyn what I did at work. Imagine the oven in your kitchen, only it's the size of a huge house, and built out of brick. Brick walls, brick on the top. On the sides of the brick wall, you have what you call chutes. The concentrate—the ore—comes down into those, and into the furnace. Sometimes a brick from the roof would fall in. You would have to replace the brick—with the flames shooting up. The heat could melt the steelwork. You'd be up on top, hanging on to one of the rods that supported the bricks. If that ever collapsed underneath you, you were in molten metal right away. You were dead. But we did that all the time. I never told her any of that. I saw three people get killed. One of them fell off 30 feet down. Another one got burned to death. Molten metal slapped on him.

"What was the third one? I can't remember. But I rode the ambulance with two of them. One of them breathed his last breath just as we went out the gate headed for the hospital. You just forget about it. Just forget about it."

EVELYN GORHAM: "I worked everywhere. I worked at the company hospital. I worked in personnel and HR.

I worked at the refinery.

I worked at the smelter.

I worked at engineering.

And I ended up working

at the SX/EW plant.

Solvent extraction and

electrowinning.

Twenty-two years

altogether."

EVELYN GORHAM

JACKIE GORHAM: "Thirty-six for me. I went underground when I was first hired on."

EVELYN GORHAM: "It's pitch-black."

Nine men at a time were lowered into the tunnels in a three-foot-by-three-foot metal cage. A hoist man controlled the speed.

Cheryl Lira-Castro got her first job with Magma at 17. She worked in the framing shed, cutting timber. Her older sister shoveled ore at Magma's mill. Her younger sister worked in human resources.

CHERYL LIRA-CASTRO: "If your parents worked for the mine, they'd help you get a job for the summer. You could work all summer, making 14 dollars an hour."

At 21, Cheryl became a timekeeper at Magma's No. 9 shaft. Each miner was assigned a number, which was engraved on a small brass plate. When a man began a shift, he would "brass in," collecting his time card in exchange for handing over his brass ID. At the end of the shift, he would ascend to the surface, return his time card, and retrieve his brass.

CHERYL LIRA-CASTRO: "At the end of the day, they're running through, you see their face, know their name, and give them their brass back. But if the brass was still there, *Where's that man?* There were guys that would call me from underground, lost. Their lamp went out, they couldn't see. They would be touching their face, screaming, crying, 'I can't see, I can't see.'"

JACKIE GORHAM: "We'd go down there and we'd go this way, turn that way, go this way, come back that way. All of a sudden we were back where we started, and I don't know how in the hell we got there."

At lunchtime, miners would pull out a small plank of wood to sit on. Some would bring a thermos of *agua de gallo*—rooster water—a spicy fortified broth. Family recipes varied. You might start with chicken or beef stock, or tomato juice, then add beans, onions, garlic, chili peppers.

MICHAEL McKEE: "Agua de gallo was hot. It lit you up."

After lunch, the men would turn off their lights, lie back, and doze for 10, 15 minutes.

Water dripped from the tunnel walls and ceiling. When the men switched their lamps back on, dozens of cockroaches that had crept out in the darkness would skitter for cover.

DAVID LIRA: "The mine makes noises. The ground heaves, it creaks. An experienced person learns to be down there by sound."

Superior's retired miners talk about "tommyknockers," phantoms they encountered in the mine. Sometimes it was just a sensation—something you felt on your body, or a presence nearby. A Magma miner named John Sixsmith told friends he saw white boots, walking around without a body. To meet a tommyknocker was not frightening. These benevolent spirits might warn you about loose rocks or an imminent cave-in.

EVELYN GORHAM: "When I started in the employment office, after I'd been in there for, I don't know, maybe six months, they wanted me to start interviewing applicants. I said, 'I can interview applicants for the smelter, for all the plant, but I don't know what the hell I'm talking about when it comes to underground.' I said, 'You want us to interview applicants to see if they're able? We should go underground.' So we did. We went through every part of underground. We climbed ladders. We went on trams. We crossed grizzlies, which is pretty scary. After that, I could paint a picture to an applicant, what they were getting into. These kids, they're high school graduates, they're college suits, summer hires, whatever. They have no clue. They're from Tucson. They're from Green Valley. Most kids that age—they think they know everything. I thought I knew everything at that age. So you paint a picture for them, tell them what the job entails. Some of them, I could just tell, they weren't going to make it. I'd tell them exactly how narrow those ladders were, how big the cages were, how they shook on the way down, how dark it was, how crossing this grizzly—which was like railroad ties about a foot apart, where all the ore drops through, tons and tons of rocks and boulders and dirt—you can go down one of those grizzlies, you can land in the car that's collecting it, end up in the smelter before anybody knows you're gone. You paint *that* picture. What it means to go down there and sweat buckets. You just tell them what it entails."

JACKIE GORHAM: "A load of steel fell on me. January the third, 1961. It busted my shinbone. There wasn't a lot of safety then. Bone came out like *this,* and the bone in back was broken in two places. I got to the hospital, they took me into X-ray, and cut away my pants. I said, 'Is the bone sticking out of the skin?' They said, 'Yeah, you wanna look at it?' I said, 'No, I don't want to look at it!' I went into surgery, and they put pins in and everything.

"The next morning, the doctor came in there, Dr. Fenman, and he said, 'Can you move your toes?' I said, 'Yeah, I can move them.' 'Let me see.' He stood there for a while, and finally he said, 'Okay.' He turned and walked off. The nurse was there. I said, 'What was going on?' And she said, 'If you couldn't move your toes, he was going to amputate.'"

EVELYN GORHAM: "You had no options. It was the company doctor. Period. This guy was in the MASH unit during the war. He was an improviser."

JACKIE GORHAM: "I spent five months in the hospital. Eleven months I was in a cast. They paid me 60 percent of my wages, then I went back to work on what they called 'light duty.'"

EVELYN GORHAM: "Not everybody who got injured got hired back, though. When I was in HR, there were a lot of people that got hurt really bad, and they were not able to go to work within the year, and there was automatic termination. They were called in and told, 'We're sorry. You're unable to return to work, and we have to terminate your employment.'"

◆ ◆ ◆

EVERY MINE HAS AN ANTICIPATED "LIFE SPAN." It takes a certain amount of time to build the infrastructure of the mine, and then there is a period during which resources are extracted. Finally, there is the period called reclamation, during which affected lands are meant to be rehabilitated: contaminants neutralized, topsoil replaced, topography restored. Mining is, by definition, an enterprise with diminishing returns. Once the resources are removed, the mine shuts down. A mine can close sooner if, for instance, commodity prices drop. According to historian Patricia Nelson Limerick,

"Mining set a mood that has never disappeared from the West: the attitude of extractive industry—get in, get rich, get out."

When Magma shut down in 1996, Superior changed. Half the town's residents left.

MILA BESICH-LIRA: "You really started to see the community take its first major nosedive."

Both of Besich-Lira's parents were laid off from the mine. They divorced later that year.

PATRICIA BROWN: "There was no one on the streets, because everyone left. The theater closed. The drugstores closed. The clothing stores closed."

But families like the Gorhams did not consider leaving.

MICHAEL McKEE: "Life goes on, you know. The diehard people weathered the storm."

With Magma closed, there were few options for employment. Some people got jobs at other mines in the area. Others found work in Florence, a half-hour drive away, at either the Arizona State Prison complex or the detention center run by U.S. Immigration and Customs Enforcement (ICE).

PATRICIA BROWN: "My sister, Barbara, worked at the prison. I worked for the one lawyer in town."

MICHAEL McKEE: "Until they killed him."

PATRICIA BROWN: "He raised gardens of roses. Rows and rows of roses. All different colors. One of the guys who worked in the garden robbed and murdered him. Cut his head off. They found the head—"

MICHAEL McKEE: "—in the mineshaft."

PATRICIA BROWN: "They found his car in Mexico."

CHAPTER 7

"When I was pregnant, each time, I knew it was a girl."

VANESSA NOSIE

Vanessa Nosie, the eldest of Wendsler Nosie's seven children, is one of six sisters. She is a single mom to three daughters,

Naelyn,

Baasé-O,

Nizhoni.

VANESSA

VANESSA NOSIE: "I always wanted Apache names. *Naelyn* means 'girl' in Apache. So when I named her with her father, we thought, *she's our first girl,* so we named her 'girl.'"

NAELYN

"When I had Nizhoni, I wanted another Apache name, but it's hard, you know, the language, the pronunciation. I worried about my kids at school. I was telling my grandma, 'I already picked a name.' At first she was like, 'You're not supposed to do that.' But I said, 'Just in case, I've been thinking: *Nizhoni*.'"

In Apache, *nizhoni* means "pretty," or "beautiful."

VANESSA NOSIE: "And she goes, *'Beautiful!* It's a girl. Beautiful.' And so she's *Nizhoni,* which she is.

NIZHONI

"Then Baasé-O. My grandparents called me Baasé. It's from a song in a ceremony where we dance with the hoop. *Baasé* means 'hoop.' She's named after me, for that song."

BAASÉ-O

The girls' father is Willie Pike, a Tonto Apache who lives on the San Carlos Reservation. When the children were young, Vanessa and Willie divorced. Vanessa and the girls lived off the reservation in Mesa, Arizona—"in the Valley," as the greater Phoenix area is called. Vanessa commuted to a job back in San Carlos at the Apache Gold Casino.

VANESSA NOSIE: "I paid out jackpots.

"Because we chose to stay out in the Valley, I worried about my daughters becoming assimilated, not knowing their identity. I took them home every chance I got."

Trips home meant visits to San Carlos, and to other ancestral lands not on the reservation.

VANESSA NOSIE: "I especially took them to Oak Flat."

NAELYN PIKE: "There's life in the city and there's life on the reservation. When you go to a reservation it's totally different. It's like a third world country. We were the only brown kids in our schools. I was known as 'that little Native girl with the really long hair.'"

VANESSA NOSIE: "Down to the middle of her thigh."

NAELYN PIKE: "I had to cut my hair to my shoulders when my great-grandfather passed away, and then for my dad's grandmother. I cut it out of respect for them. When I had long hair, I always got, 'You look like Pocahontas.' I'm like, 'I'm not no Pocahontas.' Some teachers and students would say all we do is gamble or that we are liars or stuff like that. When I was smaller, I would just look at them, like, *Forget you*. As I got older, I realized people just do it without thinking."

After her Sunrise Dance, Naelyn was possessed by a new kind of drive.

VANESSA NOSIE: "One time after her ceremony she was like, 'Mom, I want to talk.' I was in the shower. She's like, 'Mom, I want to talk to you!' I'm like, 'Can you wait?' 'No!' So I open the door. She was in her freshman year at Chandler High. She said, 'I went to the Native American Club. We were supposed to make fake Indian jewelry and we're all going to be diabetics 'cause they're just feeding us junk and sugar.'"

Naelyn wanted to start her own intertribal youth organization.

VANESSA NOSIE: "I said, 'Okay, did you write down your pros and cons? You need to write out a statement.' I said, 'Naelyn, you put in the work, I'll support you.'"

The group Naelyn started, Native Youth Unite, began meeting shortly after.

VANESSA NOSIE: "That's when she decided to move back to San Carlos to be a part of Oak Flat and everything going on with the Stronghold."

After the land transfer legislation passed, Naelyn and Nizhoni went to live with their dad. Naelyn was 14, Nizhoni 12. The Apache Stronghold movement already occupied much of their time. They transferred to the public high school in Globe, where Vanessa and Wendsler had been students. To catch the school bus, they woke up at 4 a.m. Baasé-O stayed with Vanessa.

NAELYN PIKE: "When Nizhoni and I moved back to San Carlos, we dressed very different from a lot of girls. We were looked at kind of weird at first, you know? We dressed with the trends, more shorts and dresses, sandals or heels. Living in the city, you kind of just go with the trend. But we put a lot of Native thought into it."

NIZHONI PIKE: "We wore turquoise. Naelyn wore her beads."

NAELYN PIKE: "Trends go by fast. Today I could be wearing this shirt—this is cute—but tomorrow it's like, *That is so old.* Everything is going so fast, but in San Carlos it's slower. Even in Globe, everything's different. Because we are basketball players, we wear long Nike socks, to our knees. When we were in middle school, we would wear double Nike socks, so the two swooshes would be showing. You go to Globe and that's kind of the new thing still. You see that and you're like, *Oh my gosh. So old.*

"Nizhoni likes to do fashion. Baasé-O dresses more like a Rez girl."

BAASÉ-O PIKE: "A Rez girl would wear, like, T-shirts and jeans every day."

NAELYN PIKE: "Me and Nizhoni are pretty girly. 'Zhoni is the girliest. Baasé is the tomboy out of all three of us. Me, I don't know what I am, actually. I'm a Gemini.

"There are not that many stores on the reservation. When they created the reservations, the government intended for us to be far away from everybody. Because, you know, we're 'savages.' They wanted to kill us off."

The girls chronicle their lives on social media. On Instagram they post selfies, photos of shopping excursions, driver's ed class, French class, SAT prep books. They document home facials, test new hairstyles, record trips to Starbucks to buy frothy drinks, shoot slo-mo skateboarding videos and time-lapse dance videos. There are basketball team pictures. There are photos of holidays and milestones: birthdays, honor roll ceremonies, graduation. There are photos of Naelyn's senior prom. (The theme of the prom is "The Great Gatsby." Naelyn and Nizhoni are dressed as flappers.) There are photos at Oak Flat, or, as the girls sometimes call it, "The O."

NIZHONI:
"We like indie pop,
indie rock."

NAELYN: "Hip-hop. R&B.
Baasé-O listens to rap.
Insane in the membrane . . . "

BAASÉ-O: "Old school."

NAELYN: "We like a lot of Native rap.
We just don't like music that's all about booty
and money. Nizhoni's
in love with David Bowie."

NIZHONI: "He was my first true love."

NAELYN: "That old man could've been
your grandpa."

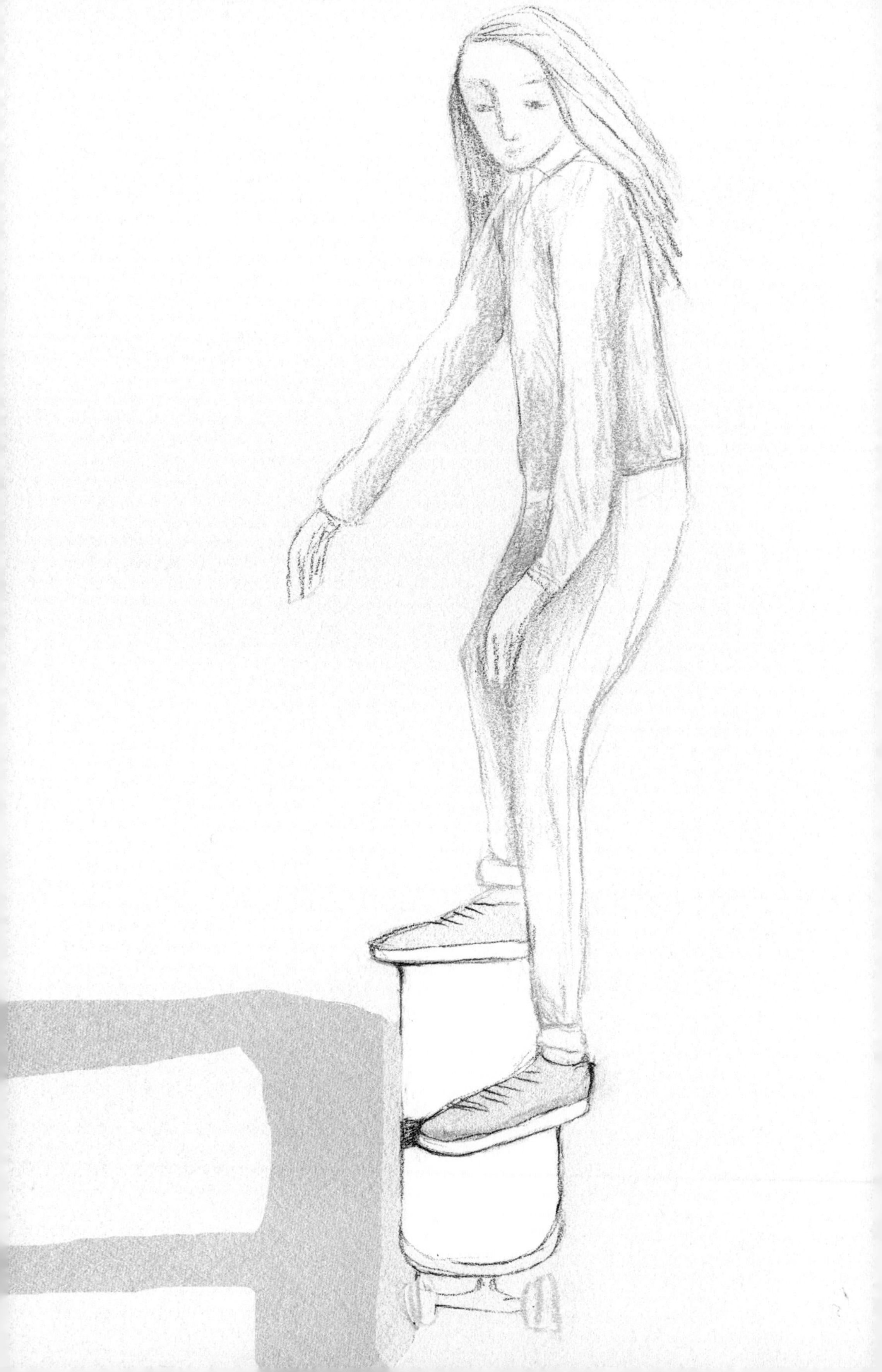

On ceremonial occasions, the girls wear traditional Chiricahua moccasins, leather to the knee with a turned-up flap at the toe, and "camp dress," loose cotton blouses with gathered sleeves and long, full skirts. Naelyn generally wears traditional dress if she is speaking in public. During the 2016 presidential race, Senator Bernie Sanders invited Naelyn to address a campaign rally he held in Tucson. After introducing herself in Apache, Naelyn spoke in English. "I come from a place called Oak Flat," she began. Not long after, she posted a photo on Instagram of an urban streetscape with high-rises. "I'm just a modern day Apache female warrior fighting for my people against corporations trying to take over mother earth!" she wrote, adding an arm-making-a-muscle emoji.

NAELYN PIKE: "Every time before I speak for a crowd, I'm nervous because I feel like, if I mess up, I mess up for my people."

◆ ◆ ◆

IN THE 1980S, Lakota social worker Maria Yellow Horse Brave Heart coined the term "historical trauma," to express the idea of "cumulative wounding across generations." Brave Heart examined the way trauma from events like the 1890 massacre at Wounded Knee and coercive Indian boarding schools had been passed down through generations of Lakota. Researchers have connected historical or intergenerational trauma to increased rates of drug and alcohol abuse, depression, suicide, and domestic violence among Native Americans.

Wendsler Nosie remembers the first time he left the San Carlos Reservation, to go to a grocery store in the town of Globe.

WENDSLER NOSIE: "Me and my sister were hiding in my mom's vehicle. Every time we saw somebody walk by, we'd duck down. During my mother's days, people were plucked. Disappeared. My mother, you know, she doesn't hug. When I try to give her a little hug, she turns away. My mother, my mother's mother, all their kids were plucked and sent to boarding schools. Prior to her time, Natives were used for medical experiments. Then, in the '60s and '70s, the Relocation system was in place. Natives were pushed to leave reservations for vocational programs in different cities. That idea was embedded in us: *Don't let these white people see you, because you could be grabbed and sent away.*"

The Bureau of Indian Affairs was created in 1824 as an agency within the War Department. In 1849, Indian Affairs was moved to the Department of the Interior, whose responsibility it became to manage "the Indian Problem." This largely consisted of removing Natives from their homelands and suggesting ways to eradicate Native culture.

"We earnestly desire the speedy settlement of all our territories," reads an 1868 Office of Indian Affairs Annual Report.

> None are more anxious than we to see their agricultural and mineral wealth developed by an industrious, thrifty, and enlightened population. And we fully recognize the fact that the Indian must not stand in the way of this result. . . . If the savage resists, civilization, with the Ten Commandments in one hand and the sword in the other, demands his immediate extermination.

But extermination, as a policy, proved to be inefficient. An educational system designed to destroy Native culture was proposed as an economical way to solve the Indian Problem. The 1868 report concluded, "It costs less to civilize than to kill."

Richard Henry Pratt fought on the Union side in the Civil War. After the Confederacy's surrender, he remained in the military, leading the Tenth United States Cavalry, a troop of former slaves and Indian scouts—Natives who fought for the United States—in Oklahoma. For three years beginning in 1875, he guarded Indian prisoners at Fort Marion, Florida. There, he formed the basis of the assimilationist educational philosophy that he eventually distilled into one blunt aphorism: "Kill the Indian, save the man."

In 1879, Pratt founded the Carlisle Indian Industrial School on the site of a former army barracks in Carlisle, Pennsylvania. Pratt was confident that Indians could be civilized. They simply needed to be stripped of their traditions and indoctrinated into the society of white men. The United States agreed, and Carlisle became the prototype for government-run schools nationwide. Children as young as three were removed from their families, often by force. The children were sent to distant institutions, where, in many cases, they remained for years at a time. They were given new names and assigned new birthdates. Their hair was cut. They were issued uniforms. If caught speaking their native languages or maintaining their religious traditions, they were punished—beaten, shackled, isolated, mouths washed out with lye soap. Indian school curricula were designed to turn Native youth into menial laborers in a white system. Girls learned to launder clothes, to hem dish towels. Boys were trained in agriculture and, in later years, auto repair and welding. Not every teacher or administrator was cruel, but physical, sexual, and psychological abuse was rampant. Children suffered from loneliness, homesickness, and infectious diseases. Many died.

In the 1930s, Wendsler Nosie's mother, Elvera, was taken from San Carlos 100 miles away to the Phoenix Indian School.

WENDSLER NOSIE: "My mother remembers the soldiers and the women who came and took the kids. Some families never saw the kids again. A lot of kids ran away from the schools, and my mom was one of those who ran away. She was about 11, 12. She ran all the way from Phoenix. She made it back to the reservation. Her grandmother would hide her when the agency came looking. They would stay in the mountains, they would stay in the creeks, until they knew they weren't being watched. But the agents caught her a second time. She ran away again, and she found her way back to San Carlos again. Finally, she was too old, so they didn't want her."

Wendsler's father was also sent to boarding school.

WENDSLER NOSIE: "He had all these great qualities of the Chiricahua Apache. He had things that he dreamed of. But alcoholism cornered him. That's the side of him I knew most—the times that he was drinking and the times that he was abusive. I remember him worrying about what tomorrow was going to bring. I saw him cry a lot. It was the same thing with my grandfather: they stripped him of everything that he was. So what could he teach his son? What is he going to teach his son while the military is pushing him around? When there were husbands who watched their wives get raped right in front of them? My father was doing what he could to get through the day. I understand why a lot of them went toward alcohol. How do you raise a son? He had four sons. How do you raise them?

"He would hit my mom. He would hit whoever was there. Since I was the youngest, I would be the one standing by my mother. My mother found healing in her children. She didn't want us to be like our father. But then, she also didn't totally blame him. The only job he could get was working with asbestos. He had other jobs, but the mine is where he worked longest. He died from leukemia. I was seven.

"My grandmother's generation. These were the people who knew the earth. They died as prisoners of war, but they had children. That generation was afraid. Then comes my generation thinking, *Hey, wait a minute, this is wrong.* I'm out here challenging things, but I'm still a little afraid. Then comes my daughter, who's like, *boom, boom, boom, boom!* And then, here comes *her* daughter, who's like, We're going *this way.*"

VANESSA NOSIE: "I've always talked to my daughters as Apaches. When you go outside, stand on the dirt, not the concrete. We could be walking into Target and we see trash blowing around. Pick it up. You're protecting the earth. I have a lot more anger than Naelyn does. Not that she's not angry. Her passion is soft, strong. When I listen to her, I feel all the hurt of my people."

WENDSLER NOSIE: "We went to Salt River on the Pima reservation. It was a youth conference. I was the keynote speaker. I told Naelyn, 'You have a lot to say, why don't you introduce me. But say what you need to say first.' She goes, 'Okay.' She talked about being a girl. She talked about our culture. I'm looking at the audience. Before you know it, everybody was crying. I forgot I was supposed to speak. That day, I turned it over to the next generation."

Elvera Nosie died in 2016. She was 88 years old.

She left seven children, including Wendsler,

47 grandchildren, including Vanessa,

124 great-grandchildren,

including Naelyn, Nizhoni, and Baasé-O,

and 30 great-

great-grandchildren.

VANESSA NOSIE: "I was 19 when I had Naelyn. They always say girls are harder to handle than boys. But I don't know, so far, so good. No trouble. I mean, I'm not naïve, my kids are teenagers. But as a family, we're traditional. My girls have their aunties, they have their uncles, they have their grandparents. I think the only problem I have is when they fight. *You took my shirt. You're wearing my shoes.*"

BAASÉ-O PIKE: "That's 'Zhoni."

VANESSA NOSIE: *"You can't take my skateboard."*

NIZHONI PIKE: "Yeah, that's Baasé. Naelyn's like, 'I'm not doing your laundry.'"

BAASÉ-O PIKE: "Like, 'I'm not going to talk to you all day.'"

NIZHONI PIKE: "Naelyn ignores everybody for the whole day."

In the summer of 2017, Naelyn enrolled at Mesa Community College. Nizhoni, a high school sophomore, got a job at Panda Express. Baasé-O, the youngest, celebrated her Sunrise Dance. In 2018, when Naelyn was 18, she got her braces off.

Naelyn says she'd like to marry an Apache man.

VANESSA NOSIE: "I tell her, good luck. She's related to everybody.

"In the Apache tradition, she's already a woman. She's supposed to be married and have kids. Once your dance is over, they paint the girl's face red, to let the community know she's an adult, she's ready to be married. It's done different ways, depending on the medicine man. Sometimes it's just a red stripe. Naelyn, her whole face, from the bridge of her nose around, was painted red."

BAASÉ-O PIKE: "Naelyn wants enough kids to make that percent one more percent."

NAELYN PIKE:

"I told my mom,

'I want ten kids.

That means ten extra Apache.

Ten extra warriors.'"

Chapter 8

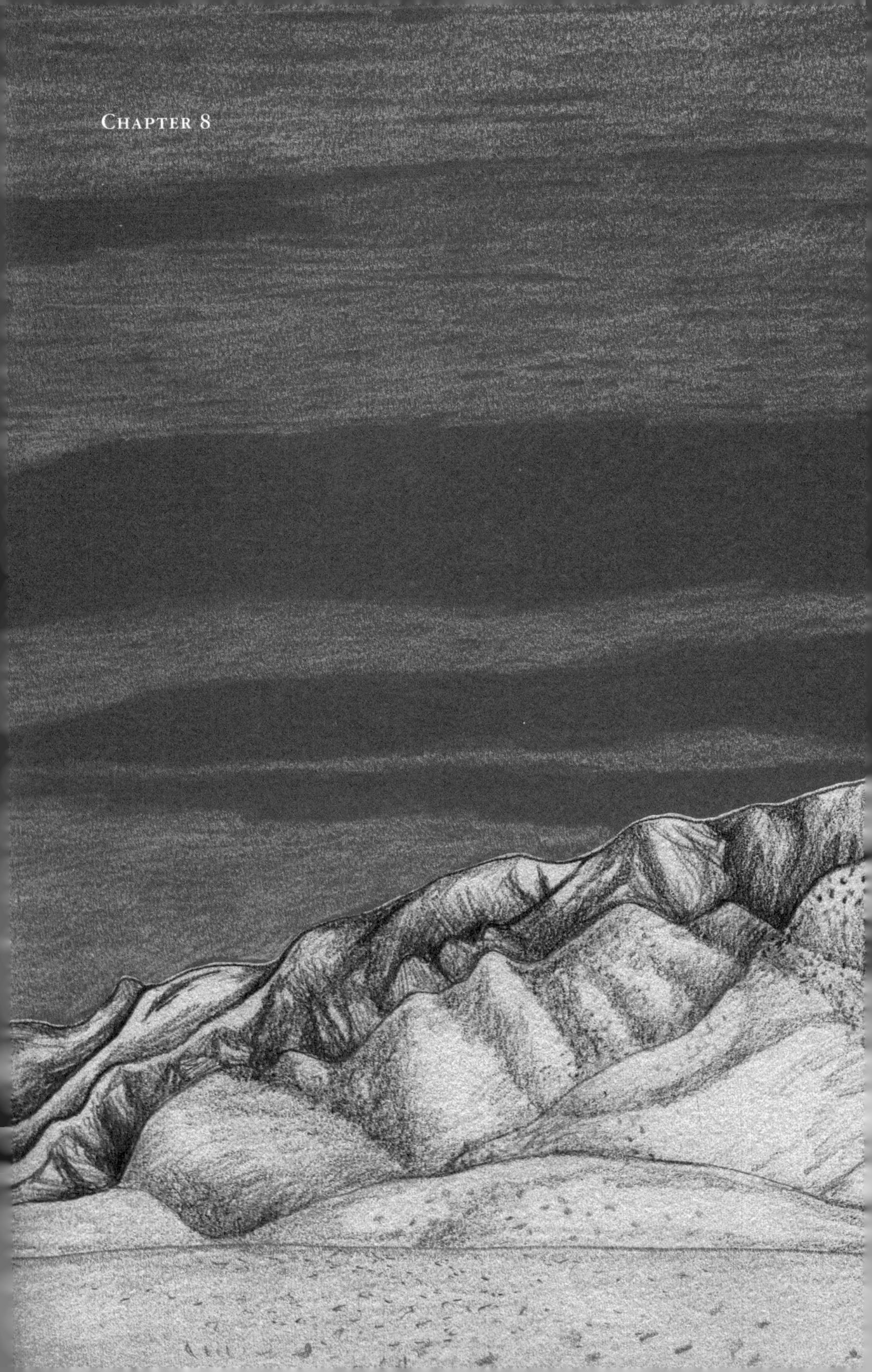

Theresa Nosie: "I knew it was time. I kept saying,

'It's time.

She's getting moody.

We've got to get ready.'"

In August 1997, Theresa Nosie sensed her daughter Alicia might be about to get her period for the first time. She was anxious to begin preparations for Alicia's Sunrise Dance.

That's when Theresa's dreams began.

THERESA NOSIE: "I started having this dream about a mountain. The mountain kept calling. It was calling Wendsler. I told him what the dream was: Wendsler was on the mountain, and he was pulling us up. I told him. 'You gotta go there.' 'All right, whatever.' Then the next day, the same dream came back. So I tell him, 'I had the same dream again.' 'Yeah, okay, okay.' Then it came again the next night."

WENDSLER NOSIE: "Theresa's Navajo, I'm Apache. So I'm kinda like, 'How are you having this dream?'

"Have you ever seen that movie *Thunderheart*?"

In *Thunderheart,* Val Kilmer plays Ray Levoi, an FBI agent who is part Sioux. Levoi is sent to the Pine Ridge Indian Reservation to investigate a murder and begins having dreams that are interpreted as visions.

Thesesa had the dream about the mountain three times. "I didn't want to wait for the fourth dream," Wendsler said. The number four has sacred significance in Apache religion. It represents the four cardinal directions, each of which is associated with a particular color. North, white; south, blue; east, black; west, yellow.

WENDSLER NOSIE: "In Apache everything's four. When she had the dream a third time, I thought, 'Man, I better go.'"

There was no question where Wendsler was going, no doubt about what mountain had appeared in Theresa's dreams.

The traditional homeland of the Western Apache was a vaguely diamond-shaped area anchored by four mountain peaks. Mount Graham, or *Dził Nchaa Si An,* as it is known in Apache, was the southernmost peak. Mount Graham looms large in Apache history and culture. The mountain is mentioned in stories, songs, and prayers. On an 1865 map of the newly created "Arizona Territory," the words "Mt. Graham" appear at the southern edge of the Pinaleño Mountains, nestled within vast expanses identified as "Chiricahua Apache" and "Coyotero Apache." The mountain was part of the Apache reservation created in 1871, until President Ulysses S. Grant reclaimed the area for the federal government by executive order two years later. Still, Mount Graham continued to serve as a refuge for the Apache. As a child, Ada Rope Jordan, the grandmother of San Carlos tribal chairman Terry Rambler, rode 80 miles on horseback from the reservation to the mountain, where she hid from authorities who were seizing Apache children and shipping them to boarding schools.

Mount Graham is the highest peak in the Pinaleños and one of the tallest mountains in Arizona. At 10,000 feet, the summit floats more than a mile above the ocean of desert that surrounds it below. Stephen Jay Gould, the late paleontologist and evolutionary biologist, called Mount Graham "a rare and precious habitat of extraordinary evolutionary interest." Gould and other scientists have referred to Mount Graham as a "sky island," an isolated ecosystem akin to the Galápagos where relic populations thrive and endemic species evolve. Nine perennial streams flow here. Threatened and endangered creatures live in five different biotic zones. In the winter, when residents of Arizona's desert towns are wearing T-shirts and hanging Christmas decorations from cacti, you can find snow on Mount Graham. Tom Waddell, the former Mount Graham wildlife manager for the Arizona Game and Fish Department, told *The Washington Post* in 1990, "A spruce fir forest in the middle of the southwestern desert is very, very unique. . . . It's an isolated museum of what was here . . . 11,000 years ago."

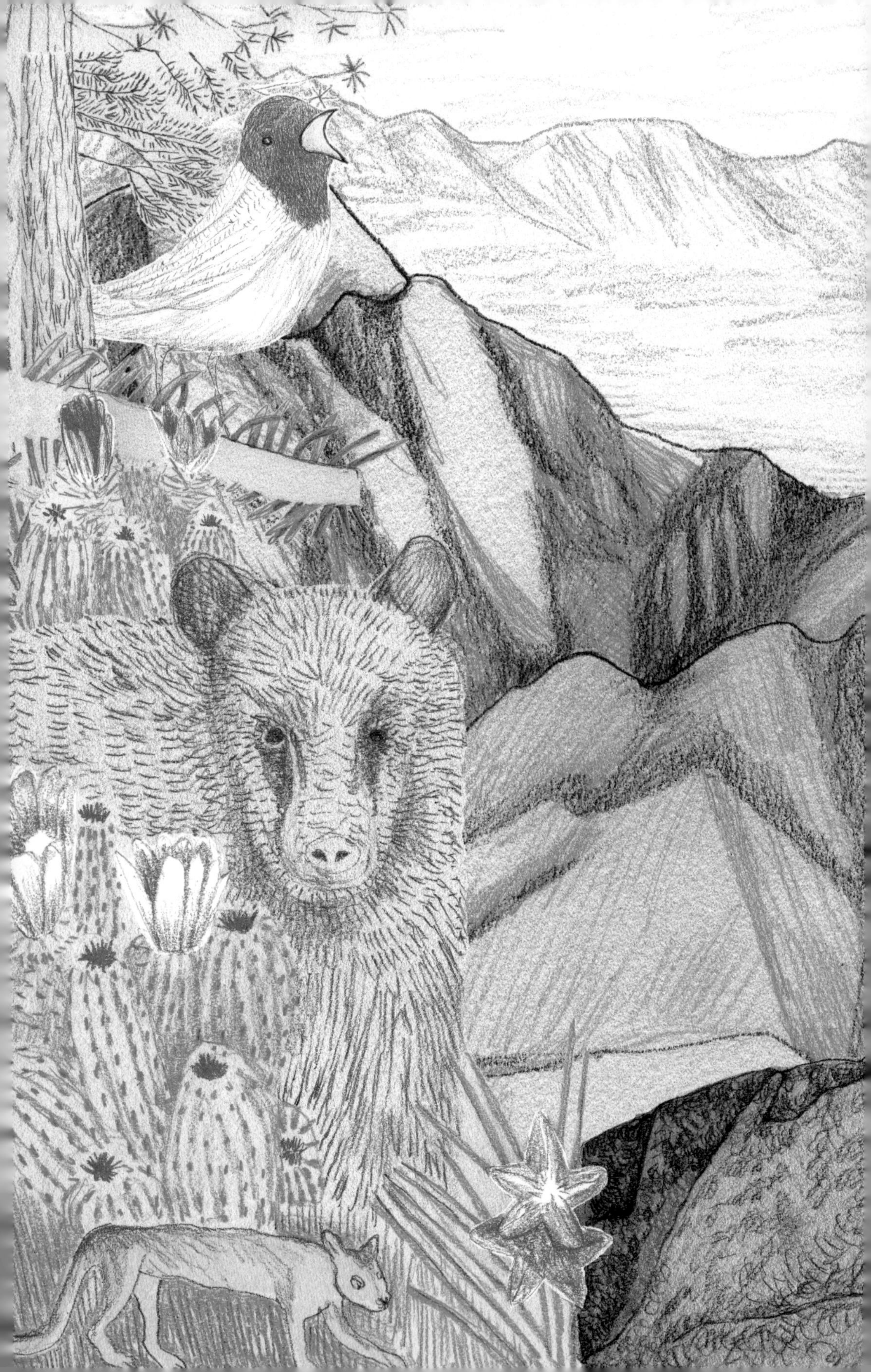

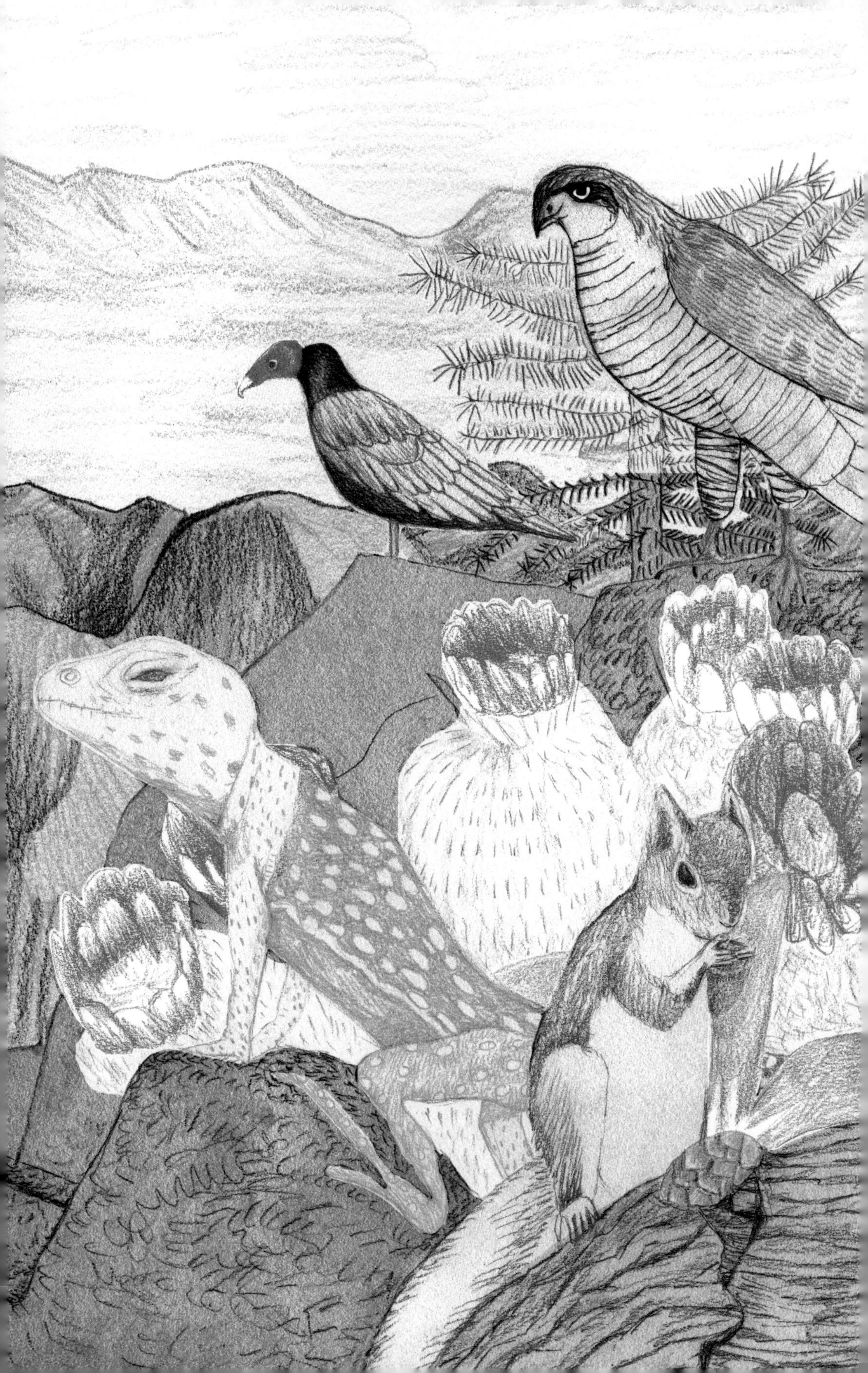

On the afternoon of August 30, 1997, Wendsler Nosie drove from the San Carlos Reservation to Mount Graham.

WENDSLER NOSIE: "When I saw the big mountain, the holy mountain, I thought, *Huh. I'm always with my kids, or Theresa.* But this time I was by myself, driving down the road."

He shrugged off the uneasy feeling and parked his truck.

WENDSLER NOSIE: "I got out and said, 'Okay. I'll pray right here.'"

A voice startled him.

WENDSLER NOSIE: "A young white girl springs up behind me. She says, 'Excuse me.' I turn around, and she says, 'You're Apache, right?' 'Yeah, I'm Apache.' She says, 'You came here to pray.' 'Yeah.' 'This is your holy mountain?' 'Yeah.' 'Wow.' I turned around but she was still standing there. So I turned back to her, and she asks me, 'Are you going to the top?' I looked at her, 'Excuse me?' And she says, 'Are you going to the top?' 'Uhh . . . yeah.' My intention wasn't to go to the top. My intention was just to stay right there. But I said, 'Yeah.' 'Wow,' she goes. So I said, 'Here I go.' I start walking. I turned back and she was kind of following me. I kept going, then looking back, and she was still there."

Wendsler climbed to the top of Mount Graham's Emerald Peak.

WENDSLER NOSIE: "I got to the top. I turn around and she was gone. Finally I said, 'Okay, I'm going to pray.'"

♦ ♦ ♦

1886. The Apache Wars had dragged on for more than three decades. Chiricahua Apache medicine man Geronimo and some 30 warriors, along with two dozen women and a handful of children, continued to slip the army's grasp, despite being vastly out-resourced and outnumbered. In April, General Nelson Miles took command of the Arizona Territory, replacing George Crook. In his 1896 memoir, Miles described the Apaches as "one of the most desperate, cruel and hardy bands of outlaws that ever infested any country."

GENERAL NELSON MILES

NELSON MILES: "The mountain labyrinths of the Apaches may be compared to criminal dens and slums of London, though on an immensely greater scale, and the outlaws to be tracked and subdued, for cunning, strength and ferocity have never been surpassed in the annals of either savage or civilized crime."

Miles conceded the great "skill and enterprise and energy" of the Apache, but he was confident that he had the tools to overwhelm "all the advantages possessed by the savages." Miles believed an effective arsenal would include not only muskets and knives, but also optical instruments: telescopes, binoculars, and heliostats.

NELSON MILES: "I had it in my mind to utilize for our benefit and their discomfiture, the very elements that had been the greatest obstacles in that whole country to their subjugation, namely, the high mountain ranges, the glaring, burning sunlight, and an atmosphere void of moisture."

Under General Miles, the U.S. Signal Corps established 14 heliograph stations in Arizona: "a network of points of observation and communication . . . on the high mountain peaks of this region," including on Mount Graham. "It was remarkable what advantage [the stations] gave us in observing the movements of the Indians or of the troops in the valleys below," wrote Miles in his memoir. A nineteenth-century heliostat was essentially a mirror mounted on a tripod. An operator could send a message to another station using a system of short and long flashes of light beamed off the mirror in a kind of visual Morse code. The larger the mirror and clearer the atmosphere, the farther the light signal could travel.

By the summer of 1886, the United States had mobilized approximately one quarter of the army's soldiers, some 5,000 troops, as well as Mexican fighters and Apache scouts fighting on the government's side, to pursue the remaining Apache fighters: 17 men. The odds against Geronimo and his followers had become insurmountable. The United States promised that if the Apaches capitulated, they would be reunited with their families. On September 3, on the western edge of Arizona's Skeleton Canyon, Geronimo surrendered. Shortly after, Naiche, the last hereditary chief of the Chiricahua Apache, surrendered, too. The Apache Wars were over. The defeated Apache were put on a train and transported to Florida, where they were imprisoned. Sent with them were hundreds of other Chiricahua Apaches who had been living peaceably on the San Carlos Reservation. Even the Apache scouts whose efforts had been crucial in securing Geronimo's capitulation were hustled onto the train and exiled to prison in the east.

"The heliostat had performed its last and best work," Miles wrote.

◆ ◆ ◆

AS WENDSLER NOSIE PRAYED at the Mount Graham summit, a storm was building. Heavy clouds blotted out the sun and darkness overtook the forest.

WENDSLER NOSIE: "When the clouds come in, you're not supposed to be there, because that's the time that the spirits walk the earth. We have rituals. You can't just say 'Amen' and you're done. You have to go through every step. I was hurrying."

It began to rain. Lightning shattered the sky.

WENDSLER NOSIE: "I was like, *One more prayer . . .* "

Thunder reverberated through the pines.

WENDSLER NOSIE: "The lightning was red, blinding me. I started walking like a blind man, trying to feel my way."

◆ ◆ ◆

After the Apaches' 1886 surrender, the military forts and heliograph stations in Arizona were abandoned. Then, 100 years after the end of the Apache Wars, there was a new proposal to place optical instruments on Mount Graham's peaks.

In the early 1980s, the University of Arizona, working with the Smithsonian Institution, began drawing up plans to build a large observatory complex to house a new generation of telescopes, including the "multi-mirror" designs that the university's Mirror Laboratory had recently developed. A multi-mirror telescope can gather as much light as a telescope with a single large mirror, and therefore peer as far into space, but it is cheaper and easier to build. The university considered close to 300 sites before deciding on Mount Graham as the location for the 13 planned telescopes. The university's officials concluded that Mount Graham's skies were clear, dry, and some of the darkest in the United States. Mount Graham was close to Tucson, an internationally recognized center of astronomical research and home to the University of Arizona's Steward Observatory. Harvard, the University of

Chicago, the University of Texas, the University of Pittsburgh, Cal Tech, Ohio State, Michigan State, the University of Toronto, and a number of other universities explored joining the project.

Astronomy probes some of the deepest mysteries of our existence. What preceded the creation of the cosmos? Is there intelligent life elsewhere in the universe? Scientists work to understand dark energy, dark matter, cosmic rays, supernovas. The more powerful a telescope, the farther into space—the farther into the past—it can see. In 1981, Steward Observatory director Peter Strittmatter told the *Arizona Daily Star* that a multi-mirror telescope on Mount Graham could help astronomers answer questions about the formation of the universe and the creation of elements like oxygen and carbon. Astronomer Donald Hall said that the most compelling reason to build the larger telescopes was to discover phenomena not yet even imagined.

From the start, controversy surrounded the Mount Graham observatory proposal. Environmentalists feared the destruction of an irreplaceable ecosystem. During the project's development phase, a rare subspecies of squirrel, the Mount Graham red squirrel, previously thought to be extinct, was found living in Mount Graham's Emerald Peak forest—the site of the planned telescopes, and the spot to which Wendsler Nosie had climbed to pray. The red squirrel was known to exist nowhere else on Earth; in 1987, *Tamiasciurus hudsonicus grahamensis* was placed on the endangered species list. Biologists, including some of the University of Arizona's own professors, began objecting to the telescopes. Earth First! activists staged protests. The Maricopa County Audubon Society condemned the project. The Sierra Club Legal Defense Fund filed a lawsuit.

Opposition also came from Native Americans. Apaches see Mount Graham, like Oak Flat, as a dwelling place of mountain spirits and a source of supernatural power. The San Carlos Apache Tribal Council passed a unanimous resolution against the telescope project. The resolution described Mount Graham's sacred springs, sacred plants, animals, and burial sites. It noted the mountain's role in the apprenticeship of young medicine men and women and asserted that the telescopes would "contribute directly to the destruction of fundamental aspects of traditional and spiritual life of the Apaches."

A group of San Carlos elders and medicine men created the Apache Survival Coalition to organize opposition to the telescopes. Wendsler Nosie, a member of the Tribal Council at the time, joined. In 1991, the Apache Survival Coalition filed a lawsuit against the U.S. Forest Service.

Native theologian and legal scholar Vine Deloria Jr. was a professor at the University of Arizona from 1978 to 1990, where he established an American Indian Studies master's degree program, the first of its kind in the United States. In an essay entitled "Sacred Lands and Religious Freedom," Deloria addressed the charge that Native Americans indiscriminately claim sacred sites. "Indians, because of our considerably longer tenure on this continent, have many more of these kinds of sacred places than do non-Indians."

WENDSLER NOSIE: "We were kicked out of these holy places. The Apache religion survived in San Carlos, with the hope of returning one day to the ancestral homelands. There was always that prophecy: the final fight between the Apache and America would be for our religion."

♦ ♦ ♦

IN 1986, many were surprised to learn that the University of Arizona had a new partner in the effort to construct telescopes on Mount Graham: the Vatican. Why would the Roman Catholic Church build a telescope, and why in Arizona?

In the early seventeenth century, Italian astronomer Galileo Galilei ran afoul of the Church for publishing work that supported heliocentrism, which proposed that the Earth orbits the Sun and not vice versa. The Inquisition tried and condemned Galileo for heresy in 1633, forced him to renounce his findings, and placed him under house arrest until his death. But the Vatican can also cite a history of engagement with science and the study of the heavens. In the sixteenth century, during the papacy of Gregory XIII, the Church wanted to refine the Julian calendar, to adjust the length of the year and secure the date of Easter in relation to the spring equinox. The Vatican built the Tower of Winds behind St. Peter's as a center for astronomical study, and, in 1582, introduced the Gregorian calendar, the system used internationally today. In the eighteenth and nineteenth centuries, the Church constructed three observatories in Vatican City.

In 1980, one man was both director of the Vatican Observatory and associate director of the University of Arizona's Steward Observatory: Father George Coyne, a Jesuit priest and astronomer. Coyne was born into a Catholic family in Maryland in 1933. He attended Catholic schools. As a young man Coyne questioned his faith, then re-embraced it. He attended Fordham University in New York City, obtaining a degree in mathematics and a licentiate in philosophy. He received his doctorate in astronomy from Georgetown in 1962 and moved on to postdoctoral research at Harvard and the National Science Foundation.

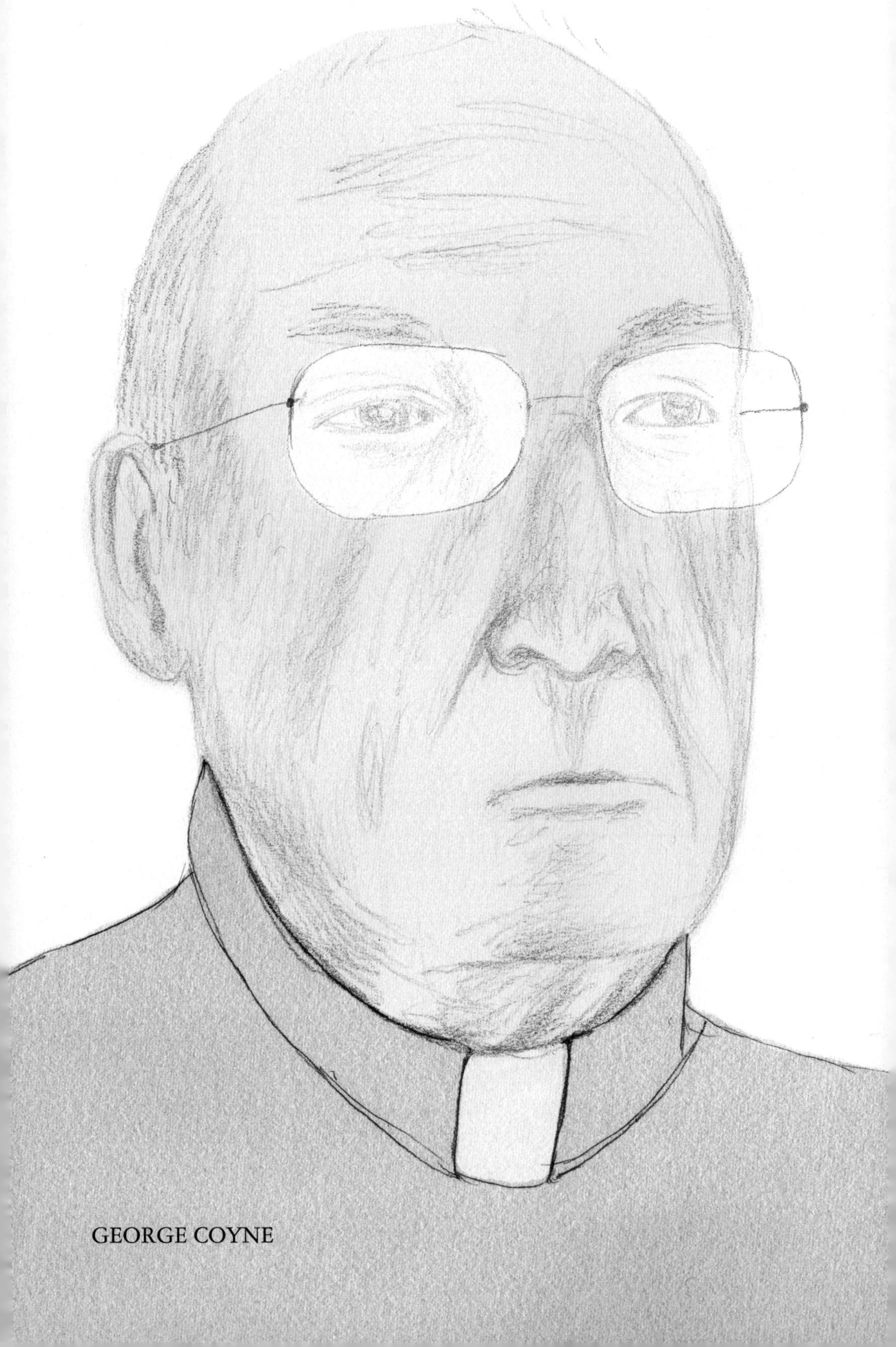
GEORGE COYNE

In 1965, Coyne was ordained as a Roman Catholic priest.

A year later, he joined the University of Arizona Lunar and Planetary Laboratory as a visiting research professor.

In 1969, he became an astronomer at the Vatican Observatory.

In 1981, Father Coyne helped establish VORG—Vatican Observatory Research Group—the research arm of the Church's operation in Tucson, Arizona.

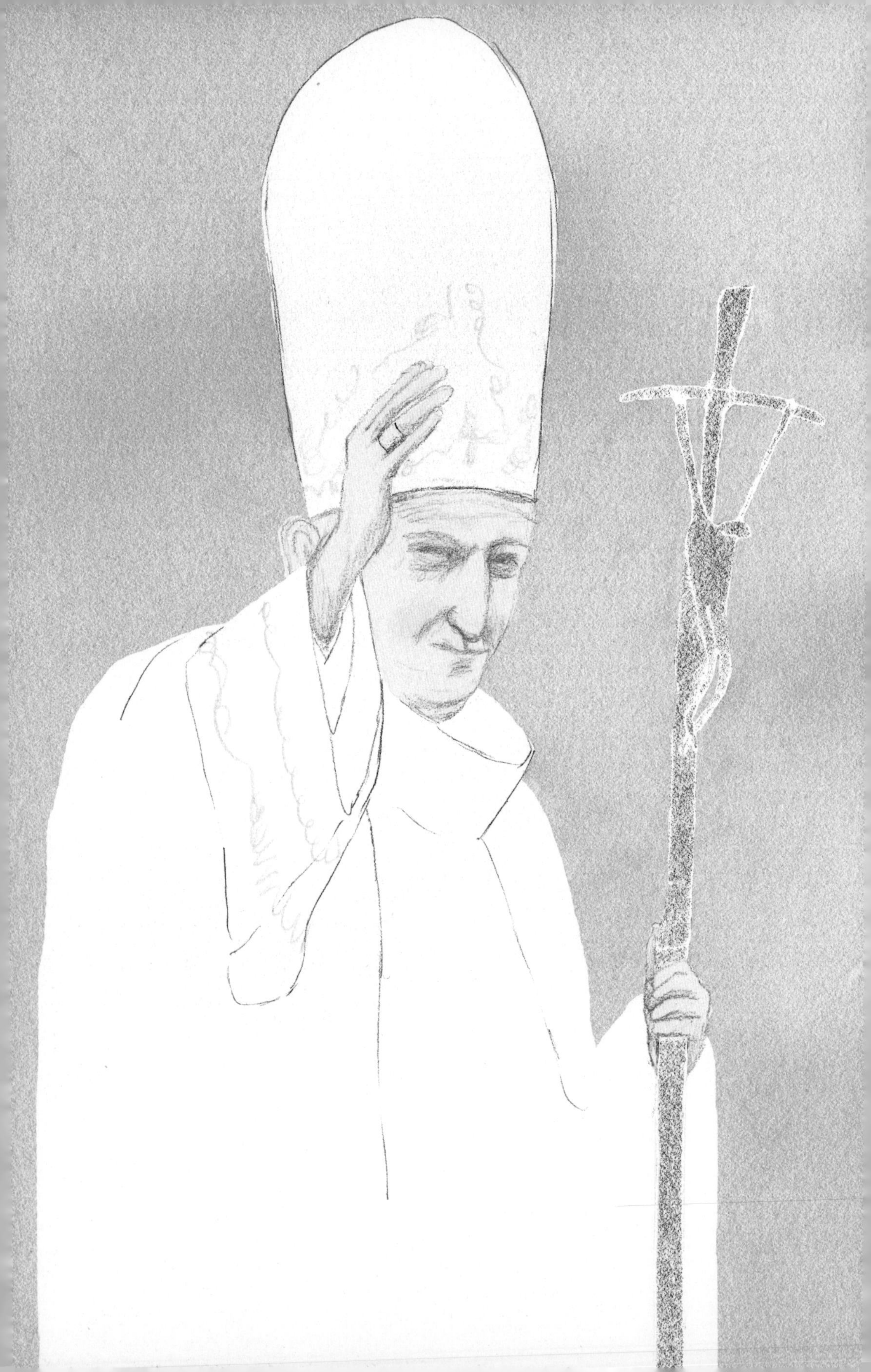

During the summer of 1987, Pope John Paul II traveled to Canada and the United States. One stop on his itinerary was the first-ever papal visit to Arizona. In Phoenix on September 14, the pope addressed a gathering of "Native peoples of the Americas" at Veterans Memorial Coliseum. In the audience were some 14,000 people from 200 different tribes. The pope praised Native Americans as "the noble descendants of countless generations of inhabitants of this land, whose ways were marked by great respect for the natural resources of land and rivers, of forest and plain and desert." The pope also acknowledged the fraught history of colonialism.

POPE JOHN PAUL II: "The early encounter between your traditional cultures and the European way of life was an event of such significance and change that it profoundly influences your collective life even today. That encounter was a harsh and painful reality for your peoples. The cultural oppression, the injustices, the disruption of your life and of your traditional societies must be acknowledged."

The pope did not explicitly address the Church's own role in Europe's history of conquest. He did not mention the fifteenth-century papal bulls that had declared war against all non-Christians, urged the seizure of their lands and resources, and advocated their "perpetual servitude."

POPE JOHN PAUL II: "I encourage you, as Native people belonging to the different tribes and nations in the east, south, west, and north, to preserve and keep alive your cultures, your languages, the values and customs which have served you well in the past and which provide a solid foundation for the future. Your customs that mark the various stages of life, your love for the extended family, your respect for the dignity and worth of every human being, from the unborn to the aged, and your stewardship and care of the earth: these things benefit not only yourselves but the entire human family."

In February 1992, the San Carlos Apache Tribe sent Pope John Paul II a letter about the Vatican telescope on Mount Graham. "Your Holiness," they wrote, the "development of your project threatens our cultural survival."

◆ ◆ ◆

THE TRIBE ORGANIZED A DELEGATION OF SIX PEOPLE, including Wendsler Nosie, to travel to Rome. They requested an audience with John Paul II. A meeting was arranged, and then, at the last minute, canceled. The pope did find time to meet with a number of San Carlos Apache who supported the telescopes. The "People's Rights Coalition" was headed by disgraced former tribal chairman Buck Kitcheyan. While chairman, Kitcheyan had denounced the Mount Graham scopes—"Since time immemorial, Mount Graham has been a sacred mountain to the Apache people," he wrote in a letter to the Forest Service in 1990—but he flipped his position after being removed from office for embezzling funds from the tribe. Following his arrest and conviction, facing fines, legal bills, and prison, Kitcheyan was presented as an Apache expert by telescope proponents. He was invited to Italy. After Kitcheyan twice failed to appear at tribal court hearings, a judge prohibited him from leaving Arizona, but his wife, daughter, and a few other supporters flew to Rome. The group visited the Sistine Chapel, were given a private tour of the Vatican Observatory, and posed for photos with Pope John Paul II.

As the Mount Graham controversy dragged on, the Smithsonian, Harvard, Michigan State, and other institutions dropped out of the project. The city council of Rome passed a motion asking the Vatican to consider the social, spiritual, and ecological damage that the telescopes would cause. The Church was unmoved. In March 1992, the Vatican Observatory issued an eight-page statement written by Father Coyne. "We are not convinced by any of the arguments thus far presented that Mount Graham possesses a sacred character."

FATHER GEORGE COYNE: "If they could show us Apaches buried under the telescope, or some clear evidence that the specific ground the telescope is on is sacred, then we'd reconsider."

◆ ◆ ◆

THE RAIN HAD TURNED TO HAIL. Wendsler Nosie needed to get off the mountain. He made his way down the slope and dropped onto a service road.

WENDSLER NOSIE: "Just when I jumped off the cliff, the U.S. Forest Service, the University of Arizona police, they all pulled up. They threw me against the car."

Nosie was interrogated and charged with trespassing, a Class 3 misdemeanor. He faced fines and a possible 30-day jail sentence.

The officers drove Nosie to the base of the mountain.

WENDSLER NOSIE: "They told me, 'Don't ever come back.' I didn't say anything. I went home."

A few days later, Nosie issued a statement. "Dził Nchaa Si An is sacred to me and my people. . . . For an Apache to be detained and cited for praying on our sacred mountain by a public university is an outrageous act." Nosie told a local newspaper, "If I have to go to jail for my religious beliefs, I will."

THERESA NOSIE: "Then he had to go to court."

On September 8, at the Graham County Courthouse in Safford, Arizona, Wendsler Nosie entered a written plea of "not guilty."

◆ ◆ ◆

IN 1823, in *Johnson v. McIntosh*, the U.S. Supreme Court ruled that Native Americans could not sell their land to private individuals. The court said that land title on the continent was first held not by indigenous societies who had inhabited the land for millennia, but by European powers that "discovered" America. Following the Revolutionary War, that title was transferred to the new nation: the United States. Native peoples were deemed to be mere occupants of the land. Writing for the court in *Johnson,* Justice John Marshall said that "principles of abstract justice" could not be factored into the decision. According to legal scholar Walter Echo-Hawk, "This is judicial code for 'something very unjust is about to happen.'" In *Johnson,* the U.S. Supreme Court created grounds for depriving Native Americans of their land. "Conquest gives a title which the courts of the Conqueror cannot deny," Marshall wrote. The decision provided legal justification for continuing expropriation of Native territory, the land grab that built a nation. Today the *Johnson* decision is regarded as infamous, on par with *Dred Scott.* But *Johnson v. McIntosh* has never been overturned. It continues to be cited as legal precedent.

The civil rights movement of the 1960s and 1970s included Native activists who fought systemic injustice against indigenous peoples. In 1978, Congress passed the American Indian Religious Freedom Act (AIRFA). The act acknowledged that Native people had historically been denied their constitutionally guaranteed right to freedom of religion, and declared, "Henceforth it shall be the policy of the United States to protect and preserve" Native religious freedom. The measure noted that access to sacred sites was crucial to Native religious practice. But AIRFA included no provision for enforcing protections. The American Indian Religious Freedom Act exists in a legal no-man's-land and is regularly disregarded.

In 1987, the Supreme Court heard arguments in the case of *Lyng v. Northwest Indian Cemetery Protective Association*. Tribes of northwestern California, including the Yurok, Tolowa, and Karok, hoped to block a U.S. Forest Service plan to pave a six-mile service road through an ancient pine forest and the sacred sites within it. They maintained that the road violated their First Amendment rights by impeding their free exercise of religion. A study commissioned by the Forest Service concluded that the road (referred to as the "G-O road" for the towns it would connect, Gasquet and Orleans) "would cause serious and irreparable damage to the sacred areas which are an integral and necessary part of the belief systems and lifeway of Northwest California Indian peoples." An attorney for California Indian Legal Services who argued the case, Marilyn Miles, said, "It would be like building an interstate through the Vatican." In lower courts the tribes had prevailed, but in 1988, the nation's highest court ruled against them.

Writing for the majority, Sandra Day O'Connor said, "Even if we assume that . . . the G-O road will 'virtually destroy the Indians' ability to practice their religion' . . . the Constitution simply does not provide a principle that could justify upholding respondents' legal claims." Chief Justice William J. Brennan's dissent found this conclusion—that destroying a religion does not burden it—"astonishing."

VINE DELORIA JR.: "People often feel guilty about their ancestors killing all those Indians years ago. But they shouldn't feel guilty about the distant past. [Recent years] have seen a more devious but hardly less successful war waged against the Indian communities."

IN OCTOBER 1992, in an interview with London's *Daily Telegraph*, Father George Coyne was asked what he would say if an extraterrestrial was contacted through his work at Mount Graham. Coyne said he would ask any alien he encountered,

Have you ever
"experienced something
similar to Adam and Eve,
in other words,
original sin?"

and

"Do you people
also know a Jesus
who has redeemed you?"

"The Church would be obliged,"
Coyne said,
"to address the question
of whether extraterrestrials
might be brought
within the fold and baptized."

Another Vatican astronomer and University of Arizona astrophysics professor, Father Christopher Corbally, agreed.

"It would be fascinating
to have a real encounter with
another intelligence. I think we'd
have to consider whether we
should baptize [the alien]."

The goal of the Vatican Observatory was not expressly to
"spread the Gospel to extraterrestrials."
But,
Corbally said,
"We would be open to that sort of thing.
Certainly, some of our efforts
should be directed toward that."
In 2008, Father José Funes, the Jesuit astronomer who succeeded Coyne as director of the Vatican Observatory, told the Vatican newspaper, *L'Osservatore Romano*, that the possibility of "brother extraterrestrials" is indeed consistent with Catholic theology.
"This does not conflict with our faith," he said,
"because we cannot put limits on
the creative freedom of God."

By 1988, the University of Arizona
had hired Washington lobbyists Patton, Boggs
& Blow, one of D.C.'s most powerful law firms. Patton,
Boggs's client list included Haitian dictator Jean-Claude "Baby
Doc" Duvalier, the Chrysler Corporation, and the governments of
numerous countries including Uganda, Pakistan, Qatar, and Paraguay.

The firm successfully lobbied Congress to pass a "special-use authorization" which exempted the Mount Graham International Observatory from environmental and cultural laws that could have derailed the project. The controversy continued, but construction began.

Eventually three of the originally proposed 13 telescopes were built on Mount Graham. Today, in addition to the Vatican Advanced Technology Telescope, the observatory complex includes two other high-tech facilities, the Heinrich Hertz Submillimeter Telescope and the Large Binocular Telescope.

Wendsler Nosie's trial was held in September 1997 in Safford, Arizona. Though the outcome of the case would turn on whether or not the state could prove beyond a reasonable doubt that Nosie had *intended* to trespass, the larger concern, according to criminal defense attorney William Foreman, who represented Nosie, was the hardship being placed on religious practice. Foreman told the court, "I see this issue as nothing less than the moral and religious health of the Apache people."

On January 20, 1998, Judge Linda Norton announced her decision. Wendsler Nosie was acquitted. He was relieved. "It shows hope," he said.

Wendsler Nosie still frequently travels to Mount Graham to pray and to participate in religious ceremonies. He believes the controversy over Mount Graham prepared him for future struggles, including the battle for Oak Flat.

Nosie views the forces that sent him to the mountain, and resulted in his arrest, in spiritual terms.

> In Theresa's dream,
> Wendsler was atop Mount Graham,
> reaching down to hoist the members
> of his family toward the
> mountain's summit.

Nosie can't explain the presence or sudden

disappearance of the woman who impelled him to Emerald Peak.

He sees her as an otherworldly phantom, a messenger who pressed

him forward in his fight

for sacred lands.

WENDSLER NOSIE:

"My life changed at Mount Graham,
with the lady who pushed me to the top.
I don't know if she was a human being."

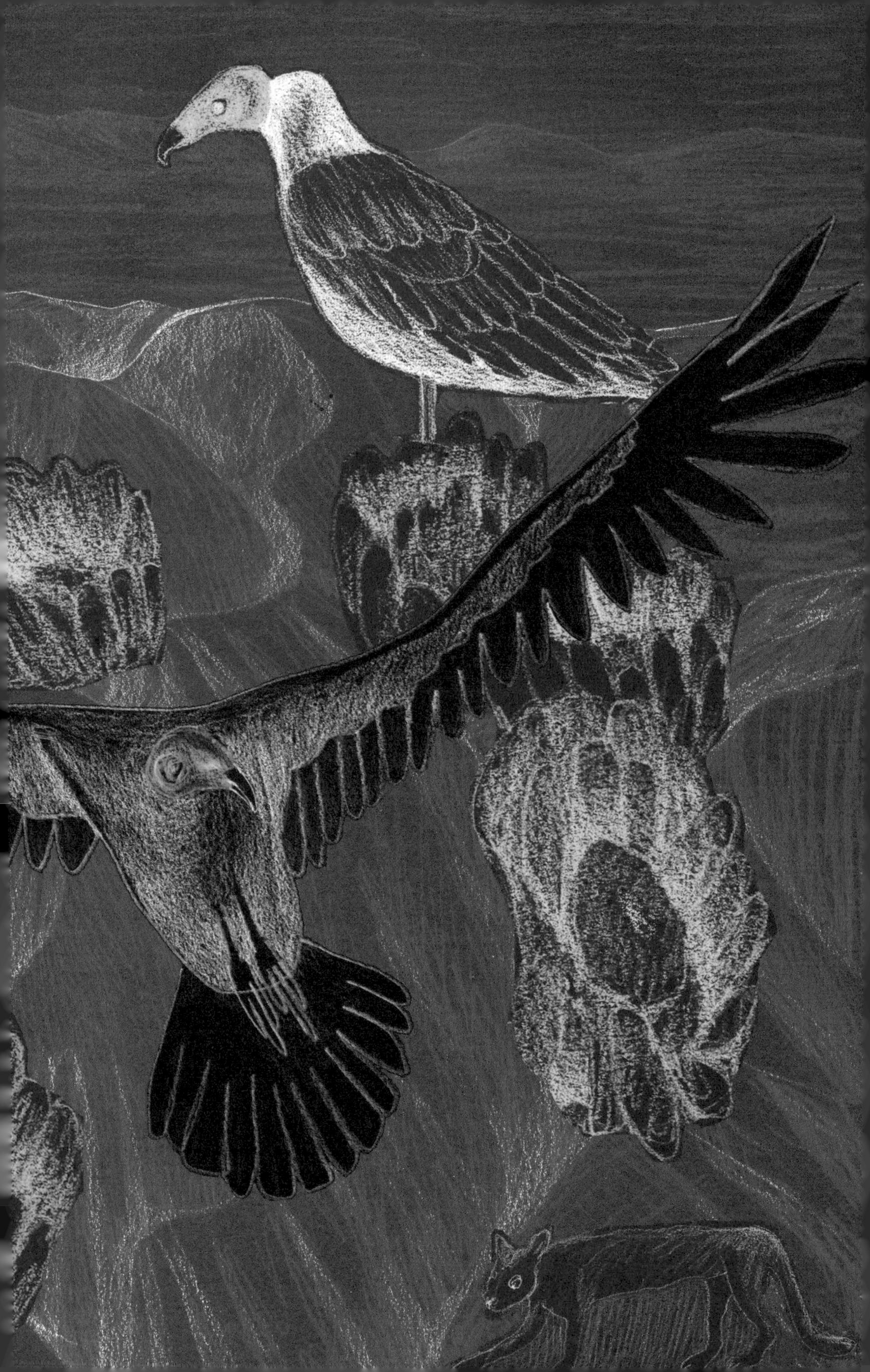

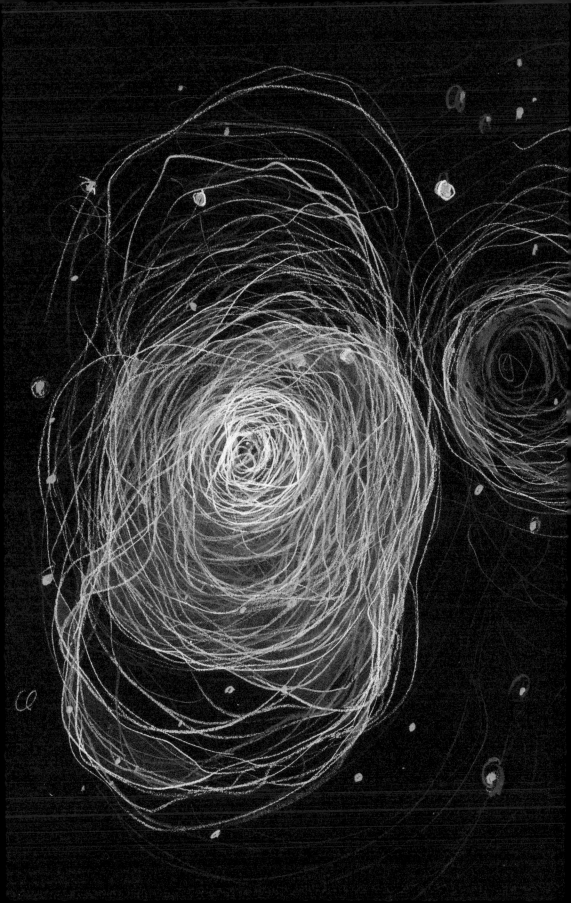

WHEN A NEW TELESCOPE captures its

first image, astronomers say it has achieved

"first light." At 9:15 p.m. one summer

night not long after the observatory's

completion, the light from Altair, the

brightest star of the Aquila constellation,

beamed onto a mirror of the Vatican

Advanced Technology Telescope on Mount

Graham. The telescope's camera snapped a

picture and "champagne flowed," the *Arizona*

Daily Star reported. The following Sunday,

the Vatican astronomers marked the occasion

with a telescope dedication Mass.

If I told you there was once a man named Goyaałé who, at 21 years old, lost his wife, three children, and mother in a brutal raid by enemy soldiers, who was inflamed by desire for justice and vengeance, who fought against crushing odds to defend the freedom of his people, who staged escape after escape from captivity, whom *The New York Times* called "crafty, bloodthirsty, [and] incredibly cruel," who rode a horse in President Theodore Roosevelt's inaugural parade—you might wonder why you have never heard of him. But if I told you that, later in life, Goyaałé was known as Geronimo, you'd see the man's face in your mind's eye. You might have already decided if you consider him a villain or a hero. You might hear the name as an exclamation—*Geronimo!*—a cry to summon bravery, or reckless abandon.

Or, you might think of the words relayed from Abbottabad, Pakistan, to Washington, D.C., just after 1 a.m. on May 2, 2011, when a group of U.S. Navy SEALs breached the compound where Al Qaeda founder Osama Bin Laden was hiding.

"We have a visual on Geronimo," CIA director Leon Panetta reported over video link to President Obama and his advisers who had gathered in the White House Situation Room to watch the secret operation unfold.

"'Geronimo,'" President Obama said on CBS's *60 Minutes* after the raid was made public, "was code for Bin Laden."

In an upstairs bedroom of the Abbottabad house, one of the SEALs fired his HK416 assault rifle, striking Bin Laden in the head. Two other SEALs burst into the room. More shots were fired.

The SEALs radioed home:

"For God and country—Geronimo, Geronimo, Geronimo."

"Geronimo E.K.I.A."

Enemy killed in action.

Apaches and other Natives were angry that the United States had used Geronimo as a code name in their mission to "hunt down" Bin Laden. One of Geronimo's descendants, Harlyn Geronimo, called it "an outrageous insult." Native rights advocate Suzan Shown Harjo told *The Washington Post* that the choice showed "how deeply embedded the [idea of] 'Indian as enemy' is in the collective mind of America."

♦ ♦ ♦

"CLAIMING IS PRESENT IN THE VERY PROCESS OF NAMING," writes historian Jean M. O'Brien. In countless American history books, O'Brien says, the naming of a place by European settlers marks the start of its official history; anything before that date is relegated to "preface." Thousands of years of indigenous culture are shoehorned into cursory preambles before the real story begins, with the appearance of white settlers. Indians are people who exist in the past tense, whose claim to the land is a distant memory.

The Mount Graham International Observatory maintains a website that includes a page on the History of Mount Graham. "The mountain," the site tells readers, "was named in 1846" in honor of Lieutenant Colonel James Duncan Graham, a senior officer in the U.S. Army Corps of Topographical Engineers. The MGIO site does not mention that Mount Graham has a different, older name—that it has long been known as Dził Nchaa Si An in Apache.

Anthropologist Keith Basso worked with Apache tribes for four decades. He was active in efforts to prevent telescopes from being built on Mount Graham. In his book *Wisdom Sits in Places: Landscape and Language Among the Western Apache,* Basso recounts his work with Apache consultants to create a map locating "each and every place that bears an Apache name within a twenty-mile radius" in a certain section of the White Mountain Apache Reservation, just north of San Carlos. At one point while visiting sites, Basso repeatedly mispronounces a certain place name. Finally, he gives up and apologizes to his Apache guide. "I can't get it," Basso says. "It doesn't matter." His guide, identified only as Charles, doesn't like Basso's comment. Charles mutters,

> What he is doing isn't right. It's not good. He seems to be in a hurry. Why is he in a hurry? It's disrespectful. Our ancestors made this name. They made it just as it is. They made it for a reason. *They spoke it first, a long time ago.* He's repeating the speech of our ancestors. He doesn't know that!

Charles goes on to describe how, in the ancestors' practice of naming a place, "They made a picture of it with words. Now they could speak about it and remember it clearly and well. Now they had a picture they could carry in their minds. You can see for yourself. It looks like its name." Apache place names generally describe the physical features of a place— rocks, trees, rivers—and might even indicate a vantage point from which to view the place. Basso describes the way an Apache elder might use place names to teach a child a lesson. The child is told a morality tale which unfolds, crucially, in a specific place. In the future, whenever the child hears the name of this place, she will be reminded of the lesson. In this way, "the land makes the people live right." Because these names depict a place at a particular moment in time, they also mark time's passage. When the place changes—a rock tumbles, a tree falls, a river dries up—the name, instead of painting a picture of the place as it is, conjures an image of how it once was. According to Charles, "The names . . . show what is different and what is still the same." In Apache, Oak Flat is *Chi'Chil'Bagoteel,* which translates to "flat with acorn trees." If Oak Flat's mesas, with their old-growth trees, were to collapse into a subsidence crater caused by mining, the place would be destroyed. The name would linger in its absence.

◆ ◆ ◆

ARIZONA IS DOTTED WITH GHOST TOWNS. They are mostly abandoned settlements that flourished with the development of new mining operations and emptied out when the mines shut down. Many have colorful names: Inspiration, Paradise, American Flag, Christmas, Bumble Bee, Fortuna, Crown King, Nugget, Tip Top, Vulture City, Total Wreck, Tombstone. In 1877, silver prospector Ed Schieffelin was warned about the risks of searching for ore in Apache country: *You go there and the only thing you'll find is your own tombstone.* But Schieffelin survived, and when he did find silver, he named the site for the warning he'd been given. For a decade, Tombstone thrived, until the mines flooded and the population moved on. In the end, the town's name was accurate.

According to Arizona historian Will C. Barnes, Swillings was the first name for the spot where Jack Swilling, Confederate soldier and prospector, formed a community in the late 1860s. For some 2,000 years, the Hohokam people had lived in the area, where they'd constructed an elaborate system of irrigation canals. Swilling recognized that the remains of the Hohokam canals could be used as the foundation of a new irrigation system in the valley. Darrell Duppa, one of Swilling's business partners, suggested that, rather than "Swillings," the place be called Phoenix: like the mythic bird who rises from the ashes, a new city would emerge from the ruins of the former civilization. The City of Phoenix was incorporated in 1881.

Today, the name Apache is ubiquitous in commercial and popular culture. The Apache Corporation is a Houston-based oil and gas company. The Boeing AH-64 Apache is a four-blade, twin-turboshaft attack helicopter used by the U.S. Army. The Apache AP is a stealth air-to-ground anti-runway missile manufactured by multinational weapons producer MBDA. There are Apache Warrior RVs and Apache motorcycles. Apache is the name for a type of safety glasses ("universal nose-bridge accommodates a variety of wearers"). Les Apaches were a violent criminal gang in Paris in the early twentieth century. In 1960, British rock group the Shadows released a single called "Apache." Record company ads warned, "Hang on to your scalps." The song's composer, Jerry Lordan, said, "I wanted something noble and dramatic, reflecting the courage and savagery of the Indian." The song hit number one in the UK. Dozens of cover versions and spin-off records followed, including a propulsive rendition by the Canadian group the Incredible Bongo Band that became one of the most sampled records of all time, the foundation of countless hip-hop songs. The Apache HTTP Server is a free, open-source Web server. The idea for the name came to one of its creators, Brian Behlendorf, "out of the blue," he later remembered. "It just sort of connoted: 'Take no prisoners. Be kind of aggressive and kick some ass.'"

In 2012, the Navajo Nation sued Urban Outfitters for trademark infringement and violation of the Indian Arts and Crafts Act when the clothing company marketed a series of its products as "Navajo." The items included socks, underwear ("Navajo hipster panties"), jewelry, handbags, and a decorative flask. Urban Outfitters countered that their company hadn't used the term "Navajo" as a trademark, but simply as a "generic name for a type of style." The company named 55 other prominent retailers

(Amazon, Barneys, Brooks Brothers, J.Crew, Levi's, Lord & Taylor, Louis Vuitton, Neiman Marcus, Nine West, QVC, Saks Fifth Avenue, Sears, and so on) that had also used the label "Navajo" without permission to market hundreds of products ("Girls' Navajo Hoodie," "Simplicity Navajo Leggings"). The list was meant to be exculpatory, the legal equivalent of a child's protest: *but everyone's doing it.* Eventually, the Navajo Nation and Urban Outfitters settled out of court, issuing a joint press release stating that the parties had entered into a "supply and license agreement and plan to collaborate on authentic American Indian jewelry in coming years."

The Navajo hold a trademark to the name of their nation; the San Carlos Apache do not. They reap no benefit from any commercial use of the name Apache.

Tribal names like Apache and Navajo are national identities today, but in many cases, these names are not how Native people refer to themselves in their own languages. The Navajo call themselves *Diné*, meaning "the People." Some historians speculate that the word "Apache" comes from a Zuni word meaning "our enemies." In their native language, the Apache call themselves *Ndee*; variations in other Apache dialects include *Inday* and *Inee*. Like "Diné" in Navajo, "Ndee" translates as "the People."

In 2014, Vanessa Nosie told the newspaper *Indian Country Today* that she prefers to refer to herself in more specific terms. "She will introduce herself with her first clan name, *Istinaniye* (Old People Standing), then by her tribal affiliation, *Inee*, and then by her tribal band—*Bendokahe*." Sandra Rambler, sister of San Carlos Apache tribal chairman Terry Rambler, told me, "I come from the Eagle clan. It's *Tukai*, Whitewater People. And I come from the *Nad Ots'usn* clan on my father's side, which is Slender Peak Standing Up People. Those are the people that are up at Oak Flat."

IF YOU SPEND TIME IN SUPERIOR, ARIZONA, you will eventually hear the tale of how the Apache Leap cliffs got their name. A group of Apache warriors were pinned to the edge of the cliffs by enemy soldiers. Rather than surrender, they jumped, plunging to their deaths in the valley below.

Residents of Superior told me the story. I've heard it from Apaches, too. I heard it from Wendsler Nosie, Sandra Rambler, and other members of the San Carlos Apache. The Apache Leap story appears in history books, in Arizona travel guides, and in newspaper articles, including articles in the Native press. The story is also cited in the text of the "Save Oak Flat" land exchange repeal legislation that was introduced in the U.S. Senate by Vermont senator Bernie Sanders and in the House of Representatives by Arizona congressman Raúl Grijalva in 2017.

The story's details often vary. Sometimes you'll hear that the incident occurred in the sixteenth century, and the Apache were trying to avoid being enslaved in Spanish gold mines. In other accounts, the enemy is another Native tribe, or a group of Mexicans, or the date is much later, and the enemies are hostile white ranchers. The most frequently told story describes a late nineteenth-century confrontation between the Apache and the U.S. Cavalry. *The Arizona Republic* recounted this version in a 1978 article. "The group of blue-uniformed men crept up a secret path. . . . Shots were fired, there were war whoops and finally Indians jumped off the cliffs and fell to the rocks below."

There is a second part to the story.

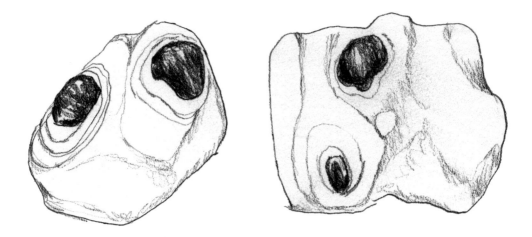

People say when the men jumped to their death, the Apache women cried, and as their tears fell to the ground, they were transformed into black stones. These black stones are known as Apache Tears. You find them in the valley beneath Apache Leap. They are obsidian, a volcanic glass formed by rapidly cooling lava. You can polish raw obsidian nuggets and turn them into jewelry, or hang them on key chains. The stones look black in your hand, but if you hold them to the light, they appear smoky and translucent. Obsidian is found on all seven continents. But for a specimen to be identified as an Apache Tear, it must come from Superior.

Apaches have long used obsidian to make tools, weapons, and ritual objects. There are Apache tales in which obsidian is used as protective armor. There is a story in which a knife made of obsidian is used to form the anatomy of a woman.

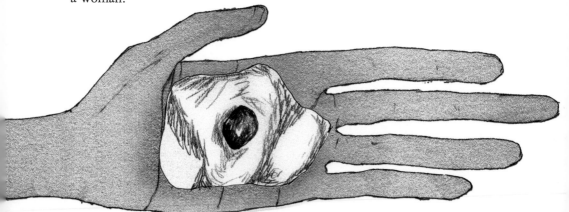

In the 1960s, Johnny Cash became interested in Native American history. He visited Arizona's Pima reservation and was given an Apache Tear. He was told the story of the warriors' mass suicide. He had his Apache Tear made into a pendant on a gold chain. Cash wrote a song called "Apache Tears," which he included on his 1964 protest album, *Bitter Tears: Ballads of the American Indian*. Cash growls the lyrics over a sighing background choir and a drumbeat that trips and drags like the gait of a tired horse.

> Hoof prints and foot prints, deep ruts the wagons made
> The victor and the loser came by here
> No head stones, but these bones
> Bring the Mescalero death moans
> See the smooth black nuggets by the thousands lying here
> Petrified, but justified
> Are these Apache Tears.

Online gem wholesalers advertise Apache Tears with a variety

of slogans and promises. "Whoever has one never has to cry again,

since the Apache women

did the crying

in their place."

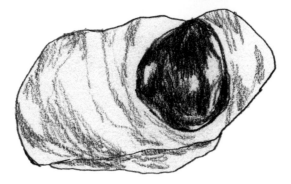

Apache Leap is a point of pride on the Superior landscape.

Residents describe watching sunsets turn the cliffs

gold and scarlet,

how when they're returning from out of town,

they see Apache Leap in the distance

and that moment marks

their homecoming.

Superior's annual town celebration, with its staged mine rescues,

drilling competitions, and parade of homemade floats, is known

as the Apache Leap Mining Festival.

Resolution Copper is the festival's principal sponsor.

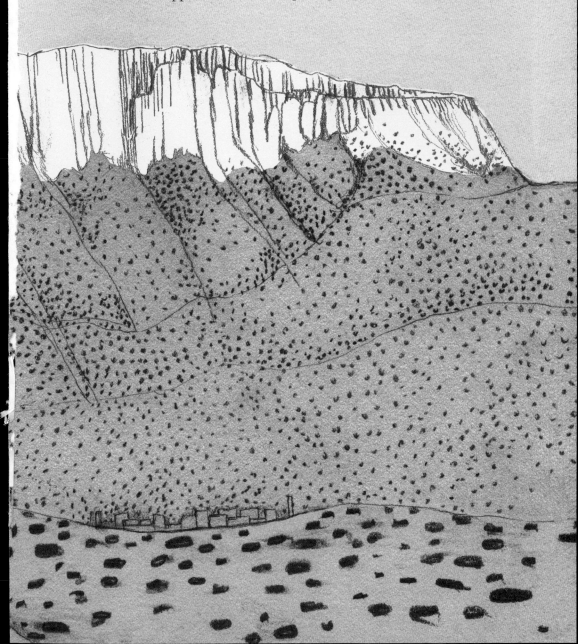

Apache Leap is 1,500 feet from what is slated to be Resolution Copper's deepest mineshaft, the former Magma mine's No. 9 shaft, which Resolution is enlarging. In a concession to public outcry, Resolution Copper has forfeited the right to extract ore directly underneath Apache Leap. The company has stated that its accommodations will "ensure that Apache Leap is fully protected in perpetuity." The U.S. Forest Service, which is charged with coordinating oversight of the Apache Leap Special Management Area, is not as definitive. In response to a question about damage to Apache Leap, Forest Service public affairs specialist John Scaggs wrote in an email, "Yes, there is possible risk. The magnitude of the mine subsidence and associated effects are under analysis."

◆ ◆ ◆

ALBO GUZMAN WAS BORN IN SUPERIOR IN 1941. That year, his father, Mike, bought a dump truck and opened a sand and gravel business. Mike Guzman was tired of working underground in the Magma Copper mine, tired of the disorienting darkness and the temperatures that reached 125 degrees. He told his son that the tunnels where he spent his days were "hot and invisible." The sand and gravel business was a success, but Mike Guzman was still restless, searching for new opportunities. Like prospectors before him, Guzman stalked the land, hoping to strike it rich.

ALBO GUZMAN: "He was always going around, looking for gold, or silver, or copper. He'd go out and look in the hills. Dig a little here, dig a little there."

Not far from the base of Apache Leap, Guzman discovered not silver or gold or copper, but another mineral that had become profitable to mine: perlite. Guzman staked his claim.

Perlite is a hydrous form of obsidian. Obsidian has low moisture content, but if exposed to groundwater over time, it absorbs the water and turns into perlite. When heated, perlite pops, like popcorn, swelling to occupy up to 20 times its original volume. Expanded perlite is light, strong, and fire-resistant, making it a versatile industrial material. Perlite is used in construction, in cinder blocks, in insulation, in ceiling tiles, in filtration systems. Perlite is used to filter beer. It's used in aerospace, marine, and ground vehicles. Gardeners use horticultural perlite to aerate soil and improve drainage. In their natural state, unprocessed obsidian nodules bulge out of a white perlite matrix like cartoon eyeballs staring out into space. Soon after planting his mine claim, Guzman discovered his perlite deposit was full of obsidian.

Albo Guzman has run his late father's sand and gravel business since 1988.

ALBO GUZMAN: "My dad said that when the United States Cavalry went up to Apache Leap and attacked the Indians, the Indians jumped off, and the squaws cried. *Apache tears.*"

Guzman transformed his perlite mine into the Apache Tear Caves.

ALBO GUZMAN: "Like a lot of people, he was looking for the thing called the mother lode. It didn't happen. The only thing that did take off was the Apache Tears."

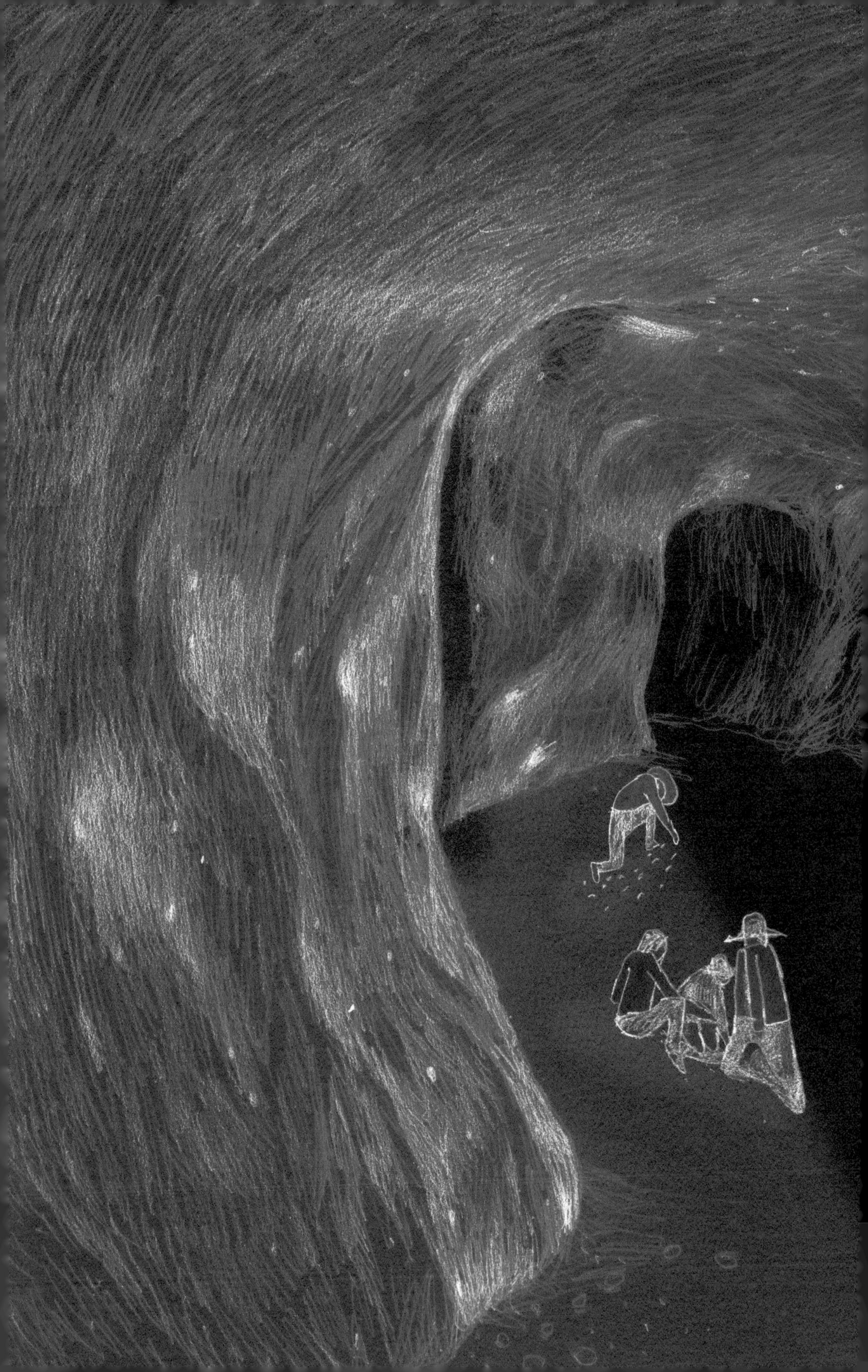

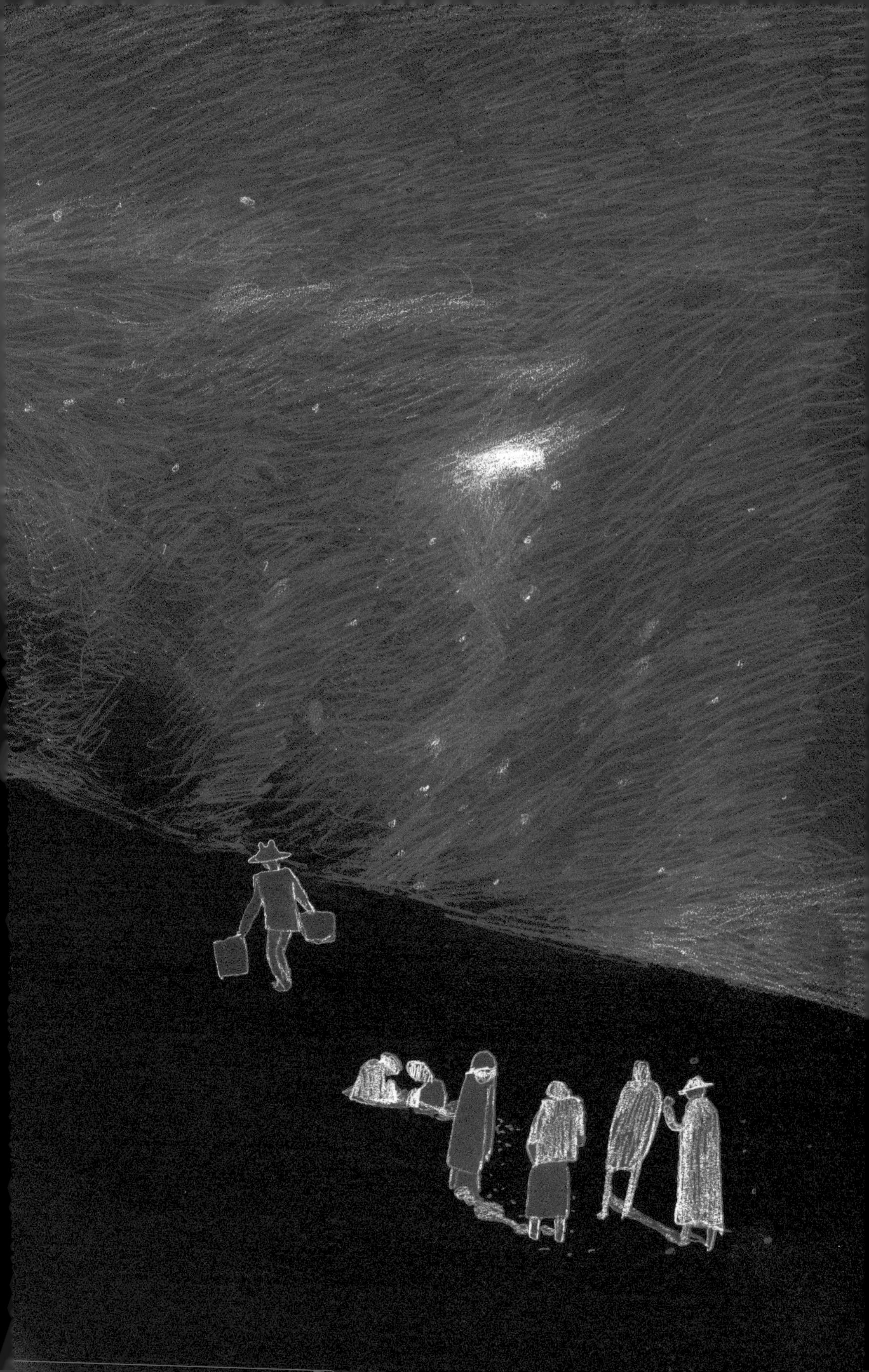

Apache Tear Caves became a tourist attraction. Mike Guzman charged visitors a dollar to spend the day filling a gallon bucket with all the Apache Tears they could find. People came from across the United States, from Spain, from Germany, and beyond.

ALBO GUZMAN: "We used to go up there with an air compressor. We would drill, and we would blast the Apache Tears all over. Then I would get on the bulldozer and I would go 'doze around, fix it up."

Newspapers picked up the story about the Apache Tears and retold it, embroidering new details. In 1967, *The Philadelphia Inquirer* wrote, "When the squaws came for the bodies of their warrior husbands they heard a soft voice murmuring in the breeze: 'Thy bitter tears shall be turned into beautiful stones, for I should not have made these cliffs so high.'"

ALBO GUZMAN: "Boy, the people went crazy. They loved it."

In 1977, *The Arizona Republic* ran a photograph of a dozen crouching figures spread out over an undulating field of white perlite, a kind of Martian wasteland. The caption read, "Crowds of Arizonans and tourists crawl over piles of earth poking and digging for Apache tears." "Recently," the paper reported, "a group of fathers and sons from Phoenix was enjoying a YMCA Indian Guide outing. They planned to use Apache Tears to make key chains."

The Apache Tear Caves closed decades ago, but the story of the stones is still told. According to Albo Guzman, the story did not originate with Native people. Guzman says his father came up with the idea of the crying women, and he invented the name Apache Tears. It was a marketing scheme.

ALBO GUZMAN: "He made it up. And it went like wildfire."

Guzman doesn't believe the original tale either, the part about the fatal confrontation and the warriors jumping.

ALBO GUZMAN: "That was made up in the 1800s. That's just an old, bullshit story."

I n 2016, protests against the Dakota Access Pipeline attracted worldwide attention. The oil pipeline was designed to run from North to South Dakota, across Iowa, and into Illinois. The Standing Rock Sioux objected to the pipeline's path on the grounds that it violated treaty rights and threatened the tribe's water supply, grave sites, and sacred land. Thousands camped out at Standing Rock to try and stop the project. For a few months, the turmoil was headline news. There was widespread outrage at the tactics that soldiers and police in riot gear had unleashed to stifle demonstrators: attack dogs, Tasers, tear gas, high-pitched sound cannons, freezing cold water in subzero temperatures, arrests, strip searches. In December 2016, the Obama administration blocked construction of the pipeline's most contested section.

A month later, newly inaugurated president Donald Trump reversed the decision. By June 2017, oil was flowing. In the tumultuous first year of the Trump administration, the media moved on. In September 2017, Standing Rock Sioux tribal chairman David Archambault II, a hero while the spotlight was trained on the controversy, was voted out of office. His challenger, Mike Faith, told the Associated Press that he, too, opposed the pipeline, but wondered if, by focusing so much energy on the protest, the tribe had inadvertently allowed other problems—troubled schools, inadequate health care, high rates of drug abuse and suicide—to fester. The protests had also diverted traffic away from the tribe's casino, a crucial revenue source. "We did what we had to do," Faith said, "but we didn't realize we were going to hurt our economy that much."

Michael Betom is tall and imposing. He wears a stud earring in each ear. In 2010, when he was 20 years old, Betom got a job in Resolution Copper's geology department. Later, he joined the company's Communities and

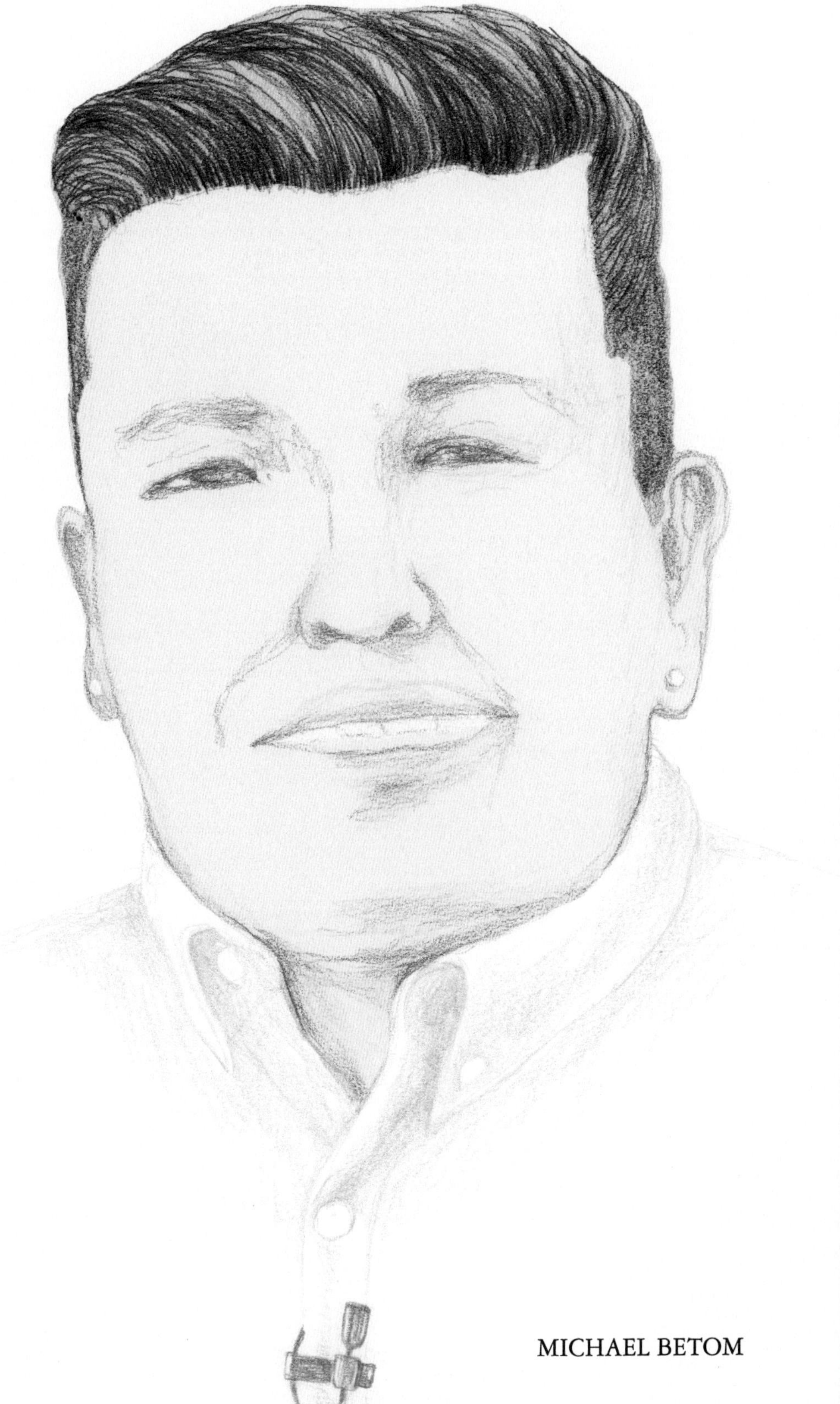

MICHAEL BETOM

Social Performance team. Betom is one of a few members of the San Carlos Apache Tribe employed by Resolution. Tribal members who work for Resolution Copper are controversial figures in San Carlos. Betom is a proud contrarian, strong-willed and opinionated. In 2018, the profile picture on his Instagram account showed him holding a toddler. They both wore dark sunglasses. Underneath the photo, his bio read, "You don't like me? Cool, I don't wake up every day to impress you!"

MICHAEL BETOM: "How would it have looked if there had been Dakota Access Pipeline workers that were Native Americans, telling other Native Americans, *There's opportunity here, let's do it!* Nothing against the people that protest, that say, 'Water is Life.' But they only want to address problems. Nobody wants to do solutions. I want solutions. I say, 'Address your problems to me so we can deal with it.'"

Betom appears in Resolution Copper's online video series "On Site with Mike," in which he is identified as the company's Native affairs coordinator. He has become a kind of ambassador for Resolution in Superior. Over the years, he has given public tours of Resolution Copper's operations in town. He brings visitors to the West Plant site to see remnants of the old Magma mine operation, including the entrance to Magma's "Never Sweat Tunnel," North America's first air-conditioned mine tunnel. At the East Plant, where the company is expanding what was the Magma mine's No. 9 shaft as well as sinking new mine shafts, visitors can take in all of Oak Flat from a viewing platform. At each stop on his tour, Betom smokes a Marlboro Light.

MICHAEL BETOM: "My primary focus is engagement of Native American tribes. There are 12 tribes that have historical ties to the area that will be affected by the mine. I developed a cultural awareness training. Any new contractor or new hire at Resolution has to sit through my cultural awareness training for an hour. I cover the history of the region and how we engage with tribes.

"My tribe opposes this project for a number of reasons. Which is valid, right? The extractive industry did a horrible job in the early years when it came to developing mines. So of course there's going to be historical trauma around Native Americans and people in general when it comes to mining. I think that the mining industry is taking a different turn now.

"After the land exchange passed, the fire came. Every news outlet bashed Resolution Copper. *The New York Times*: 'Stealing Apache land! Circumventing the process!' We didn't circumvent any process. Any time a news camera comes, they want to record 'The Man Sticking It to the Native.' That's the sexy story. There were marches. There were protests. But we rode out the tsunami. It's still going, but it's not as bad as it used to be."

Betom grew up on the San Carlos Reservation, where his mother was a police officer. His father and grandfather were miners.

MICHAEL BETOM: "They always told me, 'We're going to break your hands if you ever work at the mines.' But I said, 'It's different now. I'm not on the labor side of it.' They were still a little hesitant at first.

"I've always known this area. Before the reservation got established, Apaches migrated in that area. We're a nomadic tribe. We would come to this region—it's a great lookout—and we would look down at the neighboring tribes, see where the smoke was. We would raid the lower valley tribes. Steal women, steal horses, steal blankets, guns, whatever we could. Eventually we'd migrate back through this area and go back to our traditional homelands.

"There is a group of people that feel that this area is sacred to them. Do I have that right to say what is sacred and what is not? No."

Betom steers his van up Main Street and turns left on North Magma Ave, heading up the hill toward the West Plant. You can see train tracks and open hopper cars that Magma workers used for hauling ore. Each car bears the name of a character from the children's franchise Thomas the Tank Engine. Thomas, Percy, James. You can see a faded painting of Thomas's grinning face on the front of Engine 1. Betom warns visitors to watch out for reptiles and bees.

MICHAEL BETOM: "We have to pick and choose our battles. How do you move forward? You go to the reservation: alcohol, drugs, 70 percent unemployment rate. There are not a lot of options and opportunities. You're telling me that you're going to turn down a job that could make a long-term agreement to

train your workforce? You can do stuff with those special skills. We're creating opportunities here. I'm using this company to better my community. If that means providing employment, educational partnerships, some type of business-to-business relationship for my community, then I'm all for it. There's, like, ten departments at Resolution Copper. Each department has well over a $10 million budget. They buy supplies, contracts. Why was no money spent in San Carlos? I want to be an advocate for my community, so San Carlos can actually be at the table."

Betom has other ideas for economic development on the reservation.

MICHAEL BETOM: "Think about casinos. They're good and bad, you know? Metropolitan tribes, they do great. But we're a rural community. We don't get a lot of people coming out to our community. Sometimes we

break even, sometimes we make a little bit more. Online gaming is going to grow. How can tribes regulate online gaming?"

Betom thinks San Carlos should have capitalized on Native American tribal sovereignty to create a foothold in the marijuana business.

MICHAEL BETOM: "Now, with legalization, the ship has sailed."

He talks about building an alternative energy industry in San Carlos, installing fields of solar panels on the reservation. He envisions electric car charging stations.

MICHAEL BETOM: "I said, 'There are no Tesla stations in rural communities. Why?' So now me and my buddy are going to see if we can get Tesla to put a charging station on our reservation, so we can bring in some of those drivers."

Betom describes himself as three-quarters Apache and a quarter Navajo. When Betom's Navajo grandfather was a child, he was taken by Bureau of Indian Affairs agents to a boarding school.

MICHAEL BETOM: "They picked him up off the prairie. They put him there, cut his hair, gave him a new name. They whipped him for speaking his language."

After boarding school, Betom's grandfather was offered vocational training in Idaho as part of the government's 1956 Indian Relocation Act.

MICHAEL BETOM: "He worked in the potato fields in Idaho, digging spuds."

From Idaho, Betom's grandfather transferred to a technical program in Oakland, California, where he learned the skills of a machinist. He became the chrome plater for Oakland's Hell's Angels.

MICHAEL BETOM: "He met my grandmother in Oakland. She was from San Carlos. She was in the same program, working in a warehouse, sewing and packaging clothing. My grandparents never spoke to me in their native tongues. They wanted me to get familiar with the English language."

Resolution's East Plant sits on a gravelly plateau. The steel head-frames of two mineshafts dominate the area, each structure a kind of stumpy Eiffel Tower. On the ground, pallets are stacked with construction materials wrapped in plastic. A truck pivots and backs up, a crane lowers its arm. But most of Resolution's work is invisible at the surface. On the wooden viewing deck at the edge of the plateau, there are informational panels depicting a cross-section of the mineshafts and a diagram of "Shaft Sinking Methodology." There is a panoramic photo of the desert below, including Oak Flat. On the photo, Oak Flat's acreage is circled in blue; the predicted subsidence area is delineated by an interlocking band of red.

The viewing platform was built for Prince Andrew, Duke of York, who visited the site in 2008. As the United Kingdom's special representative for trade and investment, Andrew was in Arizona to promote UK businesses, including London-based Rio Tinto.

In 2011, Prince Andrew stepped down from his role as trade envoy following a series of scandals. The viewing platform remained. Betom decided to incorporate it into his tours.

MICHAEL BETOM: "The people that oppose Resolution have the mind-set of the old Apache way. All of southeast Arizona, all of the United States, was once Native American land. The federal government came in this region. Of course there was resistance. You were coming onto somebody's homeland. But if we don't embrace change, we get left behind."

RESOLUTION COPPER'S EAST PLANT

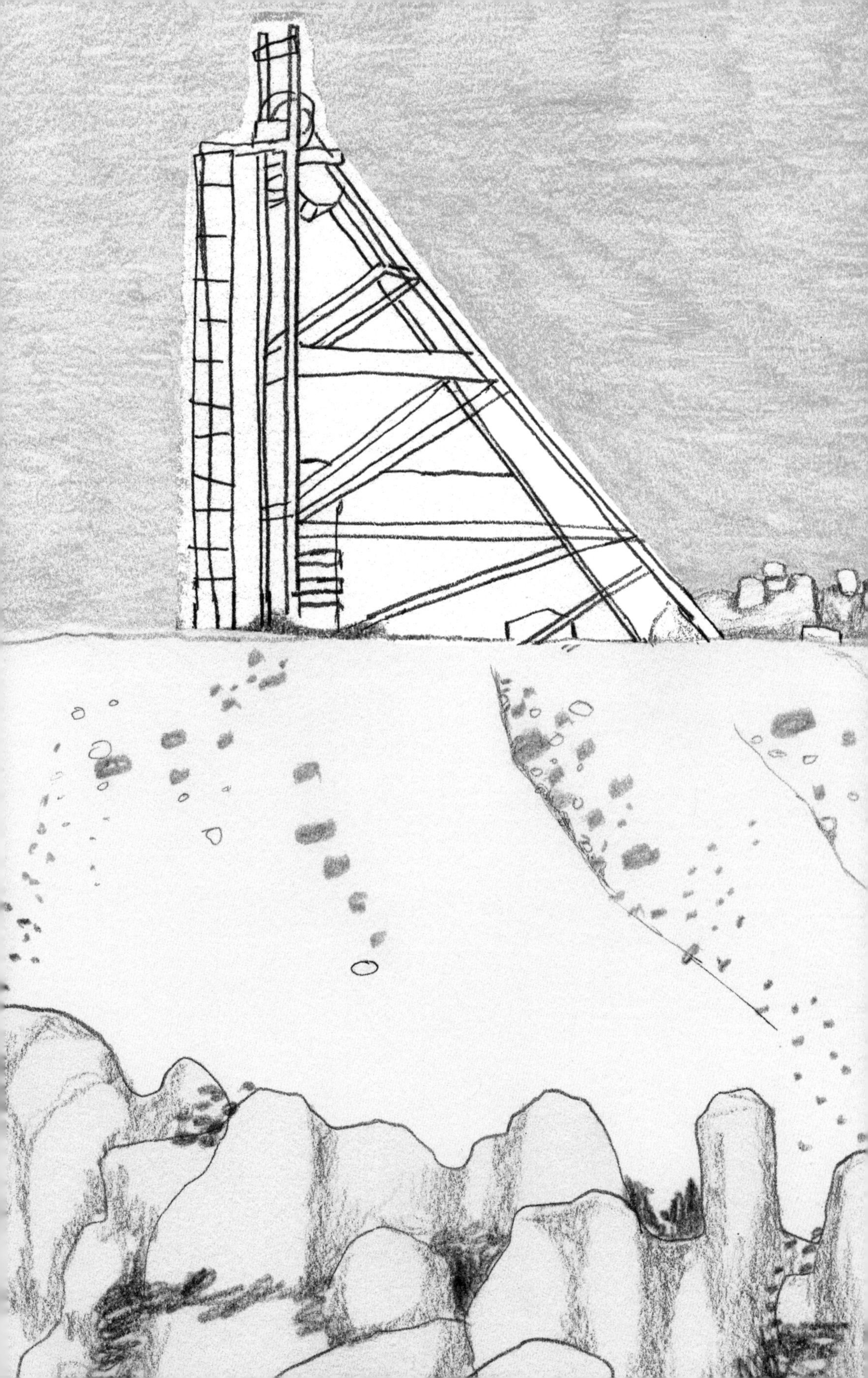

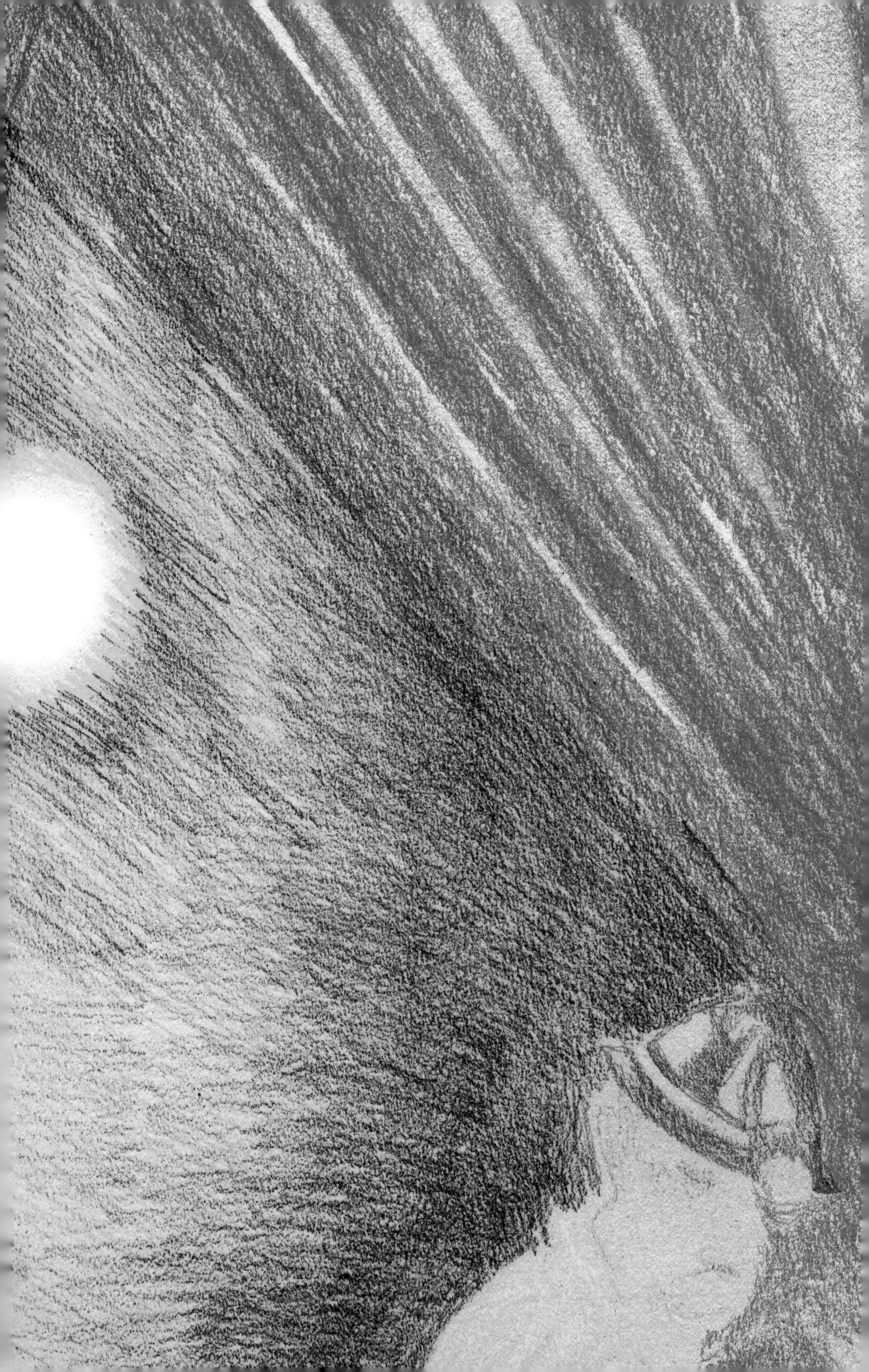

INSIDE RESOLUTION

COPPER'S No. 9 SHAFT,

7,000 FEET BENEATH

EAST PLANT

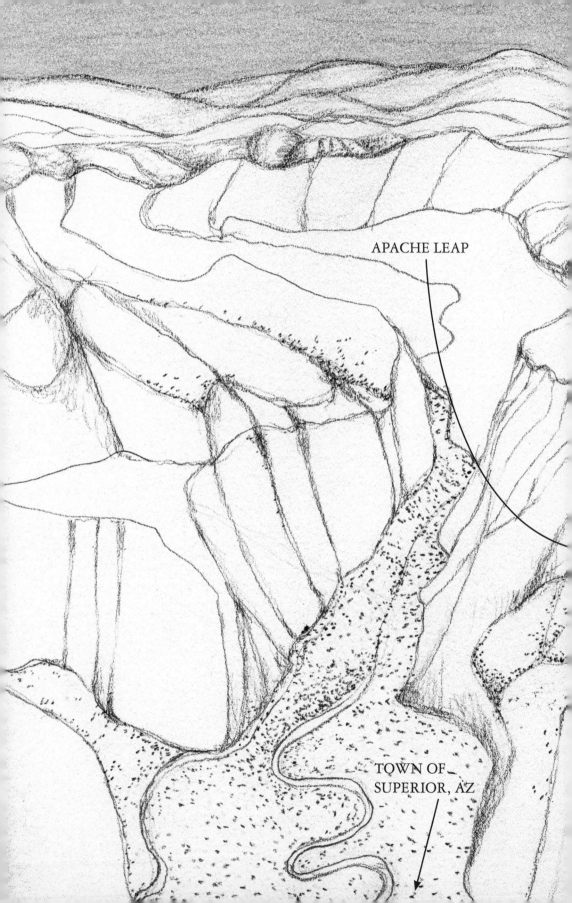

APACHE LEAP

TOWN OF
SUPERIOR, AZ

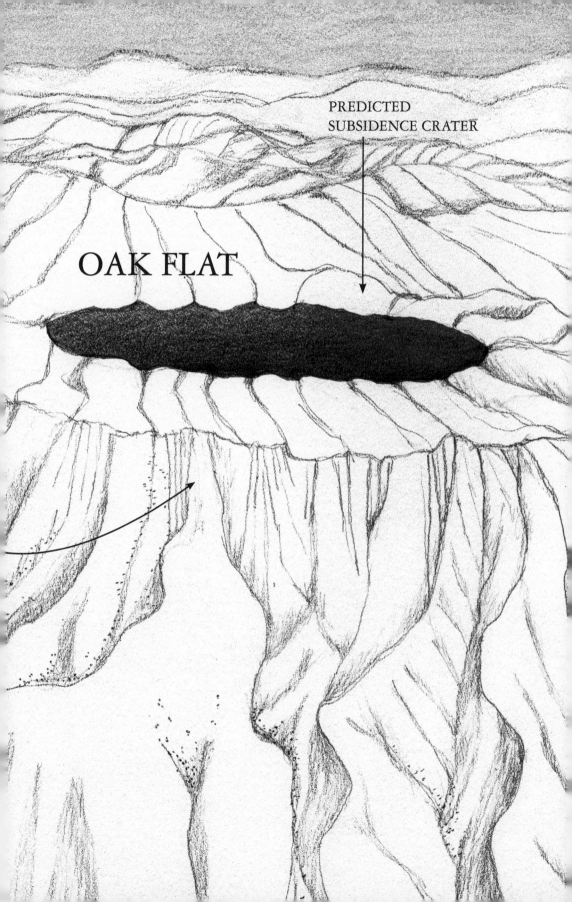

PREDICTED
SUBSIDENCE CRATER

OAK FLAT

MICHAEL BETOM: "Mining people talk about boom and bust cycles. I always say, that never affected reservations. Why? Because we've been in busts all these years. We never saw booms. This little boom here may be something we need. We've opposed other projects, other developments, and we've always lost. I used to be that reservation kid who looked for the Zorro, who looked for the Robin Hood. At the end of the day, we can romanticize Geronimo and everything he ever did, but I'm tired of living in the past."

◆ ◆ ◆

BETWEEN THEM, Betom and his girlfriend have six children, aged one to fourteen.

MICHAEL BETOM: "I'm tired of struggling. I will always have my home on the reservation. But I tell my kids all the time, I say, 'Take a look around you. Everything is designed for you to depend on the federal government. Everything is designed for you to just go to high school and become a drunk.'

"When I got into the mining industry, I traveled a lot. My girlfriend at the time couldn't cope with what I was doing. She wanted to stay on the reservation. She didn't understand what I like to call 'my American dream.' I wanted to become successful."

During Betom's senior year of high school, one of his teachers told the students that they should register to vote.

MICHAEL BETOM: "A kid in my class raised his hand, 'What should we register as?' I still remember this teacher. I will remember him for the rest of my life. He said, 'All you kids here, your families, you're all poor. So you have to register as Democrat.' He said, 'Republicans are rich.' I was sitting in my classroom, thinking, *I don't want to be poor forever. I want to be rich one day!* So I said, *Screw it. I'm going to be a Republican.*"

Betom lights another cigarette.

"If this company could have built this mine with no say from the tribes, they would have. That's the reality of it. At the end of the day, Oak Flat is going to be destroyed regardless."

Over his years at Resolution Copper, Betom has traveled with the company. He's met executives, lobbyists, and politicians.

MICHAEL BETOM: "I was at a fund-raising dinner down in Scottsdale. I'd worked with Senator McCain before and I got tickets from the company. Nobody wanted to go. So I was like, 'I'll go.' I go with my girlfriend. I'm dressed in a suit. Million-dollar home. BMWs, Lexuses, Range Rovers. We walked in the door. We're the only Native Americans there. All these white people are looking at us. Senator McCain is up there talking, talking about legislation, his platform. He goes, 'Hello, Mr. Betom' and comes down this stairway in this huge two-story house. Everybody looks over at me and my girlfriend. He comes over, shakes my hand. 'How are you doing?'

"'I'm doing good, Senator. How are you doing?'

"Senator McCain says, 'Everybody, that's Michael Betom. He works at Resolution Copper. He's a really good guy.'"

CHAPTER 11

Before the Magma mine smelter was torn down in the fall of 2018, an owl made its home inside the abandoned building. Early in the morning, you could see it glide toward the brick facade, snap its wings shut to pass through a broken window, extend them to sail across the smelter's empty interior, and pull them shut again to exit through another open window on the other side.

For nearly 100 years, the smelter's brick smokestack had been visible from nearly every place in town. You could see the smokestack from Patricia Brown's ranch house, about a mile to the south.

It was a few days before one recent Christmas. Patricia's house was strung with colored lights. The twilight sky was a dark electric blue. In the living room, the TV was on. The American flag sent home with the body of Patricia's older brother, 24-year-old Staff Sergeant Patrick "Patsy" Gorham, killed by German sniper fire in 1944, was folded into a triangle and framed. On a side table next to the sofa, a ceramic Santa Claus held York Peppermint Patties. Patricia had invited her brother and sister-in-law, Jackie and Evelyn Gorham; her nephew Mike McKee; and her 12-year-old grandson, Nathan Taylor, for pizza and empanadas.

MICHAEL McKEE: "I remember driving to the airport to listen to the radio. You'd go there for 'better reception.'"

JACKIE GORHAM: "That's what you used to say if you had a girlfriend."

PATRICIA BROWN: "A lot of people used to go 'parking' in the cemetery. Benny Escendones had a black—"

JACKIE GORHAM: "—Ford Mercury."

MICHAEL McKEE: "There was a lady who lived on Sunset. You'd drive by, honk your horn three times, and pull into the cemetery—"

PATRICIA BROWN: "And she'd come out."

JACKIE GORHAM: "Remember the telephone operator? She satisfied a lot of people here in town."

PATRICIA BROWN: "All my brothers."

JACKIE GORHAM: "She drove a Hudson. The car was like *this* [rocking motion] all the time."

EVELYN GORHAM: "We had one teacher—a lot of the football players, that's how they got good grades. She'd take them out to the creek right there. They'd get A's."

PATRICIA BROWN: "Oak Flat—"

MICHAEL McKEE: "—Oak Flat was a parking spot for the high school students."

Patricia looks at her grandson, Nathan.

PATRICIA BROWN: "That's where your mama used to park."

MICHAEL McKEE: "People weren't supposed to, but they'd hunt at Oak Flat. Deer. Bear. Domestic goats that somebody'd turned loose."

PATRICIA BROWN: "We used to picnic at Oak Flat."

MICHAEL McKEE: "And fish crawdads."

EVELYN GORHAM: "Oh, I used to go crawdad fishing with bacon up there all the time."

PATRICIA BROWN: "We'd catch 'em and throw them back in. One year, when I was in high school, some of the guys went up there because we wanted to taste frog legs. There were little tiny ones, jumping all over."

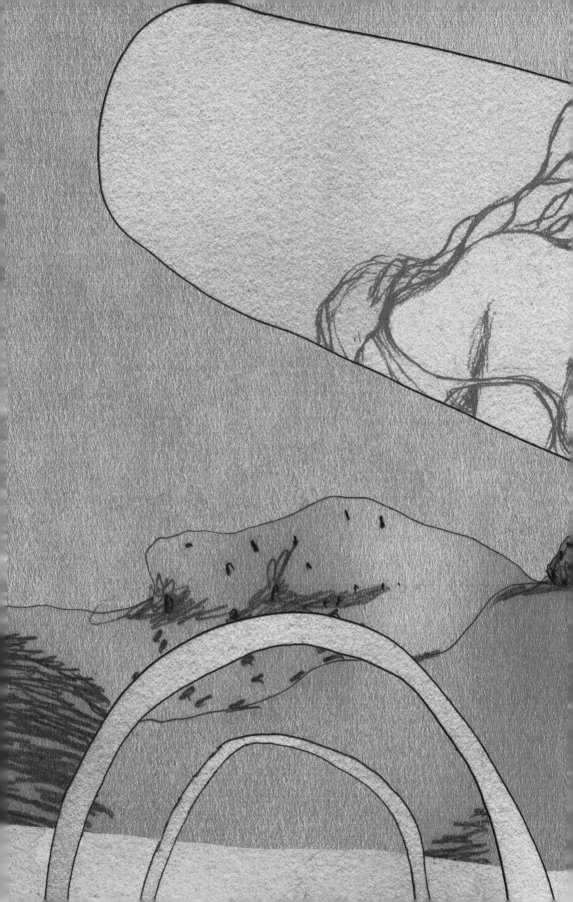

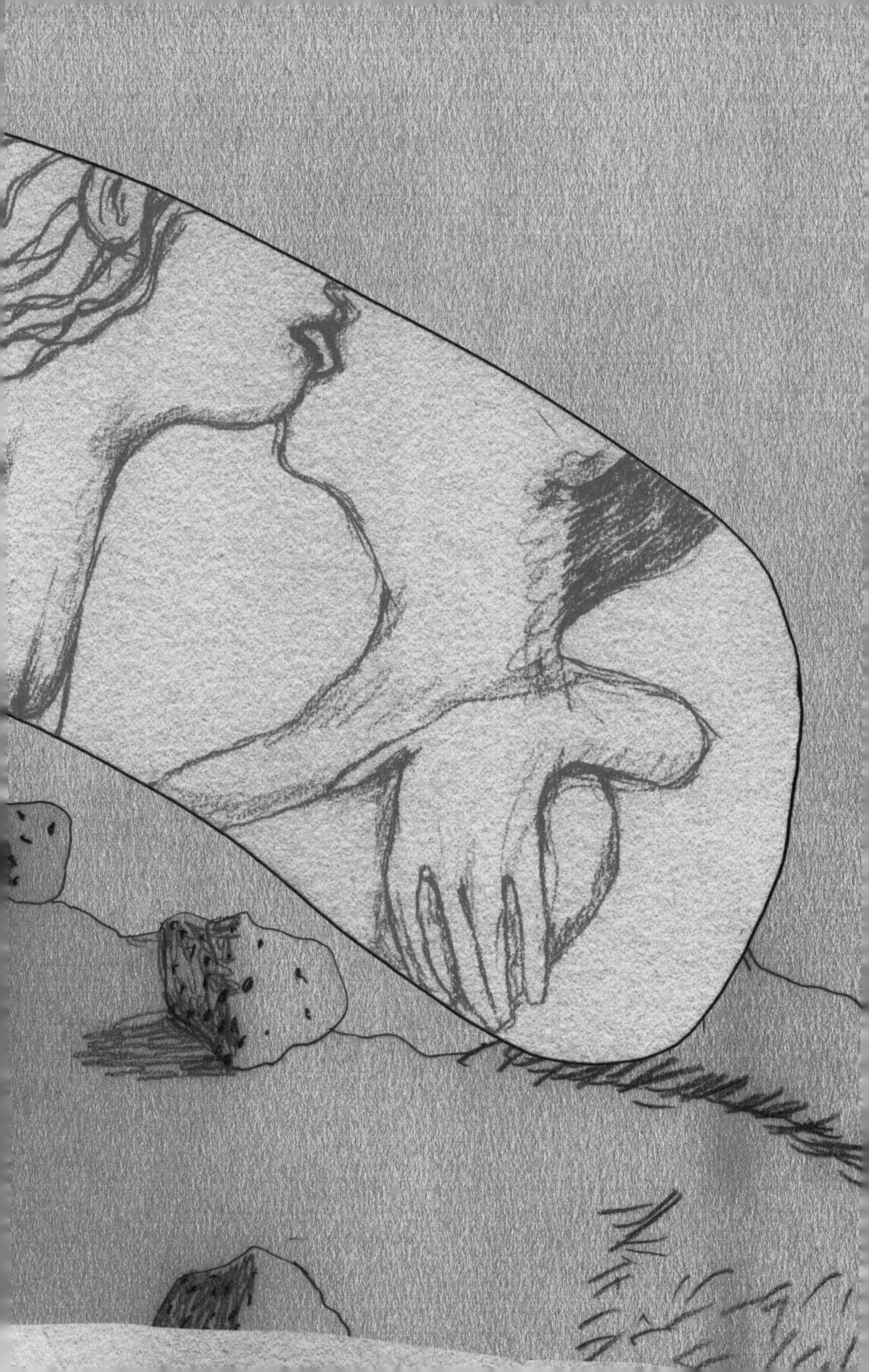

MICHAEL McKEE: "Oak Flat is big. You have an upper level, and you have two lower levels. Up top there's the big acorn tree.

"You could play baseball, horseshoes, whatever you wanted. Everybody fought to get that place."

PATRICIA BROWN: "My sister lived up at Oak Flat, and the Indians would come there to gather acorns."

JACKIE GORHAM: "The Oak Lodge had their annual Labor Day picnic up there."

PATRICIA BROWN: "First time I got married, I was 24. He was a cattle rancher here in town."

MICHAEL McKEE: "He was overgrazing all the land."

PATRICIA BROWN: "He was an alcoholic, a very abusive man. But I kept it quiet. My sisters knew because they came over one day and they saw all the bruises on my neck. But they never asked me what happened.

"With my second husband, Lorne, we'd go up to Oak Flat. We'd go up there with his tribe, all his kids, and we'd camp out all night."

JACKIE GORHAM:

"I'd drive up there just to get away from everybody."

"It was nice and quiet up there.

Away from everybody."

CHAPTER 12

In 1916, the *Arizona Republican* described Superior, Arizona, a town
barely 14 years old, as a relic. The newspaper ran a photo of abandoned
mine infrastructure captioned, "Where once man reigned supreme for a few
short years, there remains but shattered ruin and ghosts of ancient days, a
memory of El Dorado and a silver horde."

But things were looking up, the paper reported. Mining was to resume
"on a larger scale than ever. . . . The hum of activity again permeates the
place." An Australian investor had stepped in, backed with British capital,
and he planned to dig deeper and explore farther for untapped wealth.
"Thus the world may witness the tale of a city that was a prosperous, happy
community; a city that expired, a ghost city, rivaling in legendary lore
any of the great ghost cities of the west, and a city to be greater and more
prosperous than ever before."

For a few years, silver sustained Superior again. But eventually, the Silver
King of Arizona Mining Company went bankrupt. With the opening of
the Magma Copper mine, Superior had a new lifeline. The town's fortunes
zigged and zagged with copper as they had with silver. Magma Copper
struggled, but stayed open, through the Depression. Labor strikes in the
1950s and 1960s had temporarily crippling effects. ("We can't send our
children to school with no shoes," one Magma miner told the *Arizona
Daily Star* in 1959.) Again, Superior recovered, but in 1982, the price of
copper dipped below the cost of production, three miners were killed in a
cave-in, and the Magma mine shut down. Residents moved away, the
economy collapsed. The mine reopened with a limited workforce in 1990,
but six years later, Magma was shuttered for good.

MICHAEL McKEE: "You'd drive Main Street at night, and if there was a car out it was a miracle."

MILA BESICH-LIRA: "There's been controversy about Resolution Copper because there's fear. Fear because of what happened in the past."

In 2011, Elliott D. Pollack & Company, a Scottsdale-based consulting firm, produced an "Economic and Fiscal Impact Report" on behalf of Resolution Copper. The report stated that Resolution would support more than 3,700 jobs and generate nearly a billion dollars in economic activity each year of the mine's life. The Pollack report predicted a "ripple effect" of economic benefits: indirectly created jobs, taxes generated by an uptick in retail sales, new homes, and new residents. The report's conjectures were treated as facts in news articles, op-ed essays, public statements, and testimony in Congress by elected officials.

The San Carlos Apache Tribe commissioned its own analysis to examine the claims in the Pollack report. Power Consulting, a firm run by University of Montana professor emeritus of economics Thomas Power, found the Pollack report's predictions misleading and their methods flawed. The tribe's report disputed the number of jobs that the mine would create, in part because of Resolution's plan to use automation and robotic technology to keep operating costs down. The tribe's study pointed out that the Pollack report had looked only at the benefits Resolution Copper might produce and "imagined there would be no costs associated with the mine." "It is unusual," Power Consulting wrote, "to design an economic analysis that considers only pure benefits. Economics as a social science weighs both costs and benefits."

Copper mining creates an enormous amount of waste. In order to obtain pure copper from raw ore, the unrefined mineral-containing rock is pulled from the earth, ground into fine sand, and treated with water and chemicals. Resolution plans to pull 1.6 billion tons of ore to the surface for processing. The ore is approximately 1.5 percent copper. After the copper and trace amounts of other minerals have been extracted, more than 90 percent of the excavated rock will be left as contaminated waste—1.5 billion tons of waste, the company estimates. This waste, the tailings, is a kind of slurry, which may contain arsenic, lead, mercury, and other hazardous materials. The Forest Service has explored various plans to accommodate the tailings that the Resolution Copper mine would generate. One version is a facility that would be on national forest land with an embankment 10 miles long and 520 feet high. Another, also partly located on public land, would have a disturbance footprint of 8,600 acres—10 times larger than New York City's Central Park.

Tailings dams are among the largest man-made structures on Earth. They can fail, with grave consequences. On November 5, 2015, an iron mine tailings dam in Minas Gerais, Brazil, suffered a breakdown. The Fundão Dam was run by Samarco Mineração SA, like Resolution Copper a subsidiary of BHP. Thick red sludge flooded out of the dam, inundating a nearby town. Toxic mud engulfed homes, destroyed wildlife, and killed 19 people. The waste slid 400 miles through the countryside until it reached the Atlantic Ocean where, *The Guardian* reported, "it left a reddish-brown plume visible from space." Brazil charged 22 mining company executives, including 8 from BHP, with homicide. The accident was widely declared Brazil's worst environmental disaster until 2019, when about 50 miles away, the tailings dam at a different mine (the Córrego do Feijão iron mine) also failed, killing more than 230 people and submerging the land in 15 million cubic yards of waste. In 2016, Andrew Robertson, a mining consultant and designer of large tailings facilities, told *The Wall Street Journal,* "Our dams and dumps are among the highest-risk structures on Earth."

Even if a tailings facility does not suffer a catastrophic breach, its contents can seep into the ground or water supply, or filter into the air as dust particles.

Resolution Copper's General Plan of Operations outlines the company's intent to measure and monitor air and water pollution, but its assurances are wrapped in disclaimers: "to the extent possible," "Resolution Copper will take reasonable precautions." Concerns about water, air, and soil contamination do not vanish with the closure of the mine. Tailings facilities must be maintained and monitored in perpetuity long after the mining company, a limited liability corporation, has shuttered its operation and, likely, ceased to exist.

Rio Tinto, Resolution Copper's other parent company, has been criticized for human rights violations, cozying up to corrupt regimes, and environmental destruction at its mines around the world. The company has been denounced for exposing workers to radiation in its uranium mine in Namibia and for its role in the civil war in Papua New Guinea. In 2008, the government of Norway said it would divest from Rio Tinto due to the company's "grossly unethical conduct." In 2017, the U.S. Securities and Exchange Commission charged Rio Tinto with fraud for hiding the failure of its multibillion-dollar investment in a Mozambique coal mine from auditors, investors, and the company's own board of directors. In 2018,

Rio Tinto defended giving executive bonuses in a year when two of its employees died on the job. According to Danny Kennedy, former director of Project Underground, a Berkeley-based human rights and environmental organization, "Rio Tinto could be a poster child for corporate malfeasance."

Resolution Copper acknowledges that the mine in Superior, Arizona, would be a terminal operation, with a predicted 40 productive years. Nevertheless, the company maintains the mine would be a catalyst for a robust and diversified economy. The tribe's consultants disagreed. The report commissioned by the tribe contends that rather than attract economic activity, mining repels it.

> The spectacular [environmental] degradation combined with the instability associated with mining operations actually discourages individuals, families, and businesses from locating in mining towns. That is why mining communities tend to be so specialized in mining, lacking in the economic diversification that can stabilize communities in the face of commodity price fluctuations. People and business are not drawn to mining areas except for the job opportunities. When those job opportunities "flicker" or disappear, residents and businesses disappear too. That is how "ghost towns" are generated.

THOMAS POWER: "You could just look at the other small towns in Arizona's Copper Triangle. They're not coming back. Mining companies are always saying, 'I know it used to be boom and bust, but this time will be different.' It's a fantasy world they're in."

◆ ◆ ◆

IT'S SATURDAY NIGHT. Superior's Optimist Club is hosting "Fun Night," an event sponsored by Resolution Copper at the Magma Club, the former social club for Magma miners located at the base of Apache Leap, now remodeled into a community center. Inside, a mobile gambling company, onthegocasino.com, has set up poker, craps, roulette, and blackjack tables manned by tuxedoed dealers. A DJ plays classic rock as projected lights shimmer on the ceiling and local politicians make rounds. The atmosphere is friendly and festive. In an adjacent room, there are buffet tables and silent auction items: a weekend getaway package, an autographed Arizona Cardinals football helmet, bottles of wine, whiskey, and gin. The event raises money for local students who have made honor roll.

MICHAEL McKEE: "It was called Casino Night—"

PATRICIA BROWN: "—but they changed it to Fun Night because Resolution couldn't support gambling."

David Lira, Mayor Besich-Lira's cousin, got his first job at Magma, cleaning out the smelter furnace, in 1956, when he was still in high school. Over the next five decades, Lira worked at Magma as a welder, a supervisor of railroad track maintenance, and an environmental coordinator. He monitored runoff from the mine's waste dumps. Lira and his family have watched the town's fortunes rise and fall along with the mine.

DAVID LIRA: "The mining company supported the schools. As the company went, the schools went."

CHERYL LIRA-CASTRO: "When we were in school, we had all these options available to us—"

DAVID LIRA: "Choruses, choirs, symphonies, bands. Different kinds of bands—dance bands, pep bands, marching bands."

MAIN STREET, SUPERIOR, ARIZONA

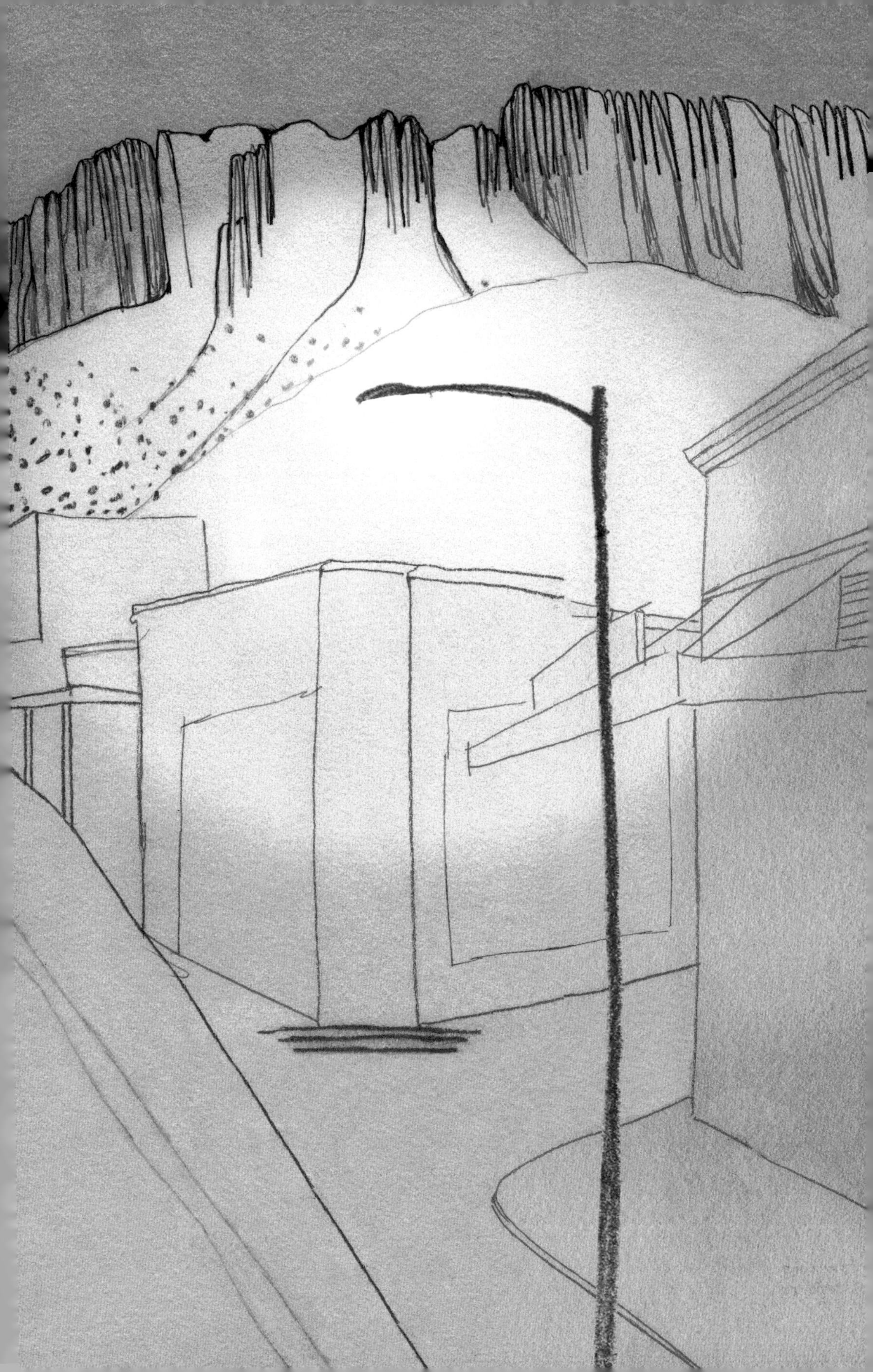

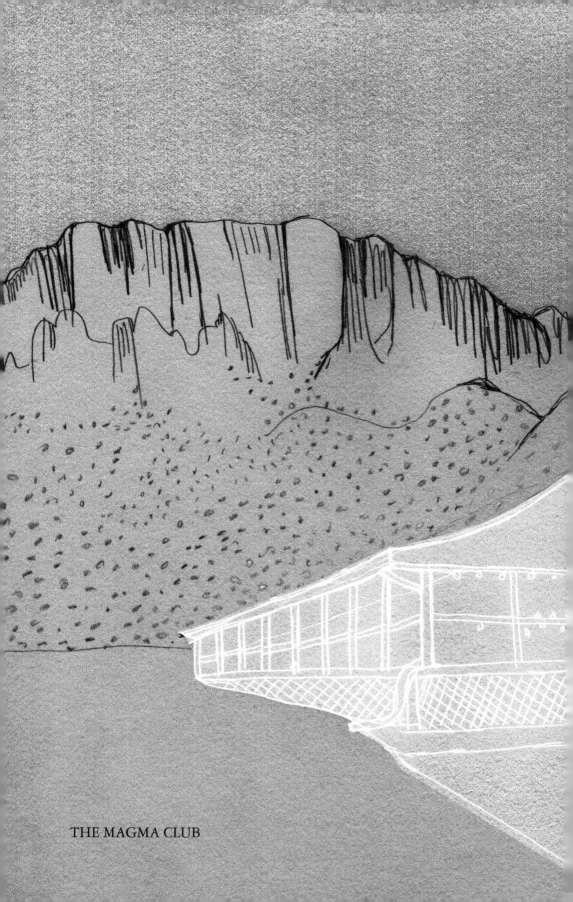

THE MAGMA CLUB

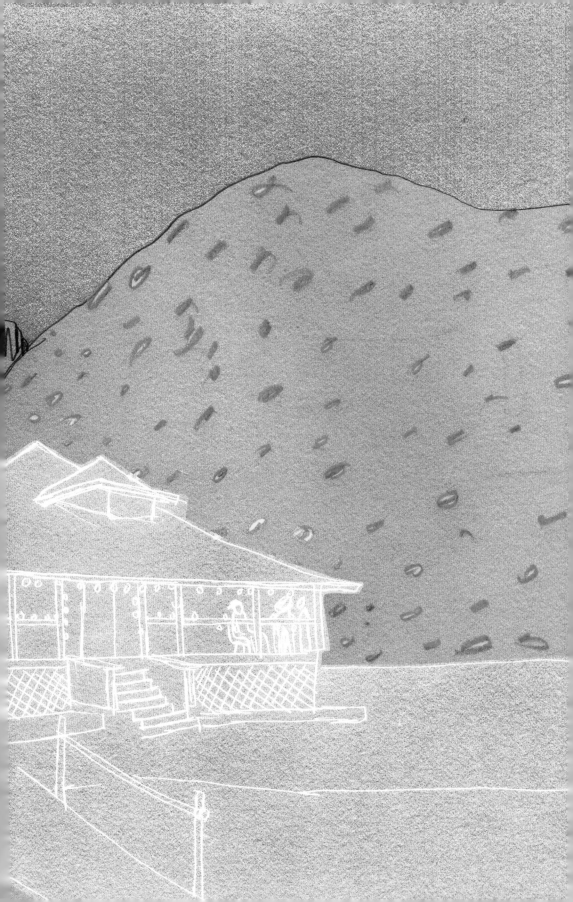

RESOLUTION COPPER OFFICES

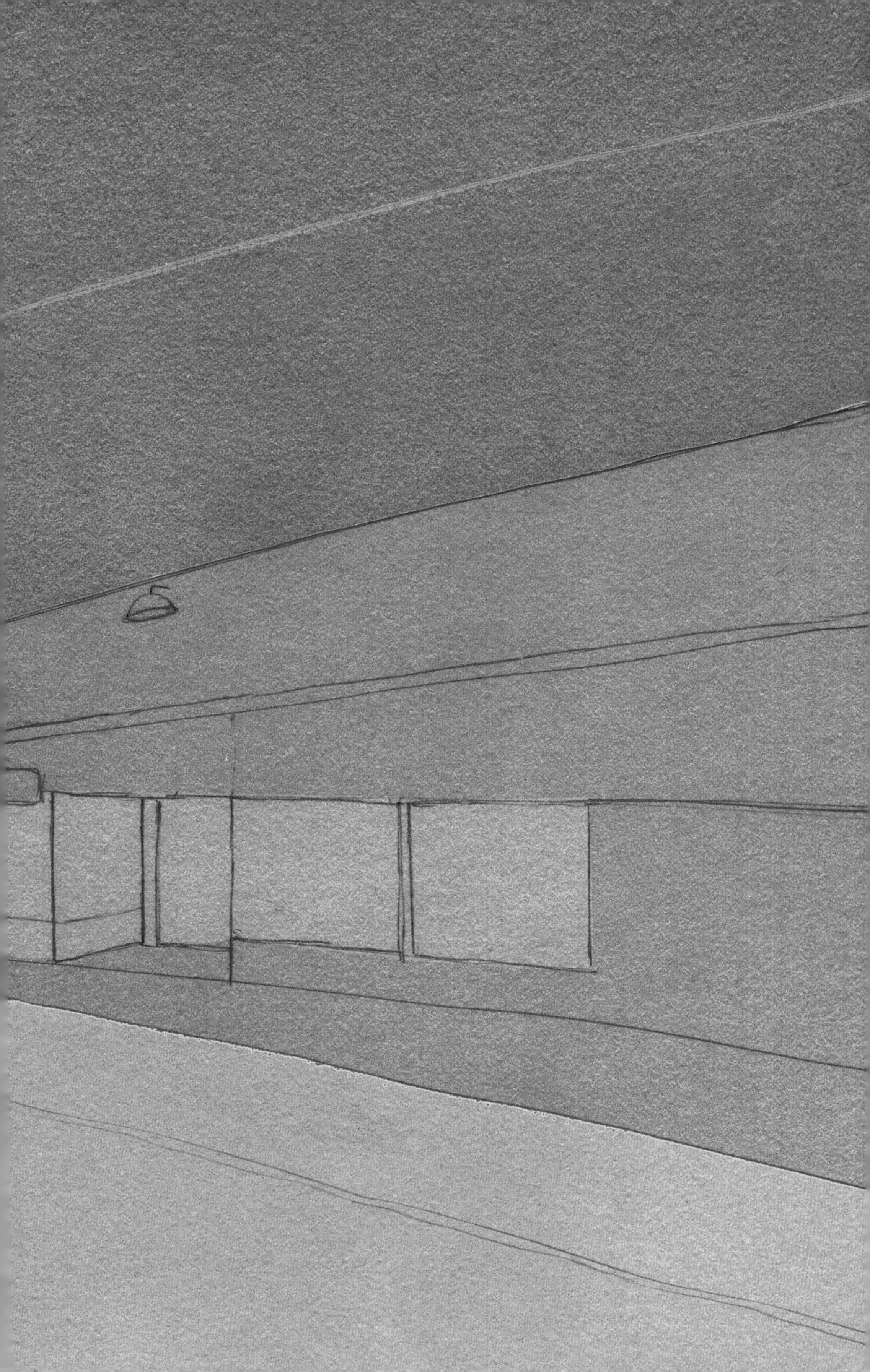

David Lira has played the saxophone since he was 12, when he would play all night in local dance bands and catch a ride home at dawn. His three daughters play trumpet, flute, sax, and piano. Evenings at home while the girls were growing up, the Liras sang together.

CHERYL LIRA-CASTRO: "In Superior High School now, there's no band. There's no art, no theater, or anything like that. There hasn't been a dance in our school for, what, 40 years? We don't even have math teachers, chemistry teachers. It's a failing school. A lot of their higher classes, kids will have to take online. They don't even have the option to take them sitting in a classroom."

DAVID LIRA: "We are starting to get an influx of artists and entrepreneurs that want to do tourist attractions. They don't want the new mine."

CHERYL LIRA-CASTRO: "What stresses me out when all these people fight against the mine—they're moved. They're gone. They want to keep the community historical. They don't know what a struggle it is right now just to raise a family here. For my daughter, just going to prom or a simple thing like going out to eat—the little things in life aren't available. Before, in the summer, you'd go work in the mines. Now there are not a lot of jobs in the community for the kids, if you don't work at Circle K. There's nothing for these kids to move forward, other than to move away."

Cheryl Lira-Castro's daughter graduated from Superior High in 2017. She enrolled in community college and got a full-time job at a Walgreens.

MILA BESICH-LIRA: "There's fear about the boom-bust cycle. There's also fear that big business gets away with everything."

MICHAEL McKEE: "People worry, *They're here today, gone tomorrow. They're a foreign outfit. Why are they selling copper to China?* You gotta remember, they're in business."

PATRICIA BROWN: "The young kids want Resolution. They want to go to work."

MICHAEL McKEE: "I'd like to see, like, 500 more people move into town. Fill in some of the empty buildings."

With the prospect of the Resolution Copper mine opening, the old MacPherson's Hotel Magma on Main Street is being refurbished. Chandeliers glitter in the lobby.

DEB McKEE: "If the new hotel opens, more people can come and stay, that might mean other small businesses, like a bicycle shop or something like that."

PATRICIA BROWN: "I've already seen people coming in, buying property."

MICHAEL McKEE: "I heard people talking about opening up a clothing store. I told them, 'We don't have one.' We have Random Boutique over there, but she don't sell Wranglers or cowboy hats or whatever. They said that they'd been going around to all the small towns looking for a place to open up. Knock on wood, I hope they come back."

DEB McKEE: "Without Resolution, I'm not sure that the resurgence would have started. Now we have some momentum going."

MILA BESICH-LIRA: "We have to prepare ourselves that it's not going to be the boom of my parents' youth or my grandparents' careers. It generates a ton of tax revenue, but not necessarily for the community. The way the mining laws are set up in the state of Arizona, they're not set up to give directly to the municipality. But what Resolution has done is said, 'Okay, what does the community need?' There are people that feel it's all false promises. But there's a larger group of people that are saying, 'We need to take advantage of this right here and right now.'

"I've had people that I respect—a lot of them are former miners, retired miners, people that maybe didn't bounce back once the mine shut down, maybe didn't qualify for the pension plan or things like that—come and say to me, 'I don't believe that you see through the smoke and mirrors of the mine.' And I say, 'I respect that you feel that way. But I don't believe that having an adversarial relationship with the mine is going to get us anywhere.'

"I'm not trying to be Pollyanna about this. I respect that these have been serious challenges for our community and it created extreme poverty at times for a lot of people. Drugs came in and, you know, really wrecked a lot of families because of the poor economic climate in the community. Those situations, they affect people. *How am I going to keep my house and take care of my children, my grandchildren? Because my kids have gone to prison or whatever.* I respect their fears.

"We have to remember that no matter how vehemently opposed you may be to mining, it's never going to go away. Our society, our lifestyles require large amounts of copper. The copper is not going anywhere. Whether it's Rio Tinto or BHP, some company is going to get it eventually. Someday a mine will open. I would like for it to open in my lifetime. I might be a very old lady by then, but I would like to say, 'I'll be there when they bring that first producing load up, ready for smelting, ready to go to production.'"

Some residents of Superior would like to move away from mining. They imagine capitalizing on the natural beauty of the area to lure residents who can work remotely or commute into Phoenix. The economy could be supported by recreation: rock climbing at Oak Flat, ecotourism, perhaps a golf course. Demand for copper could be addressed through existing mines not operating at full capacity, reduced consumption, and creative solutions like so-called urban mining, in which resources are harvested from discarded electronics, construction and demolition waste, and landfills.

Mike McKee has advice for opponents of the Resolution mine. "I tell them, 'Hey, it's gonna be 20 years before it opens up. You'll be dead, so you don't have to worry about it.'"

SUPERIOR, ARIZONA, CIRCA 1900

CHAPTER 13

Vanessa nosie:

"As soon as they

say, 'It's a girl!' the

preparations start."

WENDSLER NOSIE: "You're familiar with boxing, right? Well, that's kind of what the Sunrise Dance reminds me of. Picture it. You're dancing 64 songs. The songs are seven to eight minutes long. It's eight hours of dancing. You're lifting your feet. You're running in place. You have to withstand the heat."

THERESA NOSIE: "It's like running a marathon. She has to be ready."

During the four days of the Sunrise Dance, or *Na'ii'ees* ("getting her ready"), a girl entering puberty reenacts the Apache creation myth. Through the ceremony's stages, the girl is believed to transform into the Apache matriarch known as White Painted Woman, *Is dzán naadleeshe*. In the myth, there is a great flood and the White Painted Woman, the only human on Earth, takes shelter inside an abalone shell. When the waters recede, she emerges. The Creator, *Usen,* beckons her to a mountaintop, the first in a series of events recapitulated in the rituals of the dance. The ceremony requires hours of physical exertion, periods of fasting, perfect posture. It is a test of the girl's endurance and spiritual fortitude.

VANESSA NOSIE: "I was nine. The first in my family. When you have a huge ceremony, everybody knows you've had your menstrual. But girls aren't embarrassed. It's not embarrassing to the boys either, like, *Oh my god.* No. It's respected."

The girl's family chooses an older woman to be her godmother, a mentor who guides her through the months of preparation that will culminate in the four days of the full Sunrise Dance.

THERESA NOSIE: "You pick someone that you want your daughter to be like. You watch them for a while to see what their traits are. You give them a feather and stone. The feather is for protection. The stone is like the payment."

In the four days immediately after a girl has her first period, her body is considered "hot"—in a raw or embryonic state, rendering her symbolically pliable. The godmother massages the girl to shape her body and disposition. Baasé-O Pike went to Oak Flat for her massage.

THERESA NOSIE: "The godmother massages her while her body is hot, to form her so that her life is good."

BAASÉ-O PIKE: "You have to keep your head up, you are looking to the sun. When my godmother was massaging me, I heard Leroy, the medicine man, saying, 'Get her cheeks so she won't have wrinkles when she gets older.' 'Hit her feet four times to make her grow.'"

After the massage, the girl and her family have some six months to a year to gather everything she will need for the upcoming ceremony. Crown dancers, singers, drummers must be selected. The girl picks a partner who will be by her side for support throughout the ceremony, a girl who has already had her dance.

VANESSA NOSIE: "Her partner gives strength and encouragement. She should be someone that has a pure heart, who's still kind of innocent."

The family gathers ritual items like pollen and eagle feathers, makes a buckskin dress and a wooden cane with a curved handle.

THERESA NOSIE: "The beadwork on the buckskin symbolizes the girl. Today things have changed, but it used to be a kind of petroglyph of the girl's life."

The girl carries her cane, a symbol of longevity, tied with feathers, ribbons, and tin jingles, throughout the ceremony. She strikes it into the ground with each dancing step. She will save the cane, to use again when she is an old woman.

NAELYN PIKE: "The week before the dance itself, the girl builds her wickiup."

Long branches are bent to become the ribs of the dome-shaped shelter. Thinner branches are wrapped laterally around the boughs; where the branches cross, they are lashed together with grass twine.

THERESA NOSIE: "It has to be built a certain way, and that's her responsibility. She has to make it sturdy. You build with materials that are in the area. At Oak Flat, it's bear grass, or we bring willow and cottonwood up from the river. The godmother builds a house, too. She's probably built five or six of them by that time. Or maybe it's her first time being a godmother and she only built one when she was a girl."

That Friday, at sunrise, the ceremony officially begins. Early in the morning the girl has to make four tortillas, four frybreads, four donkey breads— a kind of extra-thick tortilla—and one ash bread, which is broken into four pieces.

NAELYN PIKE: "You cut your own wood, you make your own fire. How you make the bread is how your life will be, so you try to do it as best as you can. Someone in your family, your aunt or your mom, will tell you what to do, like, 'Oh, you need to do this,' or, 'You messed up on this.' But I never knew anyone that burnt the bread. After that, the women are cooking. There is a food exchange."

Another wickiup, draped in tarps and leafy branches, is built as a sweat lodge.

NAELYN PIKE: "The medicine man and the boys that follow him are doing a sweat. Your buckskin, your necklace, your cane, your feathers—all of that stuff is inside the sweat lodge. They're praying over them. You bring the food to the medicine man to show that you are generous. The godmother brings food, too. Then you cook for your godmother. Those breads that you made are given to the medicine man and the godparents. You exchange the food to show that you're able to cook and give to the people, to feed the people, feed your family, your children. Then you dance four songs. The godmother dresses you. She puts on your buckskin, your necklaces, your feather. You are inside your wickiup and she's dressing you. You look out and everyone's outside the door watching you, watching you being dressed. You see your aunties and your mom crying, because you're becoming a woman and the ceremony's begun. You're trying not to cry. You're supposed to be stoic! You don't want to goof around."

The girl wears a shell between her eyes and a white eagle feather in her hair. The feather is another symbol of longevity: the wearer should live long enough to have hair this color. The dressing of the girl marks the beginning of her metamorphosis into White Painted Woman.

THERESA NOSIE: "Once the godmother dresses the girl and they sing, they bring the body back to be warm again, like it was when she first had her period. When that happens nobody can touch her."

NAELYN PIKE: "Friday night there is a bonfire. You dance social dances. There are some prayer songs, but you are preparing for the next morning, because Saturday is the really big day. That day is all about prayer. Those prayers are going to stick with you and mold your life. In the morning when the sun rises, you're out there dancing."

WENDSLER NOSIE: "The ceremony begins, and once you turn your daughter over, she's in that spirit world. You can't run in there and take her back. She's locked in."

NAELYN PIKE: "You're nervous at first, but then you start praying. You're there, but you're not there."

A line of men drum and chant, recounting the story of the White Painted Woman. The girl faces the sun and dances, a steady, shuffling dance, to song after song. The jingles on her cane and dress shimmer and chime.

VANESSA NOSIE: "Every four songs is a chapter. On Saturday, they're dancing creation stories. They dance 64 songs. Thirty-two in the morning and thirty-two at night. The songs talk about when she's in the womb, when she was born. There are songs about when she learns how to crawl, and walk, and run. The songs tell her whole life until she's an old woman."

The demeanor of the girl during the four days of the ceremony dictates her lifelong character. She needs to endure the heat, the fatigue, and the hunger without complaint. The trials of the ceremony stand in for challenges she will face in life. She has a special scratching stick: with the heightened powers she possesses as White Painted Woman, she could permanently scar her body were she to scratch at her skin with her fingernails. She is not to smile, lest those lines crease her face forever.

NIZHONI PIKE: "The girl dances to the sun asking to bear children later in life. You are on your knees. Your hands are on your knees. The godmother picks them up for you and sets them, so your hands are up and you're swaying side to side."

In the myth, the White Painted Woman climbs a mountain, a red ray of sunlight penetrates her, and she becomes pregnant with the Son of the Sun.

Later, she bears a second son, the Child of the Water.

The sons of the White Painted Woman will make the world

safe for the Apache people by

killing monsters that

roam the earth.

NAELYN PIKE: "They always say to close your fingers, because if they're open, it means you'll have children at a really young age. You don't want to have children that fast! You want to live your life! Before my dance I made sure I knew every step. I didn't want to mess up. I was like, *Got to close these fingers up really hard!* My godmother was even squeezing my hand, but then my medicine man stopped us, and he was like, 'No, open her fingers.' When he said that, I was thinking, 'Gosh, everyone will think Imma be, like, some crazy girl, opening my fingers.' But during that time, my mom and I were having a lot of dreams—nightmares—of me not being able to have children. I think my medicine man felt something was wrong."

The girl's cane is planted in the ground at increasing distances from her. She runs toward and then around it four times, symbolizing four stages of life: infancy, childhood, motherhood, and old age. She runs fast and far to demonstrate her stamina.

NAELYN PIKE: "There's one point, you're running around the cane, and the medicine man will give a signal. He'll put his hands up, or say something in Apache. The girl has two baskets of gifts and treats."

VANESSA NOSIE: "Food, fruit."

NAELYN PIKE: "She's dancing and everyone surrounds her. The godfather grabs her basket and spills the nuts and peanuts, the candy and the coins, pours everything over her. He pours the whole basket over her, and everyone comes and attacks it. Everyone, the family, the friends that are there to support her, runs toward the candy and the gifts. She gives to the people to show she's generous. She's giving it all to them. Everyone is really close, surrounding you. Someone—it could be your mom or your dad, your grandpa—grabs you from underneath, because you could get trampled by all these people. I remember my adrenaline, people are so close, you don't want to fall, and you have to keep dancing."

The girl's face is marked with paint, a red chevron from one cheek to the other. She now possesses supernatural healing powers, and people line up for her blessings.

VANESSA NOSIE: "Everybody lines up. First the men line up and bless the girl, giving her strength and protection, because of the evil that's out in the world. They can also ask her to heal them. Say I was having migraines, or say I have a bad back, or I have cancer, or I have an infant. I'm sick, I ask her to heal me and take away my sickness, or to bless the infant to have a healthy, long life. In the middle of that ceremony she has that power to heal."

NAELYN PIKE: "Finally, the medicine man will tell her to run back to her home, to her camp. So she runs around the fire that they used the night before, and then she runs home."

Saturday evening, a bonfire is lit. Masked dancers arrive. They wear elaborate wooden headdresses. Their bodies are painted with geometric patterns or the silhouettes of animals. The men impersonate and embody the Apache mountain spirits known as the Gaan, also called crown dancers. The Gaan frighten away evil and bless the girl.

The last light drains from the sky. The bonfire crackles and the smell of charred wood floats through the air. The Gaan, some with heavy bellies that hang over their belts, stomp and march, twist and spin. They raise their arms and bend low to one side, to the other side. With painted wooden batons, the men slap out rhythms on their thighs. Hour after hour the dancing continues. The air is distorted by smoke and heat. The dancers begin to sweat off their paint. Their shadows are long black beams that radiate out from the fire. The wind lifts waves of glinting ash into the dark sky.

NAELYN PIKE: "The Gaan are giving blessings, they dance for the people and then they leave. The girl dances by the fire. The Gaan come back, and the girl dances behind them. The medicine man will tell her, 'This is the time you're going to dance with them.' A crown dancer will come up to you. There'll be five girls, one for each crown dancer: the Sunrise Girl, her partner, and another girl that had her ceremony. Then the godmother and the godfather will pick two other girls that have had their ceremony. They all come together. The Gaan will come and the girl spins in a circle, clockwise. Then the Gaan spins with her, and then they are one. The whole meaning of that spin is that they become one. The song ends. One girl is

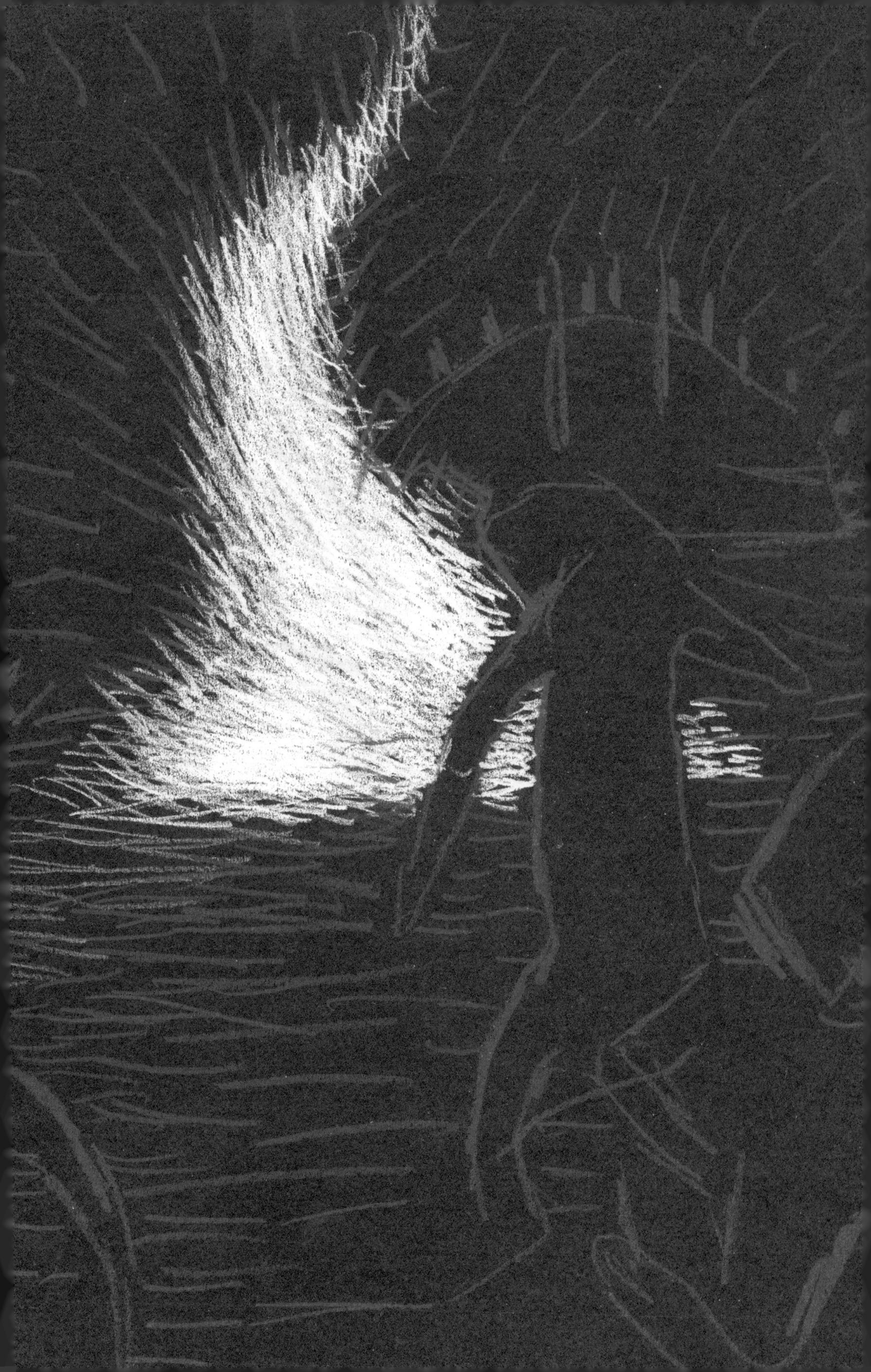

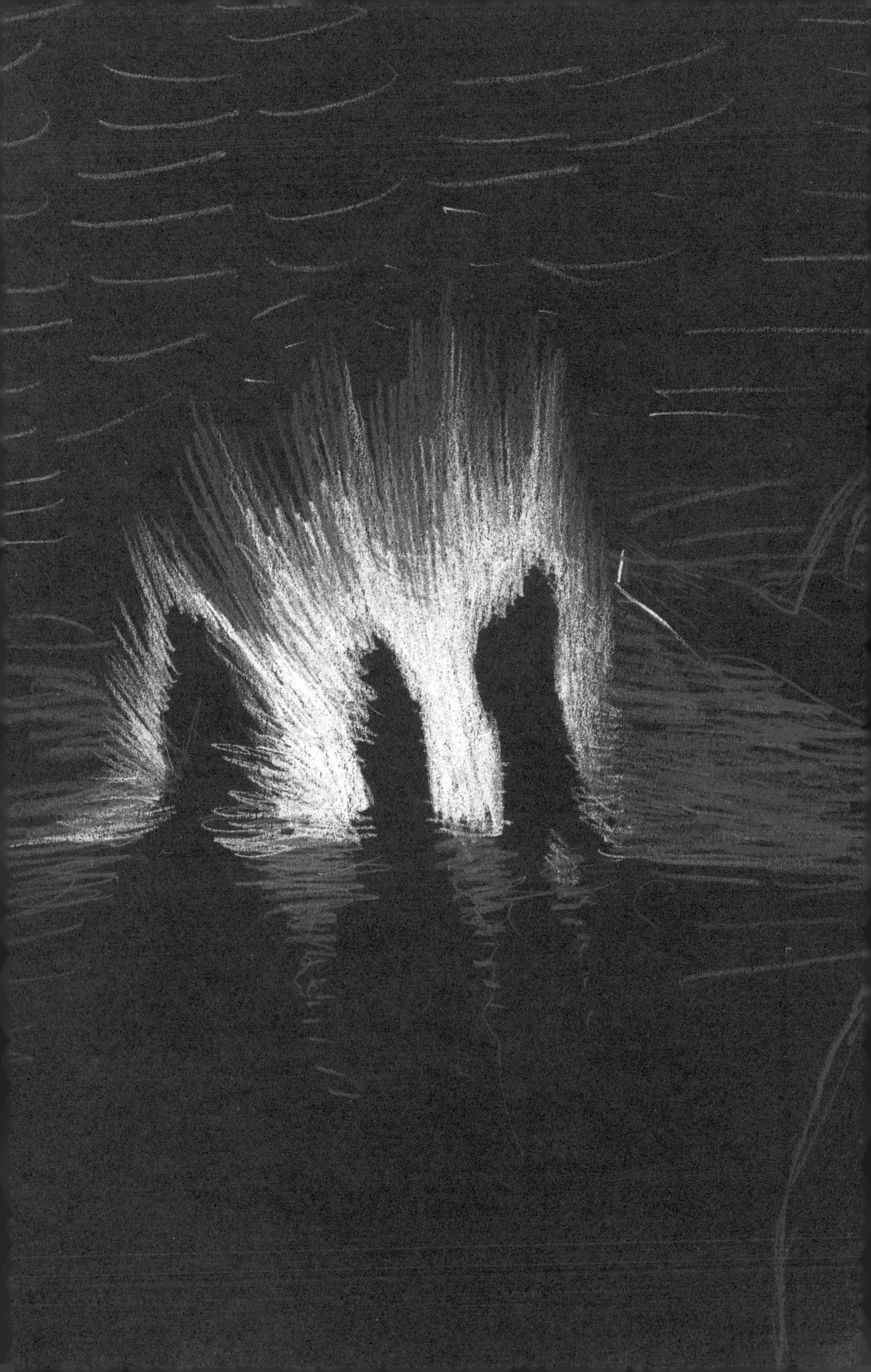

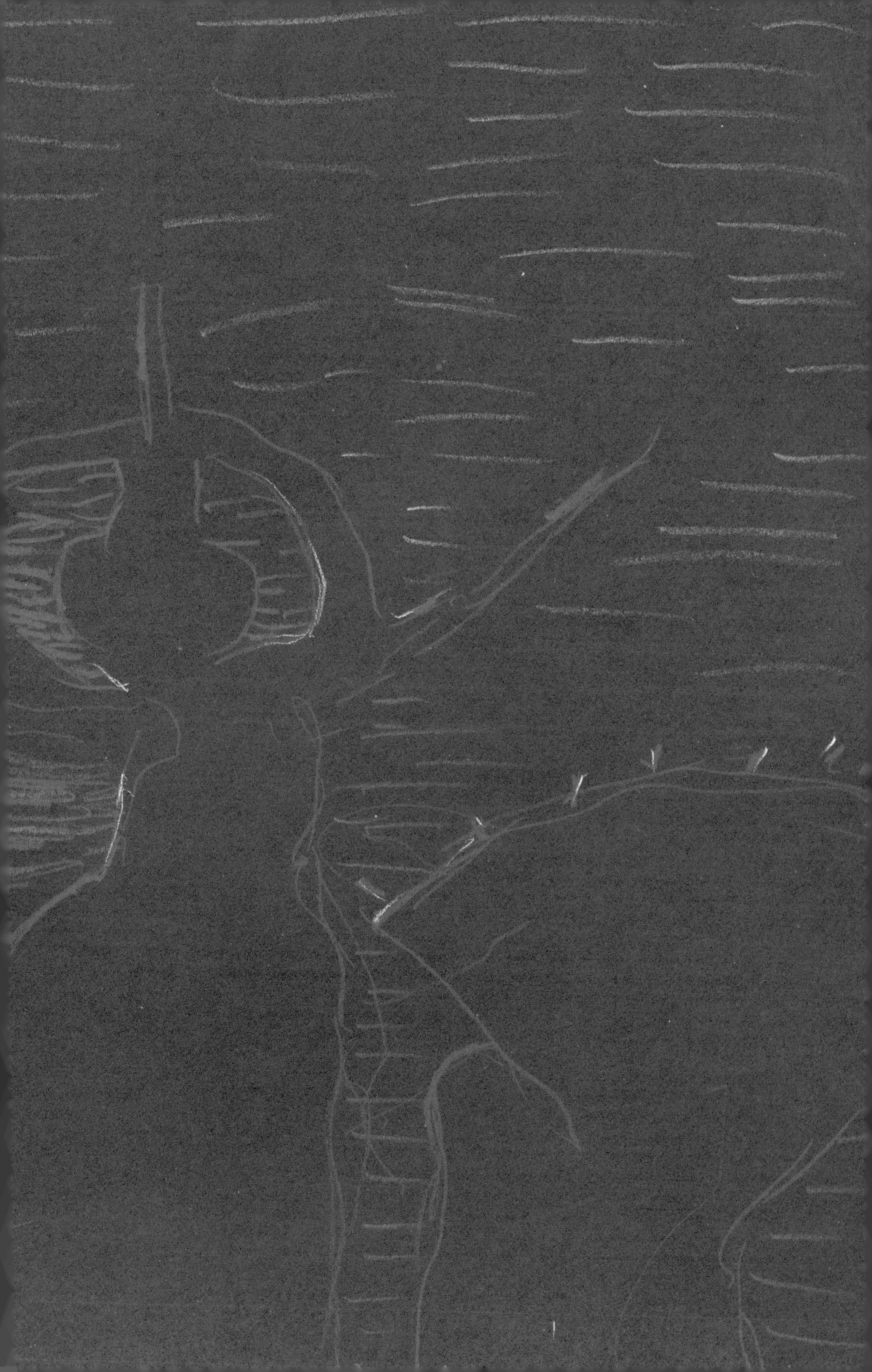

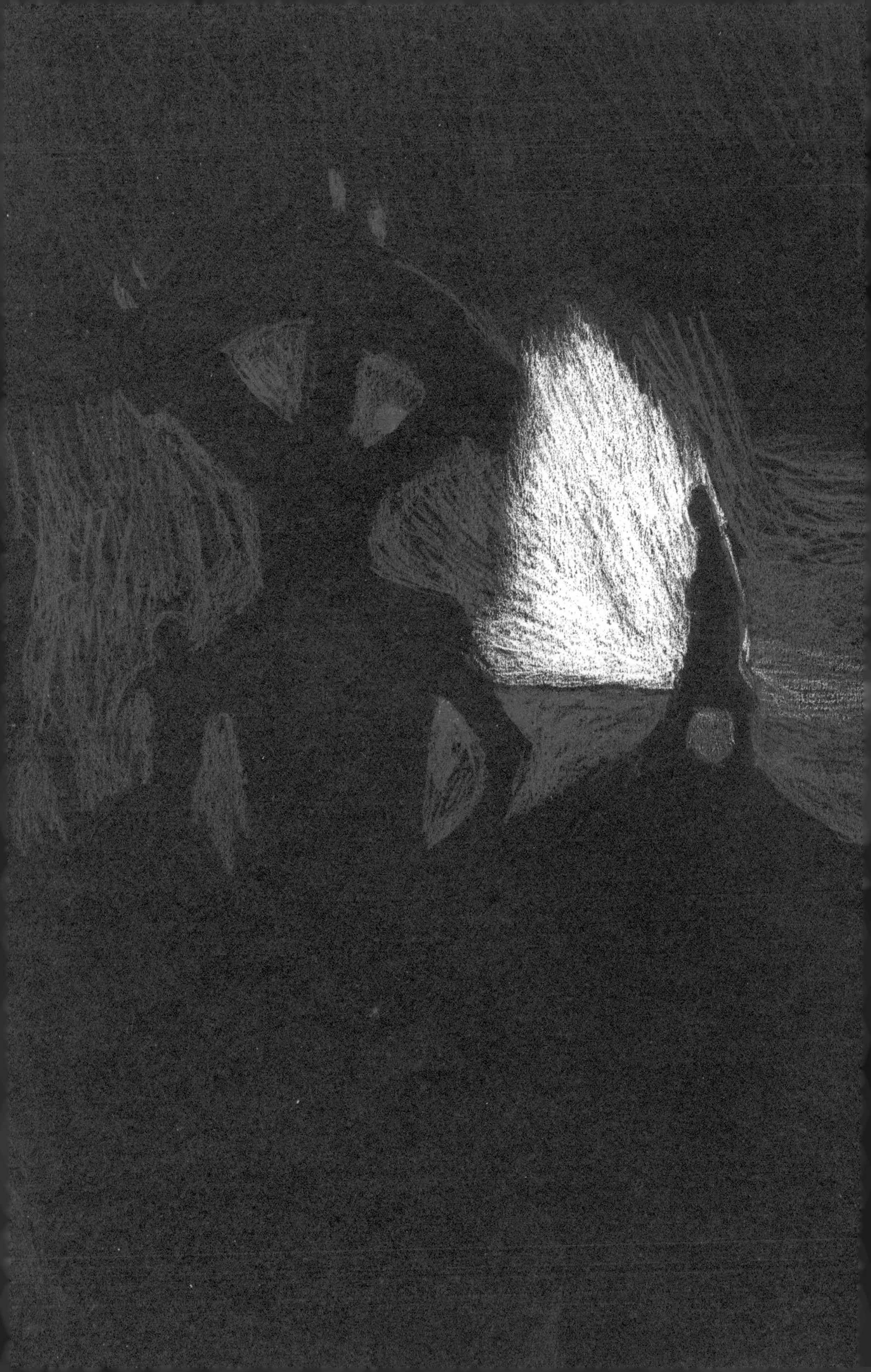

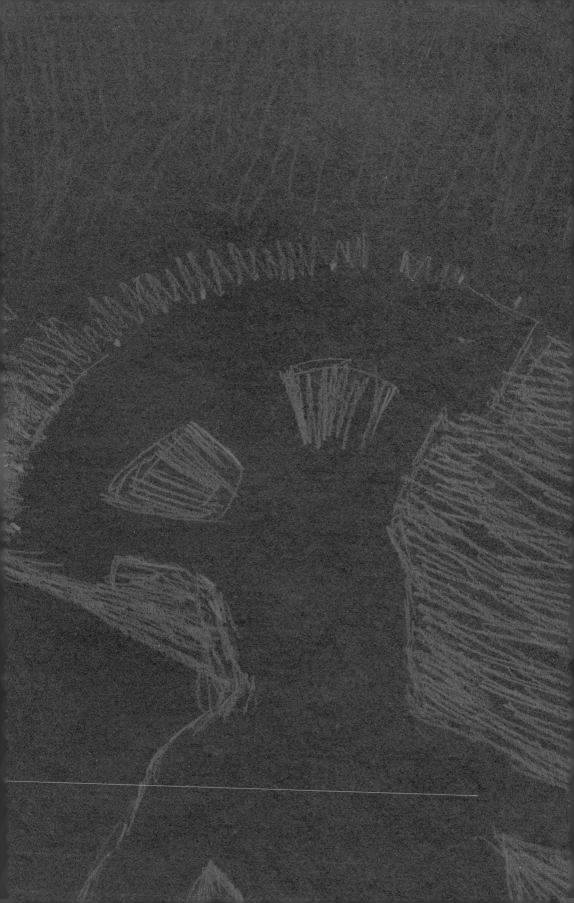

behind each Gaan. For four songs they dance to the people, and around the people, and each girl shadows a Gaan. You're dancing, and you follow every step they take: When they spin, you spin. When they slide, you slide. You're in sync. After the fourth song, the Gaan dance in a circle around everyone. They're giving their blessing to people. After that fourth song, you dance another four inside the tipi.

"Everything's so fast. The Gaan move fast. When the Gaan run, the girl has to run. When the Gaan spin, they'll spin like four times. Like, really fast. You have to spin with them, and you can't get dizzy.

"Everyone's surrounding you, so you can't really see the light that's coming from the bonfire. All you see is people taking pictures. The flashes blind you. You're just in a prayer mode."

VANESSA NOSIE: "You are in a different dimension."

NAELYN PIKE: "On Sunday the girl gets painted with *glesh*. It's white sand mixed with water and pollen."

The godfather will paint the girl, sealing in blessings for her future. He covers her face and hair and shoulders with the thick paste. He splatters paint into the air and onto the family and friends gathered around. Children reach up to catch the droplets that shower down on the crowd. Crusty dots chip off your skin and clothes.

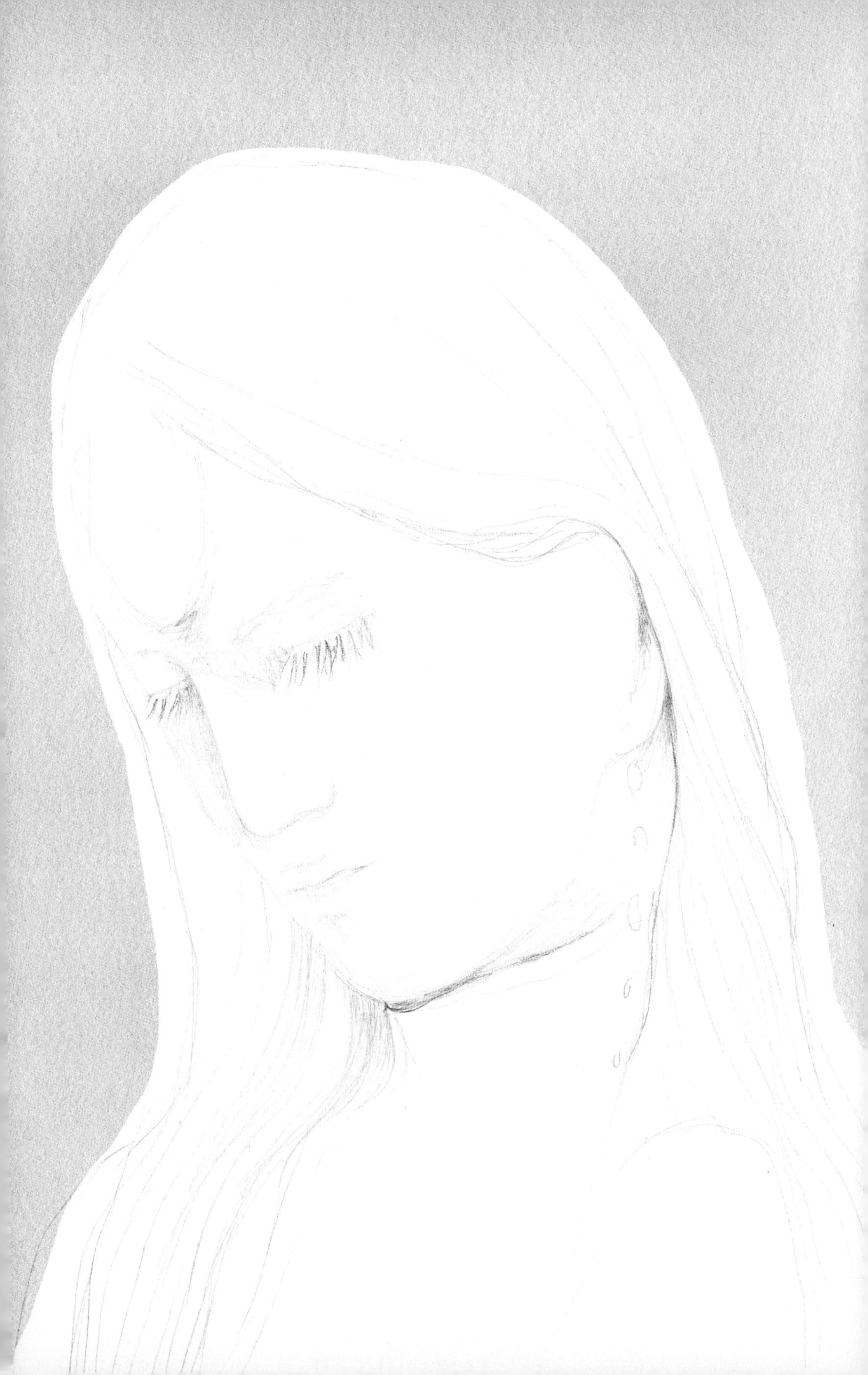

VANESSA NOSIE: "The world before was all black."

NAELYN PIKE: "In our creation story, the White Painted Woman comes out of the earth. When she emerged, she was covered in ashes. You become the White Painted Woman."

The U.S. Department of the Interior's 1883 Code of Indian Offenses criminalized Native religion:

> The "sun-dance," the "scalp-dance," the "war-dance," and all other so-called feasts assimilating thereto, shall be considered "Indian offenses." . . . These feasts or dances are . . . intended and calculated to stimulate the warlike passions of the young warriors of the tribe. . . . The result is the demoralization of the young, who are incited to the wicked conduct of their elders.

In 1870, President Ulysses S. Grant divvied up reservations, assigning them to different Christian denominations, which received instructions to "Christianize and civilize the Indian." The San Carlos Reservation was assigned to the Dutch Reformed Church. Across the United States, reservation church authorities vigorously enforced the suppression of Native religious practice. Coerced conversions to Christianity became commonplace. This became known as Grant's "Peace Policy." In a country founded on the principle of separation of church and state, "an entire race," writes Walter Echohawk, "was proselytized through the machinery of the government."

Until the Indian Reorganization Act passed in 1934, Natives caught performing religious rites could be imprisoned, their rations withheld. U.S. efforts to restrict Indian religion were inseparable from the goal of undermining tribal sovereignty and usurping tribal land. Collectively held land and the very idea of sacred land were impediments to economic exploitation.

A girl who has her Sunrise Dance at Oak Flat takes her place in a long history. She is conscious of the generations of women before her whose ceremonies were held here, often in secret.

Naelyn Pike and her family recall the final moments of her dance.

NAELYN PIKE: "That's when the mist came."

THERESA NOSIE: "A lot of different things happened during Naelyn's ceremony."

WENDSLER NOSIE: "At Naelyn's dance, it was down to five songs left. There's an excitement in the air. You could see the mist moving in. We are in this clearing and there are pine trees all around.

"Then, we were two songs away, and you could see the mist moving through the forest. Approaching. We started our second-to-last song. Right in the middle of the song, the mist came to the edge of the pine trees. And stopped."

VANESSA NOSIE: "There was a baby deer that was roaming around the dance ground."

NAELYN PIKE: "Anytime my foot struck the ground it was like I was waking up the mountain, and waking up the spirits. People told me that they could see the spirits."

VANESSA NOSIE: "Our ancestors got to hear those songs again. They got to see the Gaan."

WENDSLER NOSIE: "Naelyn was dancing. People started to wail. Some people held their hands up. Some held their hands open. I held my hands up. Then the second-to-last song was over. Nobody could speak. The medicine man started to sing the last song, and the mist starts to move. Really slow. When the song was over, the mist just went [whistles]. The mist passed over us."

THERESA NOSIE: "Then everybody noticed a hummingbird around her head—"

WENDSLER NOSIE: "—watching her."

NAELYN PIKE: "A small green hummingbird stared right at us and hovered over us.

"When you're painted, you're, like, frozen.

I was dancing, but my eyes were closed

because you don't want to get the paint inside your eyes.

They tell you to close your eyes.

The girl can't fix herself up;

the godmother wipes her eyes

with a handkerchief.

When the girl's eyes are covered, she's a girl.

When the godmother wipes her eyes,

and the girl opens her eyes,

she's not looking at the world she looked at before her dance.

"She's looking at a new world."

I n 2015, Naelyn Pike returned to Washington, D.C. Legislation calling for the repeal of the Oak Flat land exchange had been submitted in both the U.S. Senate and the House of Representatives the previous spring. Resolution Copper's pre-production operations continued to move forward, but it was still possible to undo the deal and stop the mine. On November 4, Naelyn entered a conference room of the Rayburn House Office Building.

Naelyn was the last scheduled speaker at a roundtable chaired by Congressman Raúl M. Grijalva of Arizona's 3rd District, the ranking member of the House Natural Resources Committee, who had introduced the House version of the "Save Oak Flat" repeal.

Naelyn never prepares remarks. She speaks without notes. At her second appearance before members of Congress, she spoke deliberately. Occasionally she paused and lowered her eyes, seeming to look inward as she gathered her thoughts.

NAELYN PIKE: "Oak Flat sets a precedent for all sacred sites. If this place is destroyed, this could happen to all sacred sites, like—"

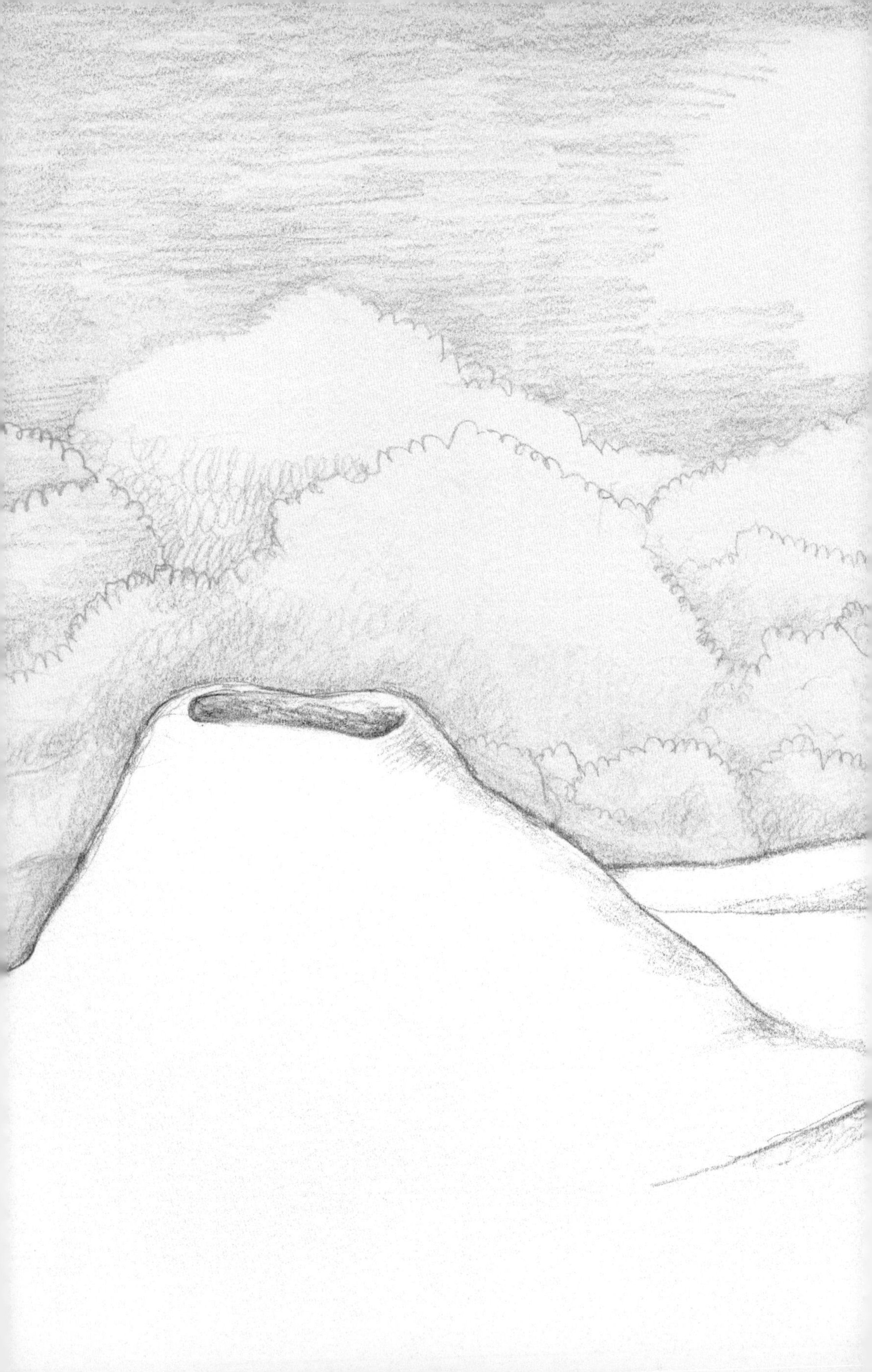

“Mauna Kea in Hawaii . . . ”

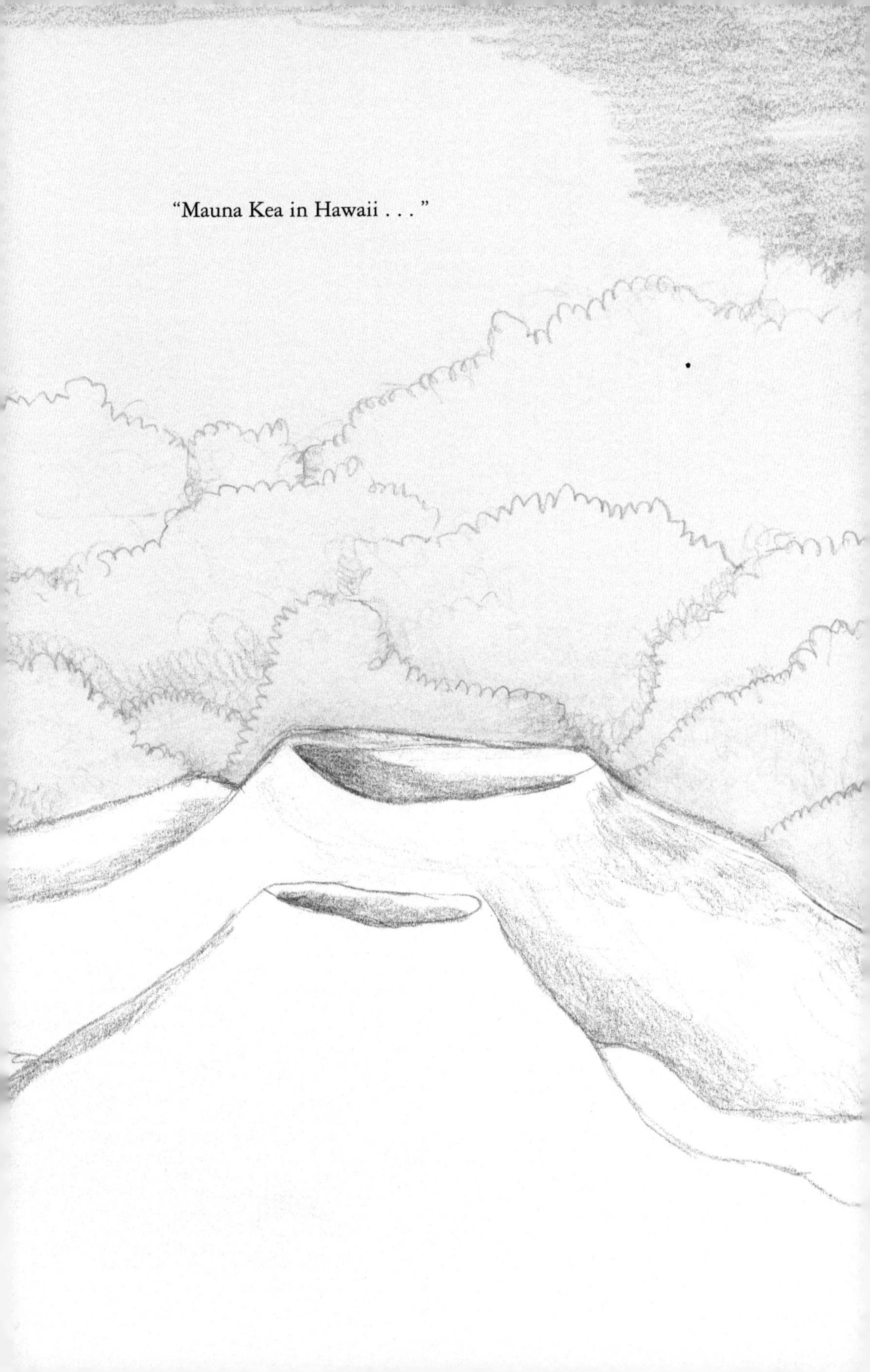

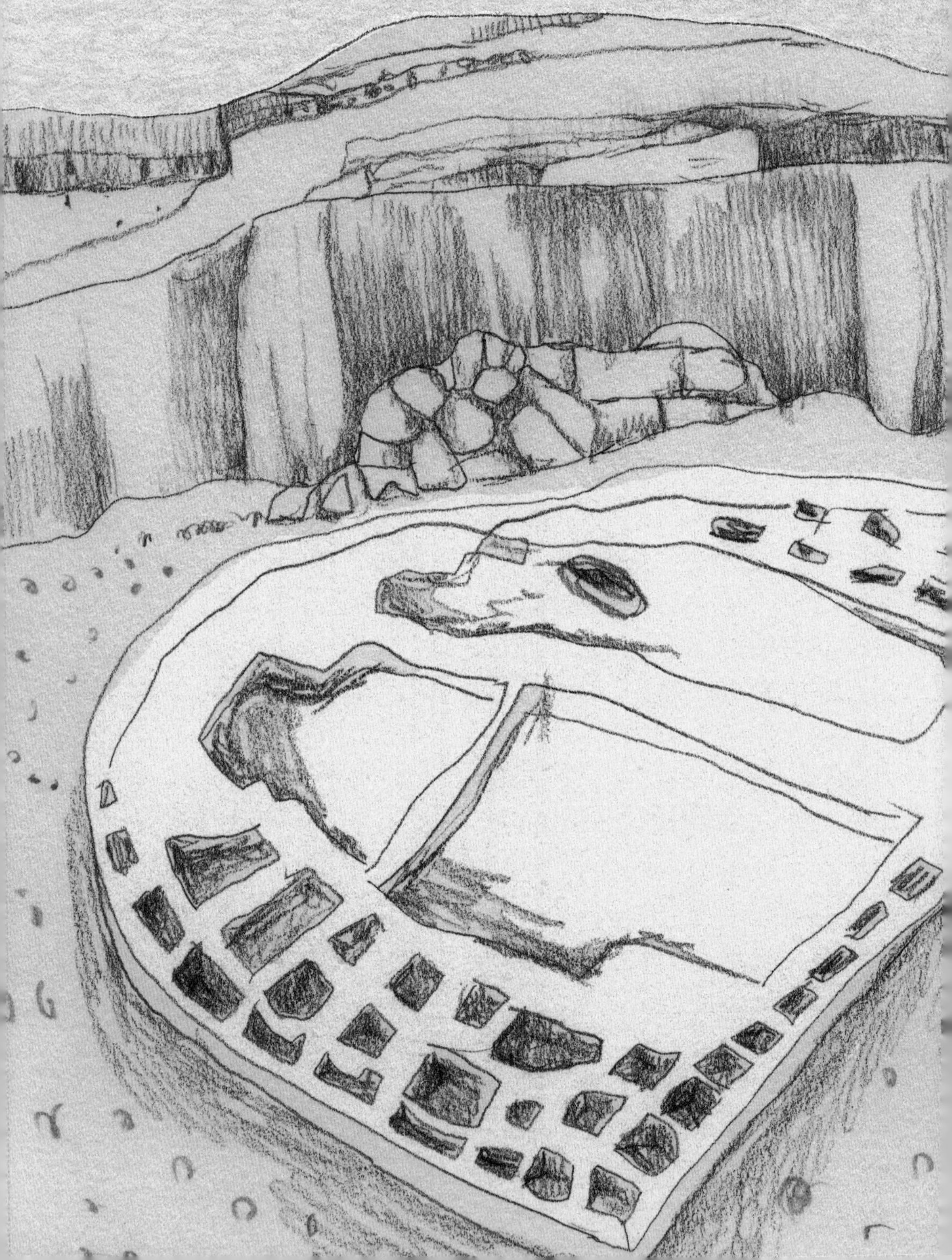

"Chaco Canyon in New Mexico . . ."

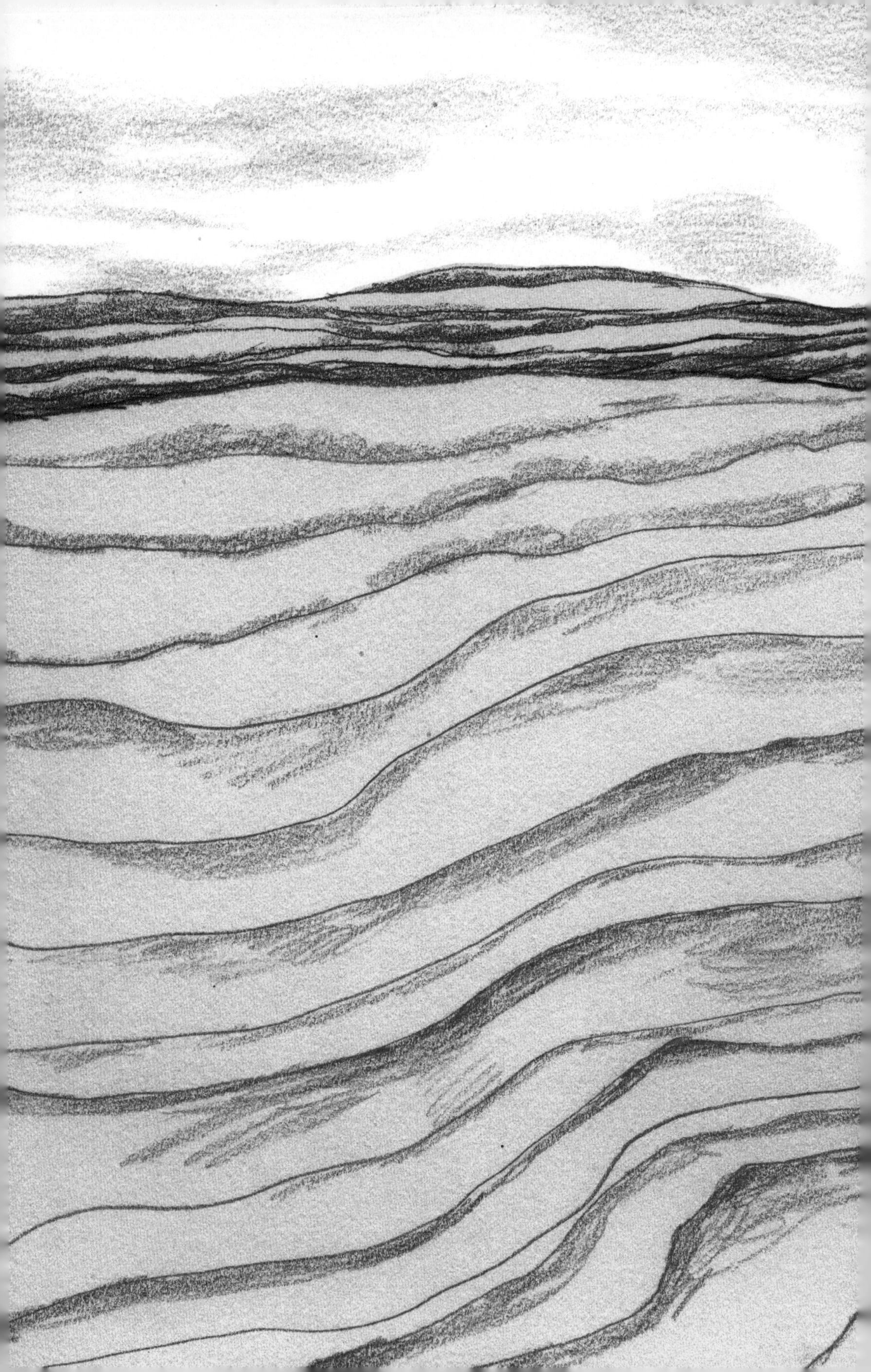

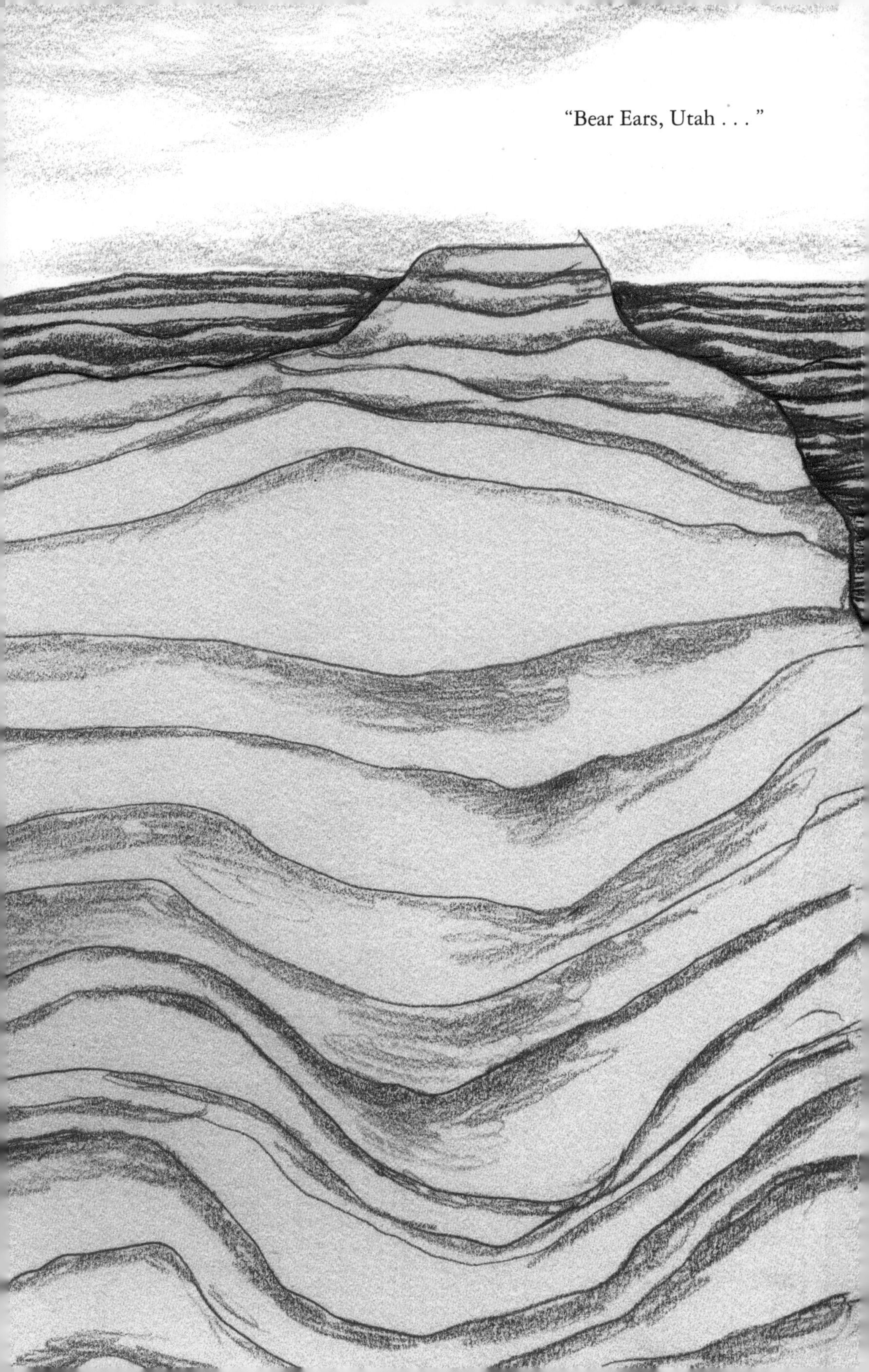
"Bear Ears, Utah . . . "

"Black Hills, South Dakota . . ."

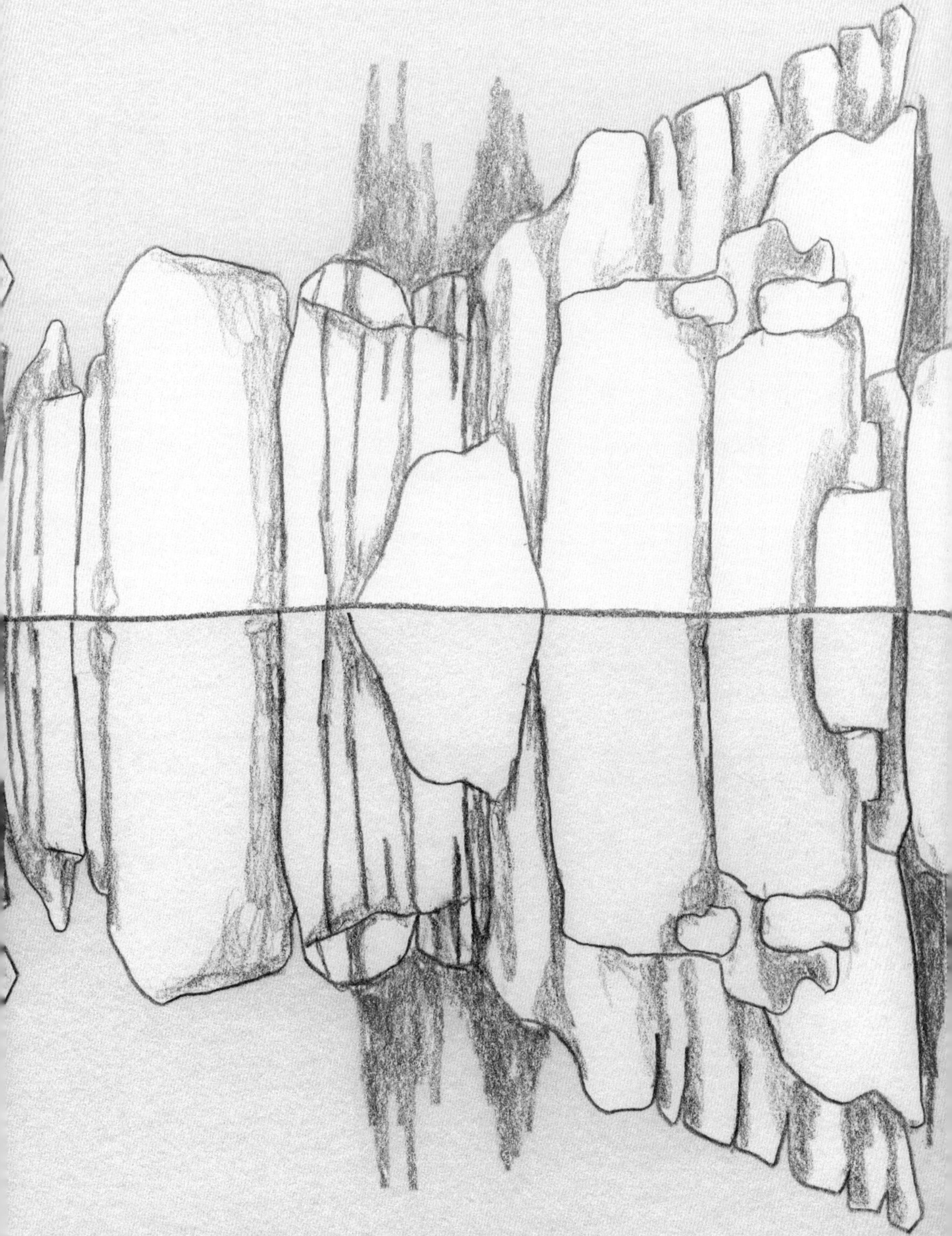

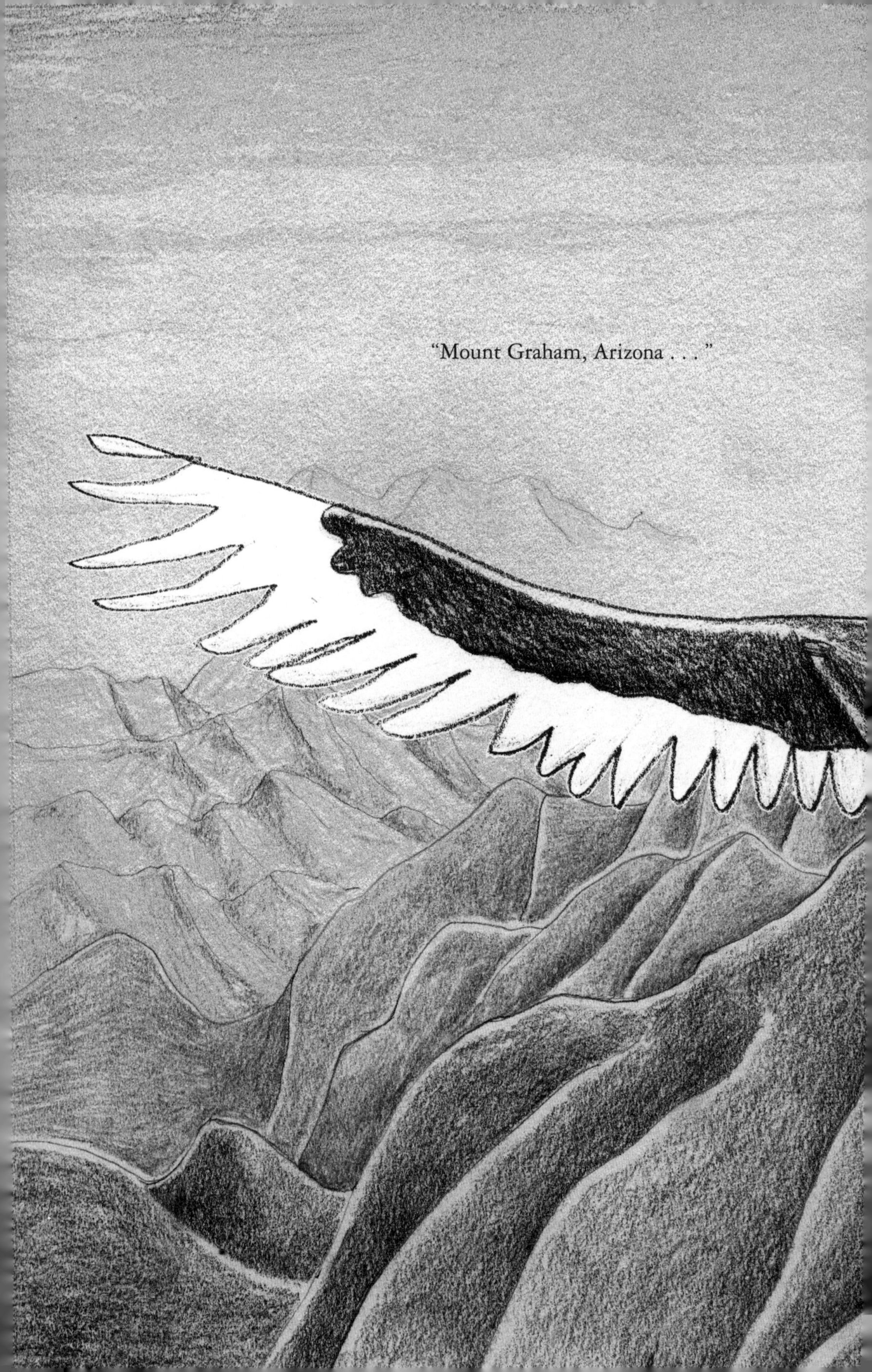
"Mount Graham, Arizona . . . "

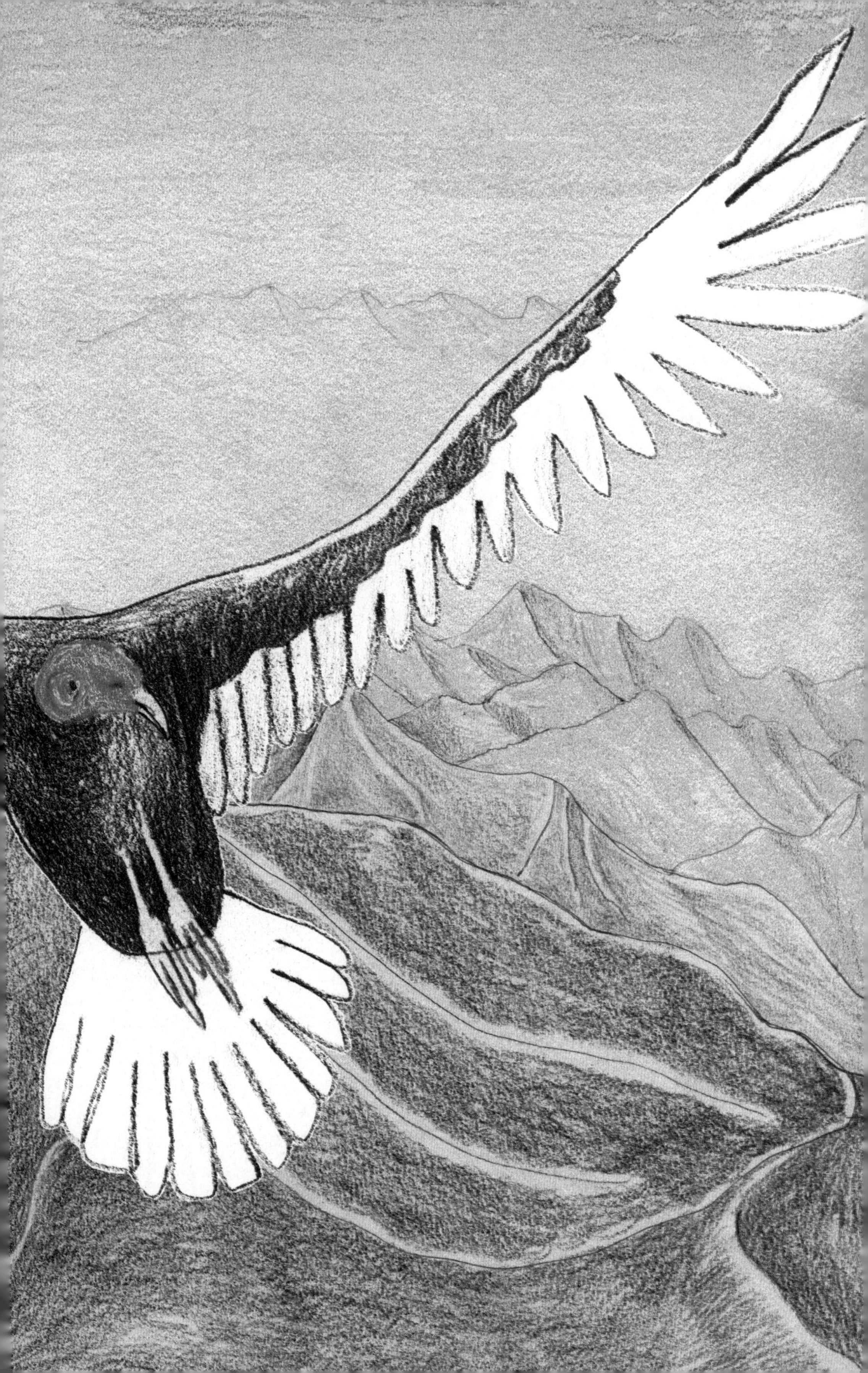

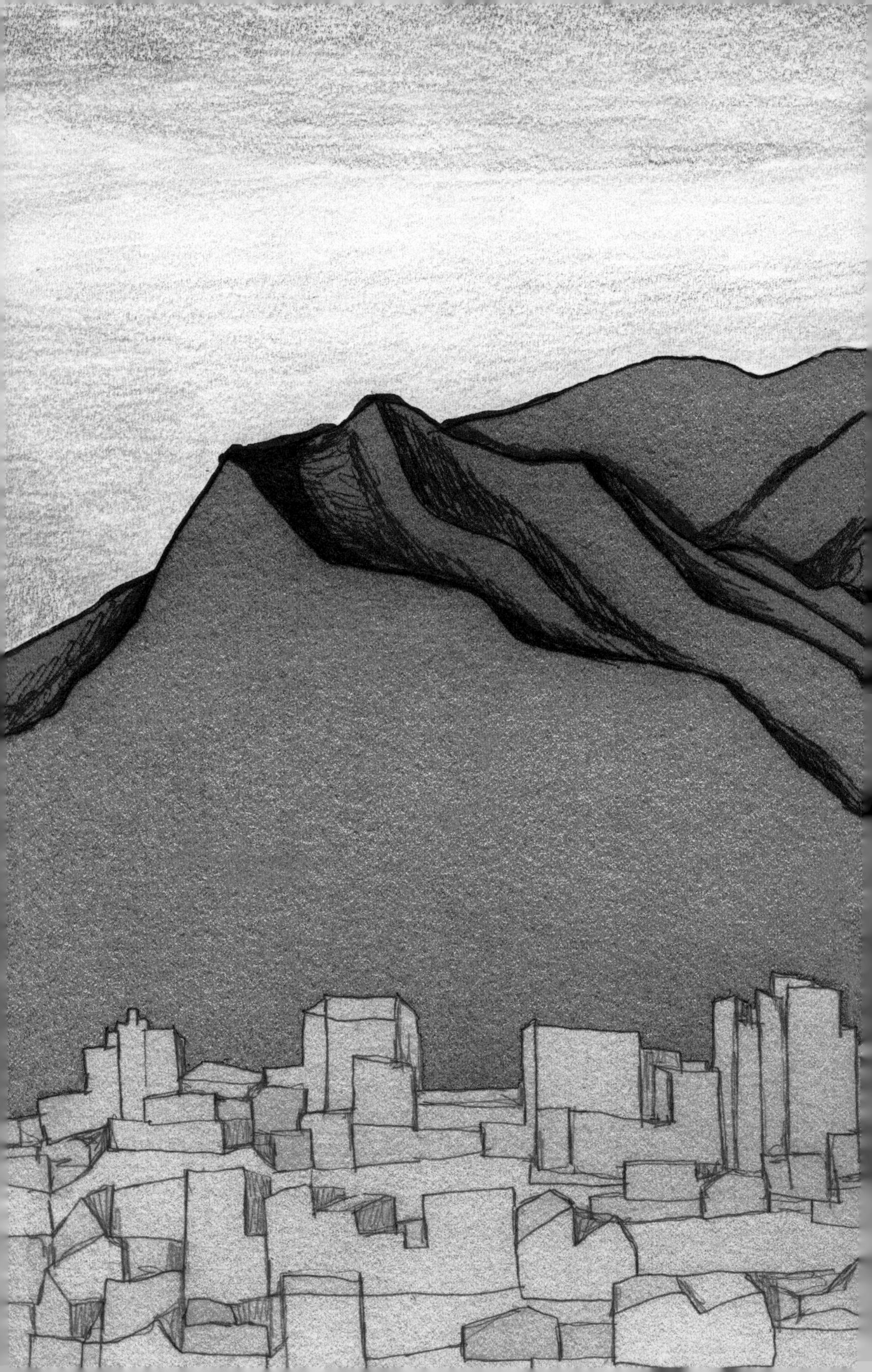

"Loop 202, South Mountain, in Arizona . . ."

"Keystone XL Pipeline in Canada

that will go through all the way to Oklahoma . . . "

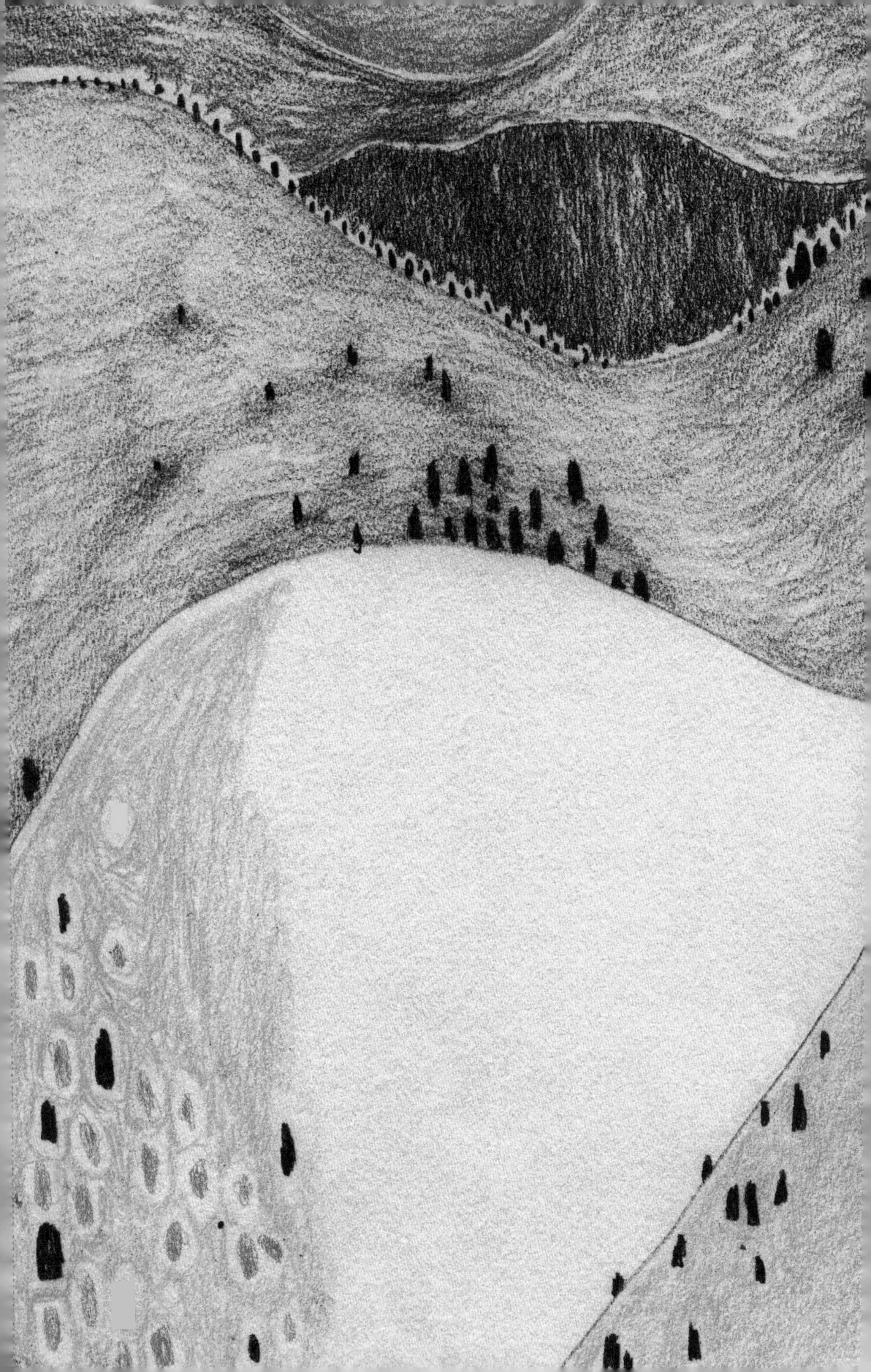

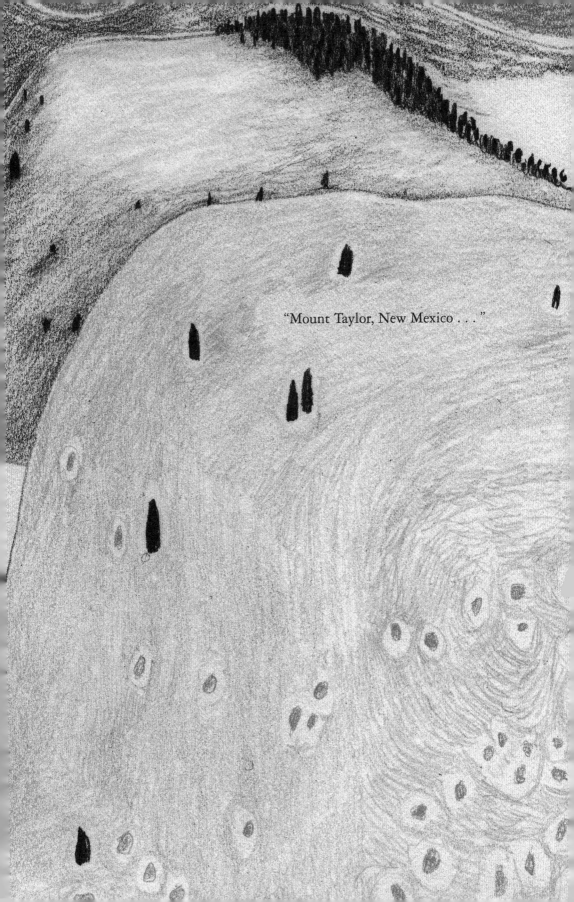

"Mount Taylor, New Mexico . . ."

NAELYN PIKE: "If these sacred lands are gone, who are we? What will we have? Mother Earth will be gone and what will we live off of? Money? No. It will not keep us alive."

Naelyn Pike, 16 years old, addressed the elected officials in the room.

"You guys need to make that right decision to protect these sacred lands."

◆ ◆ ◆

IN THE FIRST MONTHS OF THE OCCUPATION, there were always people at Oak Flat. Today, the site still bustles with activity on days of religious ceremonies, and when Apache Stronghold holds gatherings combining prayer and protest. But Oak Flat is often quiet. Years have passed since the land exchange; even if the mine becomes operational, more years will pass before Oak Flat's landscape is altered.

Opponents of the Resolution Copper mine celebrated in March 2016 when Oak Flat, identified as the *Chi'chil Bildagoteel* Historic District, was added to the National Register of Historic Places. This designation is not a guarantee that the site will be protected. According to the U.S. Forest Service, the listing "does not mean that the Chi'chil Bildagoteel Traditional Cultural Property cannot be damaged or destroyed," only that the government must "consider the effects" of the proposed mine to the "Traditional Cultural Property." Three days after the 2016 National Register was announced, Arizona representative Paul Gosar issued a press release that attacked the listing of Oak Flat as "misguided," a destructive effort by "extremist environmental organizations."

PAUL GOSAR: "Shame on the Park Service and Forest Service for ramming a bogus historic place listing down the throats of Arizonans."

"If Hollywood wanted to capture the emotional center of Western [U.S.] history," writes historian Patricia Nelson Limerick, "its movies would be about real estate. Weapons would be deeds and lawsuits, not six-guns."

RDEHIFC

♦ ♦ ♦

To shift from the status of a "project" to an active mine site, Resolution Copper still has steps to take. There are federal and state laws with which to comply. The land swap legislation requires that the Forest Service transfer the land title to Resolution Copper within 60 days of the publication of a final Environmental Impact Statement. The Forest Service can require modifications to the company's proposed plan of operations, although it lacks the authority to deny the plan outright.

Findings in the environmental review could trigger more public protest. Support for a law to repeal the land exchange could build. The price of copper could fall. Resolution Copper could decide to cut its losses and sell the property.

But momentum is in Resolution Copper's favor. The company has resources the San Carlos Apache cannot match: billions of dollars and the backing of powerful politicians.

In any event, the largest known untapped copper deposit in North America is unlikely to be forgotten.

♦ ♦ ♦

The empty infrastructure of the Oak Flat occupation has a ghostly quality. Corrugated aluminum sheets propped up as temporary walls groan as their edges scrape against each other. An oven mitt, potholders, and a ladle hang in a tree. Sometimes the occupation area can resemble a yard sale. People leave things at Oak Flat. A set of dresser drawers stands near a discarded record player, a lampshade, and a bouquet of artificial pink roses. A carved wooden hummingbird with rotating wings is perched in an empty cardboard box that once held crinkle-cut French fries. When the wind picks up, the hummingbird's wings whirl furiously.

NAELYN PIKE: "There's this famous woman warrior, Lozen, who fought with Geronimo and Victorio—she was his sister. She was Chiricahua Apache. She's someone I look up to, my hero or whatever. There's only one picture of her, and you hardly see her face. Yesterday my mom and I were looking her up on the Internet: *Lozen, images.*"

James Kaywaykla was a child during the Apache Wars. The celebrated Apache chief Victorio was his uncle. Kaywaykla knew every warrior who fought with Victorio and Geronimo. Before Kaywaykla died in 1963, he recounted his memories to historian Eve Ball. Kaywaykla described Lozen, his aunt, as uncommonly brave and possessed of superhuman power. She had "the ability to do seemingly impossible things." When Lozen prayed, arms outstretched, her "hands tingled and her palms changed color" to indicate the location of the enemy. "The closer the adversary, the more vivid the feeling." Kaywaykla recalled one incident when Geronimo's band was fleeing the U.S. cavalry. They were poised at the edge of a turbulent river:

> There was a commotion and the long line parted to let a
> rider through. I saw a magnificent woman on a beautiful
> black horse—Lozen, sister of Victorio. Lozen the woman
> warrior! High above her head she held a rifle. There was
> glitter as her right foot lifted and struck the shoulder of the
> horse. He reared, then plunged into the torrent.

NAELYN PIKE: "Women like Lozen fought like we are fighting now. But we are no longer fighting with bows and arrows. We are fighting with education, with papers, with signatures."

Members of Apache Stronghold have reported seeing drones in the sky over the occupation site. The Oak Flat encampment is occasionally vandalized.

VANESSA NOSIE: "There are times when we've come back to camp and someone has ransacked a whole tent. Things are taken or destroyed."

Baasé-O Pike remembers the day in 2016 when she came to Oak Flat to begin her Sunrise Ceremony preparations.

BAASÉ-O PIKE: "There was a guy in a maroon Dodge, taking down license plate numbers."

In an open field above the encampment, four painted wooden crosses mark four corners around an extinguished campfire, demarcating the location for the Apache Holy Ground ceremony. A feather is tied to each cross with leather cord.

NAELYN PIKE: "You know where we have our Holy Ground crosses? Someone drove right through the middle."

VANESSA NOSIE: "They tore down our sweat lodge."

NAELYN PIKE: "We've had death threats before."

THERESA NOSIE: "When it comes to Naelyn, this is just the beginning of her story."

NAELYN PIKE: "I am the oldest granddaughter of 14 grandchildren on my dad's side, the oldest of 12 on my mom's side. I'm the oldest of three sisters. I try to take responsibility.

"I used to say I hate politicians. Then I realized just being a Native person, living and breathing, that's almost like a political statement. We are supposed to be extinct."

On a mild February morning in Superior, the Sun Flour Market on Main Street is bright and pleasant. The glass storefront frames the landscape. Mayor Besich-Lira's mother, JoAnn, takes coffee orders. Mike McKee and Patricia Brown sit at a table by the window. They come here often, and on many afternoons are joined by family members and friends.

MICHAEL MCKEE: "I call it God's country."

PATRICIA BROWN: "Look at the scenery, you know?"

MICHAEL MCKEE: "The sunsets. We don't even look at the sunsets to the west. We look to the east, to see the colors changing on the mountains."

"At night when you're coming from the Valley and you get on top of Gonzales Pass, and you see the lights . . . "

PATRICIA BROWN: "You see Apache Leap.

"What used to be real pretty was the slag dump. When the smelter was working and they would dump the slag down by the smelter."

MICHAEL McKEE: "That black rock that you see down there, piled up—"

PATRICIA BROWN: "It would just light up."

MICHAEL McKEE: "It was hot molten lava."

PATRICIA BROWN: "The sky would be red."

MICHAEL McKEE: "Everything would be red."

NATHAN TAYLOR

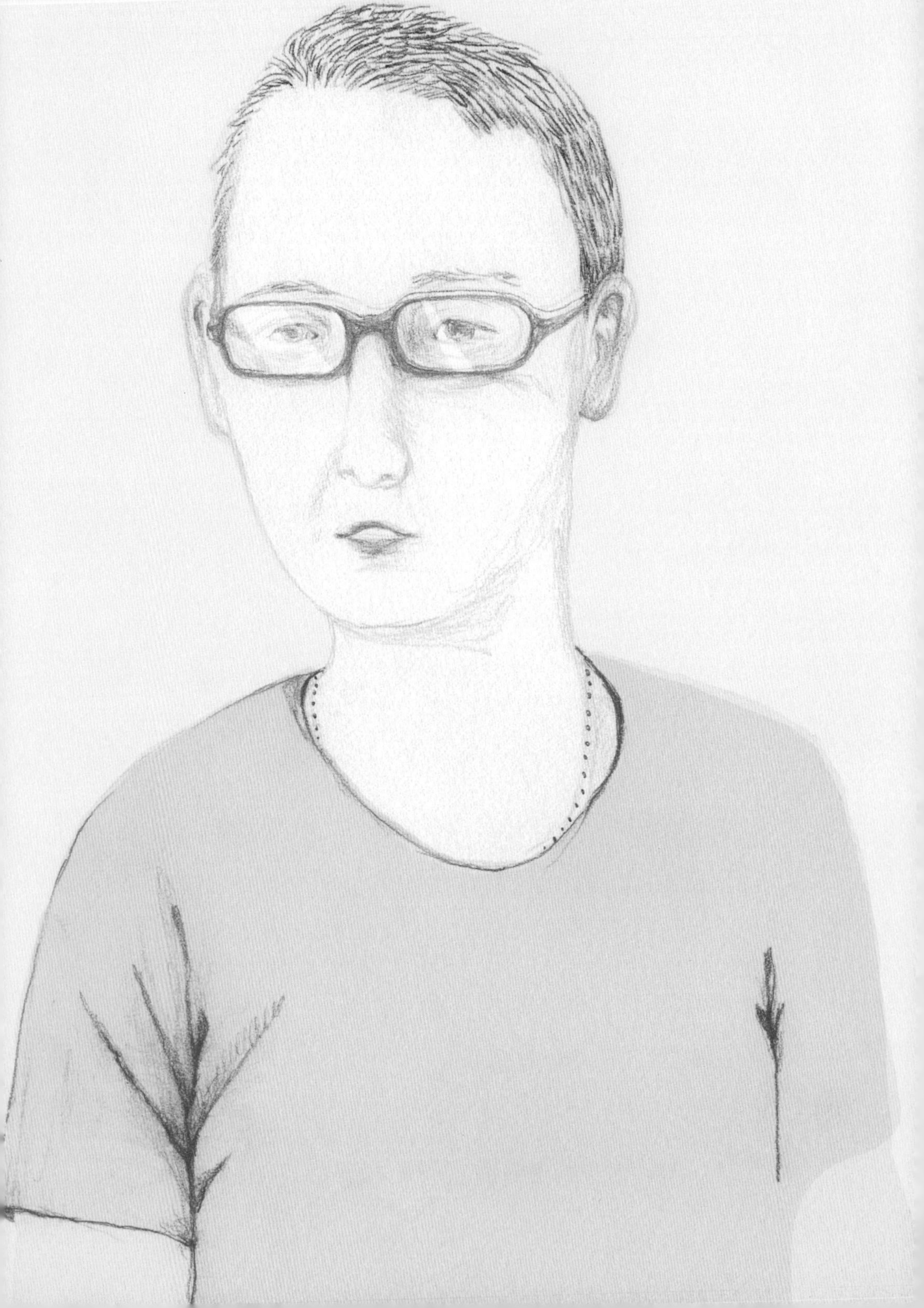

Patricia Brown's grandson, Nathan Taylor, is slender and reserved. At 12, he is president of the student body at Superior Junior High School. Nathan maintains a weather tracking station off US 177, half a mile from Main Street. During one storm, he recorded 59-mile-per-hour winds that uprooted trees, tore the roofs off homes, and knocked out power for half of Superior's residents.

MICHAEL McKEE: "He wants to go to Harvard. We hope he becomes governor."

PATRICIA BROWN: "We're already grooming him to be mayor here. When he turns 18, he's going to run for County Council."

Students in school government pledge to a constitution, which Nathan drafted.

PATRICIA BROWN: "He was just giving us a lesson on the electoral college."

Nathan isn't sure that he wants to return to Superior after college.

NATHAN TAYLOR: "It depends."

MICHAEL McKEE: "Just don't forget your hometown, that's all."

Evelyn and Jackie Gorham had two children. Their son was killed in Mexico in the 1990s.

JACKIE GORHAM: "They robbed him and shot him and left him on the side of the road and took his truck and his money."

The Gorhams' daughter and grandson live in Phoenix.

JACKIE GORHAM: "They like the big city."

In 1953, Jackie and Patricia's father, Sheriff Patrick Gorham, died at the age of 78.

PATRICIA BROWN: "Not too long before he passed away, he went to confession. He came out and he was crying."

Sheriff Gorham had been carrying a secret.

PATRICIA BROWN: "He had a second family that we didn't know about.

"In South Dakota, he got mixed up with a prostitute. She got pregnant. People from South Dakota contacted the minister in Superior. And the minister said, 'He's got 11 children here. Leave him alone.'

"The boy was Happy. Well, his nickname was Happy."

Mike nods toward Nathan. "See, he's finding out a lot of things. It's all going to be on Facebook."

What does Nathan think when he hears these stories?

NATHAN TAYLOR: "I don't know."

PATRICIA BROWN: "I think sometimes he doesn't know if it's the truth or not."

EVELYN GORHAM: "Sometimes *I* don't know if it's the truth or not."

Happy's full name was Frank Carretto. Years after Sheriff Pat Gorham died, Carretto came to Superior to meet his half siblings.

PATRICIA BROWN: "He looked just like my older brothers."

Everyone got along, and afterward, Happy would send presents to his family in Superior, jewelry and trinkets made from gold mined in the Black Hills of South Dakota.

PATRICIA BROWN: "I got these earrings from him."

MICHAEL McKEE: "Black Hills gold."

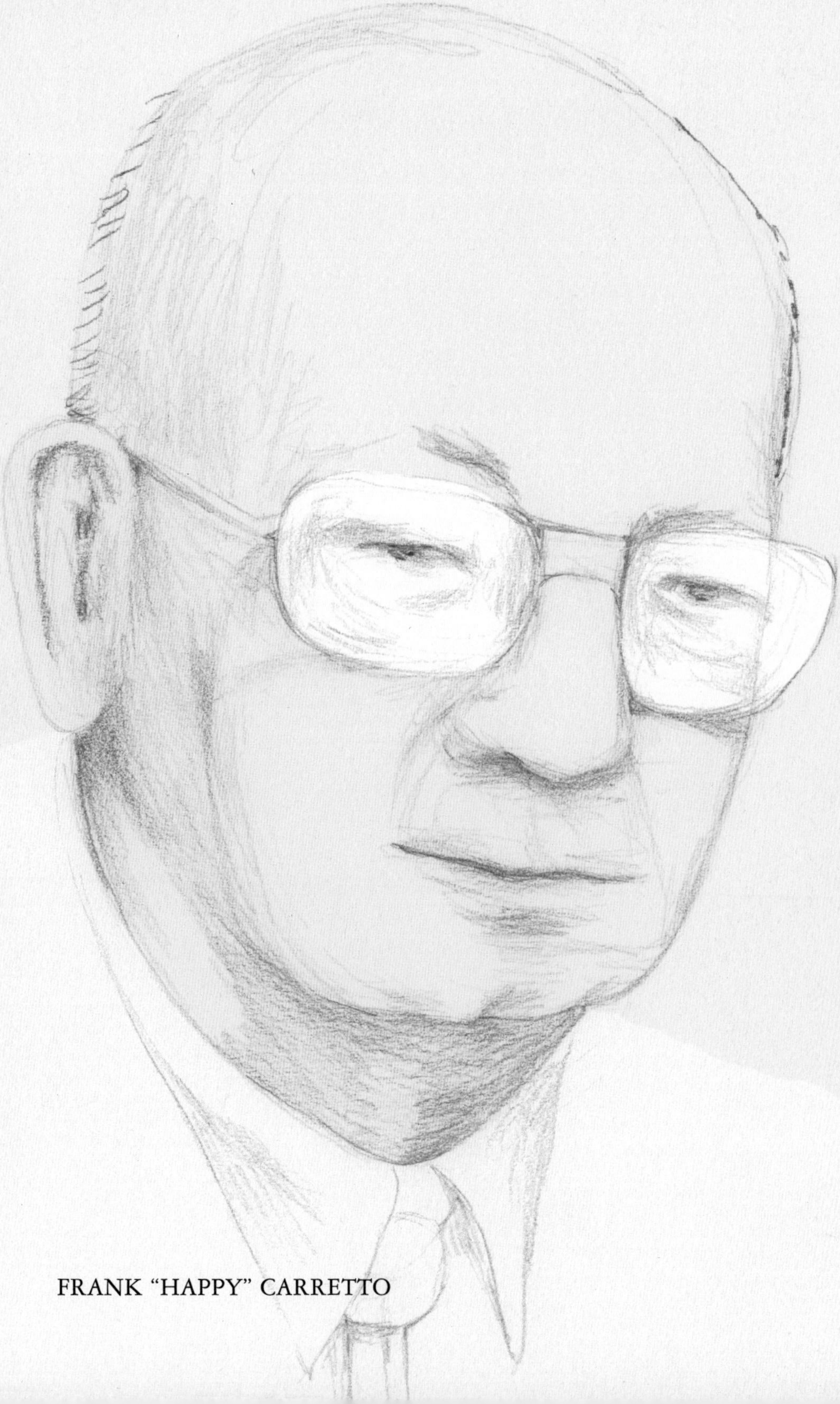

FRANK "HAPPY" CARRETTO

Many versions of the Apache creation myth

invoke obsidian, the glossy volcanic rock.

In these legends,

obsidian is sometimes referred to as "black metal."

Obsidian is associated with forces that whip over

the newly formed Earth—

black wind, black water, black thunder.

In Apache tradition,

black is the color of the east,

where the Sun rises.

At night,

the Sun is said to sink underground,

into a black hole.

Wendsler Nosie almost always wears black.

I asked him about it. He talked to me about obsidian.

He used the Apache word.

WENDSLER NOSIE: "*Bet-ch'íné* is a black stone.

The black stone helps you

to see what the eye can't see.

It helps you in sacred places.

When I close my eyes,

I find my way,

because the black stone

shows me where to go.

It helps me see the invisible."

It's dark underground.

It's dark in outer space.

We grope around, searching

for meaning

and treasure.

WENDSLER NOSIE:

"Black is the beginning.

If you go back to the beginning,

everything was dark.

You start from nothing.

Things start to come to light."

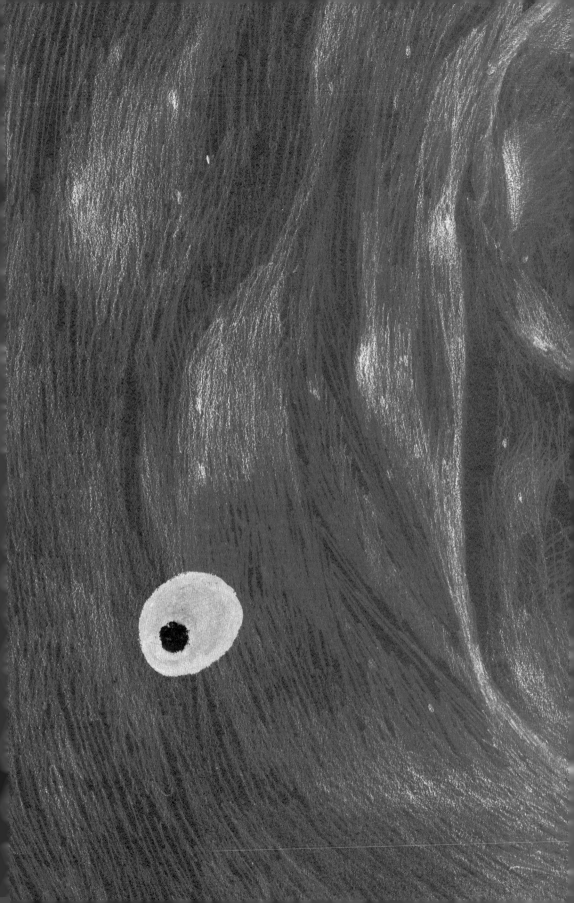

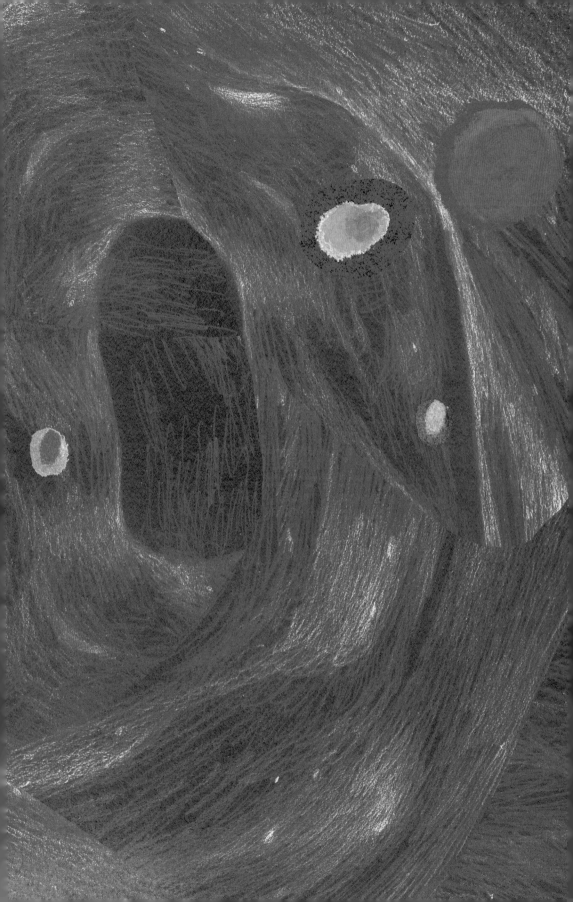

Chapter 1

9. **25 percent of the United States's annual copper demand:** This figure is one of Resolution Copper's core claims. See, for instance, "Resolution Copper Project Profile," Resolution Copper (March 2016). See also: Dan Sullivan, "Resolution Copper May Spend Billions on Mine," *Arizona Daily Star* (April 25, 2009); Senator John McCain, "Copper Mine Will Boost Economy, Protect Sacred Sites," *Arizona Central* (December 28, 2014); Steven Norton, "Mining a Mile Down: 175 Degrees, 600 Gallons of Water a Minute," *The Wall Street Journal* (June 7, 2017).

12. **deepest in North America:** Matthew Philips, "Inside the Billion Dollar Dig to Access America's Biggest Copper Deposit," *Bloomberg Businessweek* (March 14, 2016).

13. **crater in the landscape:** "Subsidence occurs when the underground excavation caves and movement of material connects all the way to the surface where a depression or deformation in the land surface is formed." Resolution Copper, General Plan of Operations (May 2016), 91.

13. **two miles wide and a thousand feet deep:** "Alternatives Evaluation Report," Environmental Impact Statement (draft): Resolution Copper Project and Land Exchange, Tonto National Forest, U.S. Forest Service (Phoenix: November 2017).

14. **40 years:** Resolution Copper says that the mine would have a forty-year operational life. Resolution Copper, General Plan of Operations (May 2016), 16.

Chapter 2

16. **"When I went to Washington, D.C.":** Naelyn Pike's quotations throughout the book are from in-person and telephone interviews conducted between 2015 and 2017 unless otherwise noted.

19. **"presents an enormous opportunity":** Senator John McCain III, "Statement by Senator John McCain on Protest of Resolution Copper Land Exchange in Washington, D.C. Today" (July 22, 2015).

19. **$61 billion into the economy:** In the report that the San Carlos tribe commissioned, Power Consulting addresses the assertion that the Resolution Copper mine would generate $61 billion dollars over its lifespan. "This is grossly misleading. It is the equivalent of saying that the pay associated with the mining jobs will be about $4 million per job instead of saying that the pay will be $75,000 per year. No one, certainly no economic analyst, would state the pay associated with a job in terms of the cumulative pay over 50 or 64 years."

The tribe's consultants take issue with other choices that produced the numbers in the Pollack Report. For instance, the Pollack Report states, "Costs associated with environmental and engineering issues and the cost of their correction were not included in the study." In other words, as the tribe's consultants write, "The environmental cost will be assumed to be zero." This is just one of a number of limitations the Pollack Report placed on its analysis, dramatically affecting the picture the report paints.

In short, the tribe's consultants characterize the Pollack Report's design as deeply problematic: "The design of the Pollack Report is non-economic, even anti-economic, in the sense that it takes a major industrial operation that has considerable costs associated with it and turns it into an 'angelic' activity with no costs. By design the Pollack Report conveniently dodges almost all of the important policy implications associated with permitting the proposed mine." ("Exaggerating the Net Economic Benefits of the Proposed Resolution Copper Mine, Superior, Arizona: A Critical Review of Resolution's

Economic Impact Analysis," report prepared for the San Carlos Apache Tribe, Power Consulting, Inc., Missoula, MO: September 9, 2013, 36.)

19. **"If you can imagine five Super Bowls"**: Emily Bregel, "Massive Mine Proposed at Oak Flat, Sacred Tribal Land," *Arizona Daily Star* (September 8, 2013).

19. **"Hope is on the horizon"**: John McCain, "Why I'll Vote for Resolution Copper," *Arizona Central* (October 15, 2014).

20. **the day's agenda:** Subcommittee on Public Lands, Forests, and Mining, Committee on Energy and Natural Resources, U.S. Senate, November 20, 2013 (Washington: Government Printing Office, 2014).

20. **sent regrets and a prepared statement:** Ibid.

20. **"Some of these bills"**: Senator Joe Manchin III, Ibid.

20. **Native tribes:** The terms "Native American," "American Indian," and "Indian" have been called out as problematic for their origins in a colonialist system. Nevertheless these terms are often used within indigenous communities. In this book I use the words that the people I interviewed use to describe themselves. These include the above terms, as well as "Native," "indigenous," "Apache," "*Ndee*," "Navajo," and "*Diné*."

21. **"a place filled with power"**: Prepared Statement of Terry Rambler, Chairman, San Carlos Apache Tribe, Senate Subcommittee on Public Lands, Forests, and Mining (November 2013).

21. **Naelyn rose and faced the senators:** Video of the hearing is archived on the Senate Committee on Energy and Natural Resources website. Retrieved from: **www.energy. senate.gov/public/index.cfm/hearings-and-business-meetings?ID=9CBAE850 -8824-4EE5-B8B2-985AAB1C5490** (accessed June 2019).

21. **photographs of Naelyn:** "Attachments to Testimony of Terry Rambler," Senate Subcommittee on Public Lands, Forests, and Mining (November 20, 2013).

22. **"My name, Naelyn, means 'Apache woman'"**: Ibid.

24. **Another defeat:** John McCain said the Resolution Copper land exchange legislation was one of the "three or four most frustrating things" he ever navigated in Congress. Ryan Randazzo, "Uncertain Path," *Arizona Republic* (October 12, 2014).

24. **"The Land Exchange was included in Section 3003"**: Terry Rambler, "Raiding Native Sacred Places in a Defense Authorization," *Indian Country Today* (December 10, 2014).

24. **President Barack Obama signed it into law:** The Obama Administration objected to the Resolution Copper land exchange when it was proposed as freestanding legislation. After the passage of the 2015 NDAA with the rider that included the land exchange, Obama's secretary of the interior Sally Jewell put out a statement: "I am profoundly disappointed with the Resolution Copper provision, which has no regard for lands considered sacred by nearby Indian tribes. The provision short circuits the long-standing and fundamental practice of pursuing meaningful government-to-government consultation with the 566 federally recognized tribes with whom we have a unique legal and trust responsibility. Although there are consultation requirements in the legislation, the appropriate time for honoring our government-to-government relationship with tribes is before legislating issues of this magnitude. The tribe's sacred land has now been placed in great jeopardy." ("Statement by Interior Secretary Sally Jewell on the National Defense Authorization Act for Fiscal Year 2015," Washington: December 19, 2014.)

25. **"Light the fires and join the occupation"**: Apache Stronghold flyer, "Occupy Oak Flat" (January 23, 2015).

25. **On a February morning in 2015:** Miriam Wasser, "Occupy Oak Flat Refuses to Back Down in Protest Against Resolution Copper," *Phoenix New Times* (February 24, 2015).

25. **defending his people from a ferocious bear:** Lou Cuevas, *Apache Legends: Songs of the Wind Dancer* (Happy Camp, CA: Naturegraph Publishers, Inc., 1991), 124–27.

25. **they conducted a prayer ceremony:** David Zlutnick, "Apaches Fight Mining Company Over Land," MSNBC Originals (April 9, 2015).

25. **"we're in the fight":** Roger Hill, "The Apache Way: The March to Oak Flat," *Truth Out* (March 4, 2015).

27. **"A groundswell is building":** Lee Allen, "Oak Flat Protesters Plan March on Washington to Protest Apache Land Grab," *Indian Country Today* (June 4, 2015).

27. **"We are committed to shining light":** Terry Rambler, "Raiding Native Sacred Places in a Defense Authorization," *Indian Country Today* (December 10, 2014).

28. **Native American college scholarship:** According to the company's website, "The Resolution Copper Native American Scholarship is a one-time grant of $3,000. . . . Applicants must supply a Certificate of Indian Blood." Retrieved from **resolutioncopper. com/wp-content/uploads/2019/02/2019_RC_Native_American_Scholarship.pdf** (accessed June 2019).

28. **"as many Native Americans as possible":** John McCain, "Setting the Record Straight on the Resolution Copper Mine Project," Facebook post (August 27, 2015).

28. **15,000 members:** 15,393 as of August 2014. Sandra Rambler, "Tribe Looking to Increase Enrollment," *Eastern Arizona Courier* (August 14, 2014).

28. **About 10,000 live on the 1.8 million acre San Carlos Reservation:** "San Carlos Apache Tribe Primary Care Area (PCA), Statistical Profile 2018," Bureau of Women's and Children's Health, Arizona Department of Health Services (Phoenix: January 8, 2019).

28. **70 percent unemployment:** John McCain, "Why I'll vote for Resolution Copper," **azcentral.com** / *Arizona Republic* (October 15, 2014).

28. **including 59 percent of children under 12:** "San Carlos Apache Tribe Primary Care Area (PCA), Statistical Profile 2018" (January 8, 2019).

28. **tests positive for drugs or alcohol at birth:** Kathleen W. Kitcheyan, San Carlos Apache Tribal Chairperson, Oversight Hearing on the Problem of Methamphetamine in Indian Country, Committee on Indian Affairs, United States Senate, Washington (April 5, 2006).

28. **16 years shorter than non-Natives in the state:** Jennifer Pullen, "Health Status of American Indians in Arizona," Making Action Possible for Southern Arizona (Tucson: March 20, 2017).

28. **more than a billion dollars:** "Project Facts," Resolution Copper (April 10, 2014).

28. **some $7 billion more:** Matthew Philips, "Inside the Billion-Dollar Dig to America's Biggest Copper Deposit," *Bloomberg Businessweek* (March 14, 2016).

28. **$144 billion worth of copper:** Ray Stern, "A Copper Mine Near Superior and Oak Flat Campground Is Set to Destroy a Unique, Sacred Recreation Area—for Fleeting Benefits," *Phoenix New Times* (April 22, 2015).

28. **profits from operations of $16 billion:** BHP, Annual Report (2018), 69. Retrieved from **www.bhp.com/investor-centre/annual-report-2018** (accessed June 2019).

28. **$18 billion in profits from operations:** Rio Tinto, "2018 Full Year Results" (February 27, 2019).

36. **"Support the Save Oak Flat Act"**: Legislation to repeal the land exchange legislation has been introduced in the U.S. House of Representatives and in the Senate. As of this writing, neither of the bills has reached a vote. See H.R. 666 Save Oak Flat and S. 173 Save Oak Flat Act, both introduced January 1, 2019.

36. **"This is our sweat lodge"**: Wendsler Nosie's quotations throughout the book are from in-person and telephone interviews conducted between 2015 and 2018 unless otherwise noted.

37. **chairman David Archambault II . . . Ashley Nailihn Susan**: Vincent Schilling, "Miss Native American USA, Ashley Niliaanh Susan, Shows Solidarity at Oak Flat March," *Indian Country Today* (March 1, 2017).

37. **Jane Sanders . . . made a speech**: Katherine Locke, "Jane Sanders Visits Oak Flat," *Navajo-Hopi Observer* (March 22, 2016).

40. **Public Land Order 1229**: President Dwight Eisenhower, PLO 1229, 1955. Reaffirmed by President Richard Nixon (PLO 5132, 1971).

40. **old-growth Emory oak trees**: About this area of Oak Flat, John Welch writes, "The stunningly beautiful, approximately 40-acre grove of majestic Emory oak trees known as Oak Flat is the most significant American Indian site within the proposed RCM [Resolution Copper Mine] impact area. Ancestors of all 10 RCM-affected tribes left behind material traces of their occupation and carried forward memories and stories." (J. R. Welch, "Earth, Wind, and Fire: Pinal Apaches, Miners, and Genocide in Central Arizona, 1859-1874," *SAGE Open,* Volume 7, Issue 4 (December 22, 2017), 1.

40. **Stone ruins**: It's not clear what these ruins indicate, or to what era they date. Apache people were nomadic and did not generally build stone buildings. A number of other Native peoples have ties to Oak Flat. (See Welch, 2017, 2–3.) According to archaeologist Tom Wright, "The area has not been systematically surveyed. It's been surveyed in bits and pieces over the last 40 something years. So there's some knowledge about it but it's not systematic." (Telephone interview with Thomas Wright, August 2016.)

40. **"the best set of Apache archaeological sites"**: Zach Zorich, "Planned Arizona Copper Mine Would Put a Hole in Apache Archaeology," *Science* (December 10, 2014). In a telephone interview in March 2017, John (J. R.) Welch added, "There isn't any other place that I know of in the world that has this type of an Apache presence signaled. [The traces] look just like you would expect them to look from photographs of clusters of Apache houses in the 1800s and early 1900s."

41. **"Fingers long and pointed"**: Diego Archuleta, "To the Editor of the New York Times," *The New York Times* (January 26, 1859). The author of this letter, Diego Archuleta, was a U.S. Indian agent. Archuleta's (long) letter goes on: the Apache are "the greatest obstacle to the operations of the mining companies and traders. . . . [W]hipping these wild tribes . . . into submission, and driving them into reservations . . . with the penalty of death sternly enforced if they pass their limits, is the only prompt, economical, and humane process."

41. **"the tiger of the human species"**: Major General George Crook, "The Apache Problem," *Journal of Military Service Institution of the United States,* Volume 7 (New York: G. P. Putnam & Sons, 1886).

41. **"All Indian men of that tribe"**: Brigadier General James H. Carleton, letter to Colonel Kit Carson (October 12, 1821). Reprinted in *Condition of the Indian Tribes: Report of the Joint Special Committee, United States Congress* (Washington: Government Printing Office, 1867), 100.

41. **"If I can but have troops"**: Brigadier General James H. Carleton, letter, *Reports of the Committees of the Senate of the United States for the Second Session Thirty Ninth Congress* (Washington, Government Printing Office: 1867), 140.

43. **some six million acres**: Welch, 12.

Chapter 4

44. **the model for the sculpture was Wes Studi**: Telephone interview with sculptor Craig Goseyun (April 25, 2017). Goseyun created the bronze "Hoop and Pole Game Dancer" for the casino.

44. **Slot machines ding, buzz, and simulate the sound of smashing glass**: The manufactured soundscape masks the absence of human conversation.

44. **photo of Geronimo**: A caption, handwritten on the photograph that has been enlarged to poster size reads, "Geronimo, Chief of the notorious band of Arizona Apache Indians, photo by Ed Irwin, 1847."

46. **golden-orange poppies**: Poppies are copper indicator plants. A. Chaffee and C. W. Gale III, "The California Poppy (*eschscholtzia mexicana*) as a Copper Indicator Plant: A New Example," *Journal of Geochemical Exploration,* Volume 5, Issue 1–2 (1976), 59–63.

46. **cemetery for Apache veterans**: According to Kevin Gover, director of the Smithsonian National Museum of the American Indian, "American Indians serve in their country's armed forces in greater numbers per capita than any other ethnic group." (Kevin Grover, "American Indians Serve in the U.S. Military in Greater. Numbers Than Any Ethnic Group and Have Since the Revolution," *Huffington Post,* May 22, 2015).

46. **Mormon, Pentecostal, Baptist, Roman Catholic**: Following years of forced conversions, many Apaches today have spiritual practices that include both Apache traditions and those of various Christian denominations.

46. **"San Carlos! That was the worst place"**: Ace Daklugies's oral history in Eve Ball, *Indeh: An Apache Odyssey* (Norman: University of Oklahoma Press, 1980), 37.

48. **"San Carlos won unanimously our designation"**: Third Officer stationed at Old San Carlos, 1883–1884, U.S. Army Report on "Sanitary Condition of the Army," 1893. Cited in Paul and Kathleen Nickens, *Old San Carlos* (Images of America series), Arizona Historical Foundation (Charleston: Arcadia Publishing, 2008), 9.

48. **the army strictly limited periods of deployment**: Paul and Kathleen Nickens, 55.

48. **"Indians shall not be allowed to leave their proper reservations"**: *Statutes of the United States of America, Passed at the First Session of the Fifty-Second Congress, 1891–1892* (Washington: Government Printing Office, 1892), 195.

49. **"routinely hunted down and killed"**: Donald L. Fixico, *Treaties with American Indians: An Encyclopedia of Rights, Conflicts, and Sovereignty,* Volume 3 (Santa Barbara, CA: ABC-CLIO, 2007), 168.

49. **required to wear identification tags**: Richard J. Perry, *Apache Reservation: Indigenous Peoples and the American State* (Austin: University of Texas Press, 1993), 134.

49. **"first concentration camp still existing to this day"**: Retrieved from: www.sancarlosapache.com/San_Carlos_Culture_Center.htm (accessed May 2019). My citation in the text edits a small typo on the website: "1871 [. It is] the first . . ."

52. **one of ten San Carlos families chosen**: Ralph Mohoney, "Best of All, an Inside Bath: Wood-Cutting, Water-Carrying Things of the Past for Apache Indians in Mutual Help Plan Homes," *Arizona Republic* (November 23, 1964).

52. **"designed to blend well with the landscape on any reservation":** "New House Plan Service to Spur Indian Building," Bureau of Indian Affairs (Washington: November 5, 1965).

52. **assumed most of the work . . . while Paul was away:** Winn Purchase, "New Homes on the Range: Apaches Bustling at Building Bee," *Arizona Daily Star* (August 2, 1964).

52. **"Mrs. Nosie drove a pickup":** Ibid.

52. **She planned to grow fruit trees:** Ibid.

54. **"not insurmountable":** "Guide to Mortgage Lending in Indian Country," Office of the Comptroller of the Currency, U.S. Department of the Treasury. Retrieved from **www. occ.gov/publications/publications-by-type/other-publications-reports/country. pdf** (accessed May 2019).

54. **the federal government holds legal title:** Sabrina Tuttle, federally recognized Tribal Extension Program agent, San Carlos Apache Reservation, and assistant professor, Department of Agricultural Education, "The San Carlos Apache Reservation Quick Facts," University of Arizona College of Agriculture and Life Sciences in cooperation with the U.S. Department of Agriculture (2014). Retrieved from: **indiancountryextension. org/sites/indiancountryextension.org/files/publications/files/u6/San%20 Carlos%20Apache%20Quick%20Facts%20Oct08.pdf** (accessed June 2019).

54. **made banks reluctant to grant loans:** Tribes can apply for government grants that guarantee the loans in case of default. However, individual applicants still need to qualify for these loans, and many low-income applicants do not. The United States still funds various housing programs on reservations, but, by all accounts, a housing crisis in San Carlos (and throughout Indian Country) continues.

54. **"They're the only flowers":** Theresa Nosie's quotations throughout the book are from in-person and telephone interviews conducted between 2015 and 2017.

58. **"We are decades behind":** Wendsler Nosie Sr., San Carlos Apache tribal chairman, "Hearing on Reauthorization of Native American Housing Assistance and Self-Determination Act," Subcommittee on Housing and Community Opportunity of the Financial Services Committee, U.S. House of Representatives, Washington (June 6, 2007).

59. **"She asked me to ask you: 'What happened?'":** Ibid. I have edited this line of Nosie's testimony slightly for clarity. The transcript reads, "So she asked me the question to ask you: what happened?"

Chapter 5

62. **A smartphone uses about 15 grams of copper:** Bianca Nogrady, "Your Old Phone Is Full of Untapped Precious Metals," BBC (October 18, 2016).

62. **exteriors clad in copper to form an electromagnetic shield:** Kriston Capps, "The Dark Architecture of National Security," *CityLab* (June 8, 2017).

See also: Leland H. Hemming, Architectural Electromagnetic Shielding Handbook: *A Design and Specification Guide* (New York: John Wiley & Sons, 2000), 95.

62. **Weapons systems rely on copper:** "Strategic and Critical Materials 2015 Report on Stockpile Requirements," Under Secretary of Defense for Acquisition, Technology and Logistics, Department of Defense, Washington (January 2015).

63. **electric car uses triple that:** Frank Holmes, "This Commodity Is Going to Be a Huge Beneficiary of the Shift to Electric Cars," *Business Insider* (April 19, 2016).

See also: "Copper Demand for Electric Cars to Rise Nine-Fold by 2027: ICA," Reuters (June 13, 2017).

63. **26 million tons:** 23.9 million metric tonnes, Ibid.

See also: "Copper," Mineral Commodity Summaries, U.S. Geological Survey (February 2019).

64. **When commodity prices rise:** Alison Stewart, "The Growing Black Market for Copper," National Public Radio (April 10, 2008).

When I lived in Red Hook, Brooklyn, my morning commute included crossing a somewhat desolate pedestrian walkway over the Brooklyn Queens Expressway. It was common to find the walkway strewn with home electronics that had been busted open, gutted for their copper wire, and discarded.

64. **Organized crime rings loot:** "Copper Thefts Threaten U.S. Critical Infrastructure," Intelligence Assessment (Unclassified)," FBI Criminal Intelligence Section (Washington: September 15, 2008).

65. **some of these homes later exploded:** Jon Tevlin, "The New Underground Currency," Minneapolis *Star Tribune* (April 12, 2008).

Chapter 6

66. **smelter stands on a hill overlooking town:** The 1924 smokestack and smelter complex was demolished by Resolution Copper in 2018.

68. **"The only people in town we don't know":** Michael McKee's quotations throughout the book are from in-person and telephone interviews conducted between 2016 and 2019.

69. **"But then, we're starting to know them":** Patricia Brown's quotations throughout the book are from in-person and telephone interviews conducted between 2016 and 2019.

70. **photo contests:** "There Is Still Time to Enter the Superior Chamber Photo Contest: Cash Prizes to Be Awarded!" *Copper Area News* (December 18, 2017).

70. **First Pregnancy Care Center:** Claire Grochocki, Letter to the Editor, "Resolution Copper Makes Donation to Family First," *Copper Area News* (November 27, 2017).

70. **and a nature club in local schools:** Superior Unified School District. Retrieved from **www.superiorusd.org** (accessed May 2019).

70. **fire department, police department, and other emergency services:** James Hodl, "Superior Town Council Accepts a Mutually-Beneficial Agreement with Resolution Copper; Mining Company to Pay Superior $1.65 Million for Police, Fire Services Through 2021," *Copper Area News* (February 13, 2016).

70. **invoices Resolution Copper:** Town of Superior, Town Council Meeting Minutes (January 11, 2018).

70. **"too late when he got there":** Jackie Gorham's quotations throughout the book are from in-person and telephone interviews conducted between 2016 and 2019 unless otherwise noted.

73. **"a cave-in?":** "Local Field News," *The Hazleton Sentinel* (November 16, 1886). "Yesterday morning Peter Gorham, a laborer in the Hartford mine, Ashley, was instantly killed

yesterday morning [sic] by a fall of top rock. Not long ago Gorham was severely hurt in a similar manner, being badly cut and bruised by a fall of rock. He leaves a wife and six children. The unfortunate man was about 50 years of age, a good citizen universally esteemed."

76. **"killed in France in the Battle of Saint Lô":** According to Jackie Gorham, "Patsy never married. He carried a picture of his horse with him." Four days before Staff Sergeant Patrick "Patsy" Gorham Jr. was shot by a German sniper in August 1944, he wrote a letter home: "I really got to see a lot in the last month, most of the sights would have made Jeff Smith's stomach turn." Jeff Smith was Superior's mortician. Staff Sergeant Patrick Gorham Jr., graduate of Superior High School class of 1938, was awarded a Silver Star, a Bronze Star, and a Purple Heart.

77. **black lumps of silver:** David F. Briggs, "Superior, AZ: An Old Mining Camp with Many Lives," Arizona Geological Survey (Tucson: December 2015).

77. **a new name: Superior:** "Magma: Among Greatest Producers in Arizona," *Arizona Republican* (November 23, 1916).

77. **established in 1910:** Magma Copper Company archives, Arizona Historical Society, Tucson, Arizona.

77. **1.3 million tons of copper:** David F. Briggs, "History of the Magma Mine, Superior, Arizona," *Arizona Daily Independent* (July 19, 2015).

78. **Patrick Gorham was offered the job:** Gorham was sheriff of Superior from 1918 to 1950.

79. **a man known as Star Daley was arrested:** "Lord's Prayer Prelude to Hanging of Murderer and Rapist," *Arizona Daily Star* (May 8, 1917). Star Daley was a pseudonym for Van Ashmore.

79. **"recited the Lord's prayer in unison for him":** Ibid.

79. **"Everyone posed for pictures":** Photograph of the lynching of Van Ashmore/aka Star Daley in Mesa (Ariz.) in 1917. Arizona State Library, Archives and Public Records. History and Archives Division, Phoenix, #97-1361.

80. **"the house of ill repute":** Deb McKee's quotations throughout the book are from in-person and telephone interviews conducted between 2016 and 2019.

In her book *The Legacy of Conquest: The Unbroken Past of the American West* (New York: W. W. Norton & Co., 1987), Patricia Nelson Limerick writes, "In the broad sweep of Western history, it may look as if a united social unit called 'white people' swept Indians off their lands; that group, as the history of prostitution shows, was not a monolith at all but a complex swirl of people as adept at preying on each other as at preying on Indians" (p. 51).

85. **"I worked in the Belmont later":** Mila Besich-Lira's quotations throughout the book are from in-person and telephone interviews conducted between 2016 and 2017.

86. **hasn't screened a film since 1979:** Trey Ross, "Hayden Sees Its Dying Days," *Arizona Sonora News Service* (April 20, 2017).

86. **emitting illegal levels of lead and arsenic:** "ASARCO LLC Settlement," United States Environmental Protection Agency (Washington, November 3, 2015). See also: Leslie Kaufman, "Asarco Pays $1.79 Billion to Fix Sites," *The New York Times* (December 10, 2009).

86. **install pollution control technology:** "ASARCO LLC Settlement" (2015).

86. **Fourteen million tons of tailings:** "Leading Practice Reclamation at Resolution Copper Mining: Claiming the Future by Reclaiming the Past," Resolution Copper (2014).

86. **"That was before the days":** Cheryl Lira-Castro's quotations throughout the book are from in-person and telephone interviews conducted between 2016 and 2018.

86. **"in the pit" of the Ray mine:** The Kennecott Copper Corporation opened the Ray mine in 1952. In 1986, the mine was purchased by ASARCO.

87. **"The heat is unbelievable":** Evelyn Gorham's quotations throughout the book are from in-person and telephone interviews conducted between 2016 and 2019.

92. **"be down there by sound":** David Lira's quotations throughout the book are from an interview at his home in Superior in 2016.

92. **"tommyknockers":** Tommyknockers are described in the *Proceedings of the Mining and Metallurgical Society of America* (Issues 304–11, New York: Mining and Metallurgical Society of America, 1956): "Most of you know the *tommyknocker*. . . . They are friendly gremlin-like characters that came over with the Cornish mineworkers who migrated to California in the decade following the big gold strike of the late 1840s."

95. **"Mining set a mood":** Limerick, 100.

Chapter 7

96. **"When I was pregnant":** Vanessa Nosie's quotations throughout the book are taken from in-person interviews conducted between 2016 and 2018.

101. **"There's life in the city":** Interview with Vanessa Nosie, Nizhoni Pike, Naelyn Pike, and Baasé-O Pike. Phoenix, 2016.

102. **"We wore turquoise":** Interview with Vanessa Nosie, Nizhoni Pike, Naelyn Pike, and Baasé-O Pike. Phoenix, 2016.

103. **"A Rez girl would wear":** Interview with Nizhoni Pike, Naelyn Pike, and Baasé-O Pike. Phoenix, 2016.

106. **"I come from a place called Oak Flat":** Naelyn Pike, campaign rally for Bernie Sanders, Reid Park DeMeester Outdoor Performance Center, Tucson (October 9, 2015). Senator Sanders also featured Naelyn's photo on campaign brochures.

106. **"cumulative wounding across generations":** Maria Yellow Horse Brave Heart, *"Wakiksuyapi,* Carrying the Historical Trauma of the Lakota" (New Orleans: Tulane University School of Social Work, 2000), 21–22, 245–266.

107. **"None are more anxious":** "Report to the President by the Indian Peace Policy Commission," Commissioner of Indian Affairs (Washington: Government Printing Office, 1868), 33.

107. **"It costs less to civilize than to kill":** Ibid, 42.

108. **Union side . . . Fort Marion:** Various biographical details come from Pratt's memoir, Richard Henry Pratt, *Battlefield and Classroom: Four Decades with the American Indian, 1867–1904* (New Haven: Yale University Press, 1964).

108. **"Kill the Indian, save the man":** Pratt pronounced his original phrase, "Kill the Indian in him, and save the man," during a 1892 speech at George Mason University. The speech is reprinted in Richard H. Pratt, "The Advantages of Mingling Indians with Whites," *Americanizing the American Indians: Writings by the "Friends of the Indian," 1880–1900* (Cambridge: Harvard University Press, 1973), 260–271.

108. **new names . . . new birthdates:** *Away from Home: American Indian Boarding School Experiences, 1879–2000* (editor: K. Tsianina Lomawaima, Phoenix: Heard Museum, 2000) is one of many books on Indian boarding schools. The book includes recollections of former students and was published in conjunction with the long-running exhibition "Remembering Our Indian School Days: The Boarding School Experience" at the Heard Museum in Phoenix, Arizona.

108. **washed out with lye soap:** Eve Tulene Watt, with Keith Basso, *Don't Let the Sun Step Over You* (Tucson: University of Arizona Press, 2004), 54.

108. **auto repair and welding:** Lomawaima, 35. As it turned out, the Indian boarding school system also had the unintended consequence of building relationships between Natives from different backgrounds, creating alliances that later supported indigenous activism. According to Ruthie Blalock Jones (Delaware/Shawnee/Peoria), "[The schools] were started to stamp out the Indian from Indian people, you know, make us all into white people, and you know, it didn't work. Actually . . . it was the exact opposite: it made us stronger as an Indian people. It made us more aware and more proud of who we were."

109. **"the agency":** refers to the Bureau of Indian Affairs.

111. **Elvera Nosie died in 2016:** "Elvera Nosie (April 1, 1928–July 16, 2016)," Lamont Mortuary (Globe, AZ: July 2016).

111. **124 great-grandchildren . . . 30 great-great-grandchildren:** Ibid.

Chapter 8

117. **Mount Graham, or *Dził Nchaa Si An*:** I am indebted to the work of Joel T. Helfrich on the conflict over telescopes on Mount Graham. Helfrich's dissertation: "A Mountain of Politics: The Struggle for dził nchaa si'an (Mount Graham), 1871–2002" (University of Minnesota, 2010) is an excellent piece of scholarship and a muscular argument for the rights of indigenous people.

In addition, Joel introduced me to Janet Witzeman, who generously provided me with a vast trove of difficult-to-find primary source documents collected by her late husband, Bob Witzeman (1927–2014). Witzeman was a physician and deeply committed to conservation. He was involved in both the effort to stop telescopes from being built on Mount Graham and the movement to prevent Resolution Copper from building a copper mine at Oak Flat.

117. **within vast expanses identified as "Chiricahua Apache" and "Coyotero Apache":** Richard Gird, "Official Map of the Territory of Arizona. With All the Recent Explorations," *Gird's Official Map of the Territory of Arizona* (San Francisco: A. Gensoul, Pacific Map Depot, and Lith. Britton & Co., 1865). See also: Helfrich, 64.

117. **executive order two years later:** "Executive Orders Relating to Indian Reservations: From May 14, 1855 to July 1, 1912" (Washington: Government Printing Office, 1912).

117. **Ada Rope Jordan . . . rode 80 miles on horseback:** I heard this story from Ada Rope Jordan's daughter, Delores Jordan, an aunt of Terry Rambler. Ada Rope Jordan, or *Du'na'Chaa'haa* (She Who Cries), was the daughter of the famous Apache scout John Rope, or *Tlol'Dil'Xil* (Black Rope).

117. **"a rare and precious habitat of extraordinary evolutionary interest":** Stephen Jay Gould, *Eight Little Piggies: Reflections in Natural History* (New York: W. W. Norton & Co., 1995), 44.

117. **"sky island":** Ibid, 41–51.

117. "11,000 years ago": Jon Lancaster, "Astronomers, Biologists Clash Over Observatory Plans," *The Washington Post* (March 8, 1990).

121. "one of the most desperate": Nelson Appleton Miles, *Personal Recollections and Observations of General Nelson A. Miles* (Chicago: Werner Company, 1896), 480.

121. "The mountain labyrinths": Ibid.

121. effective arsenal would include: Ibid, 481.

121. "I had it in my mind": Ibid.

122. "a network of points": Ibid.

122. "It was remarkable": Ibid, 482.

122. By the summer of 1886, the United States had mobilized: For an account of the last days of Geronimo's resistance and final capitulation, see Edwin R. Sweeney, *From Chochise to Geronimo: The Chiricahua Apaches, 1874–1886* (Norman: University of Oklahoma Press, 2012).

122. 17 men: The figure 17 comes from the oral history of Ace Dakluglie, recorded by Eve Ball and published in *Indeh* (Norman: University of Oklahoma Press, 1980), 101. James Kaywaykla's account, also recorded by Ball and published in *In the Days of Victorio: Recollections of a Warm Springs Apache* (Tucson: University of Arizona Press, 1970), 184, confirms this number. Kaywaykla lists the name of each of the 17 people. Still, Kaywaykla says, "Under our loose organization it is difficult to estimate. For men came and went, as scouts and as messengers. [Whatever the number, it] was infinitesimal in comparison to the hordes of cavalrymen and Tarahumaras that the U.S. and Mexico used harassing the Apaches" (Ball, *In the Days of Victorio,* 181).

122. "The heliostat had performed": Miles, 525.

123. cheaper and easier to build: Warren Leary, "Astronomers to Look for Planets around other Stars," *Arizona Daily Star* (February 13, 1978). See also: Jacques M. Beckers and Bobby L. Ulich. "The Multiple Mirror Telescope," *Telescopes for the 1980s* (Palo Alto: Annual Reviews, Inc., 1981), 63–128.

123. close to 300 sites: "Site Testing, The Early Days," Mount Graham International Observatory, Arizona Board of Regents (Tucson: 2019). Retrieved from: **mgio.arizona. edu/mount-graham-site-testing-era** (accessed May 2019).

123. concluded that Mount Graham's skies were clear, dry: For more on the history of Mount Graham's selection as a site for astronomical research see: **mgio.arizona.edu/ mount-graham-site-testing-era** (accessed June 2019).

123. some of the darkest in the United States: In 1972, Tuscan and Pima County passed the City of Tucson/Pima County Outdoor Lighting Code restricting artificial lighting. The ordinance states in part: "The purpose of this code is to preserve the relationship of the residents of Tucson/Pima County to their unique desert environment through protection of access to the dark night sky. Intended outcomes include continuing support of astronomical activity."

    The law has been updated as recently as 2012 but most of the original language is intact.

124. farther into the past: There was copious press coverage throughout the development of the Mount Graham International Observatory, beginning with the project's exploratory stages. For instance, see: "Scientists Looking for Home for the World's Biggest Telescope," *The Tribune* (Seymour, IN: August 16, 1984).

124. **Strittmatter told the *Arizona Daily Star*:** Peter Turner, "Bigger Is Better in Fixing a Knowing Gaze on the Heavens," *Arizona Daily Star* (August 31, 1981).

124. **not yet even imagined:** Ibid.

124. **filed a lawsuit:** Douglas Kreutz, "Red Squirrel Ruling Postponed by Judge," *Arizona Daily Star* (November 28, 1989).

125. **"contribute directly to the destruction":** Resolution No. 90-68, San Carlos Apache Tribe (San Carlos, AZ: July 10, 1990).

125. **In 1991, the Apache Survival Coalition filed a lawsuit:** *Apache Survival Coalition v. U.S.,* United States Court of Appeals, 21 F.3d 895. (9th Cir. 1994).

125. **"Indians, because of our considerably longer tenure":** Vine Deloria Jr., "Sacred Lands and Religious Freedom," Special Issue on Freedom of Religion, *Native American Rights Fund (NARF) Review,* Vol. 16, No. 2 (Summer 1991).

126. **Why would the Roman Catholic Church build a telescope, and why in Arizona?:** Numerous phone calls and emails to the Vatican Observatory and the Vatican Advanced Technology Telescope seeking comment on this story went unanswered.

126. **The Inquisition tried and condemned:** Hugh James Rose, *New General Biographical Dictionary,* Volume 7, B. Fellowes (London: 1848). See also: Alan Cowell, "After 350 Years, Vatican Says Galileo Was Right: It Moves," *The New York Times* (October 31, 1992).

126. **questioned his faith, then re-embraced it:** "Father George Coyne Interviewed by Richard Dawkins." Footage of 2008 interview recorded for Dawkins's television program *The Genius of Charles Darwin* for Channel 4 in the UK. The interview was not aired.

126. **degree in mathematics and a licentiate in philosophy:** George Coyne, S.J., faculty page, Le Moyne College, Syracuse, New York. Retrieved from: **www.lemoyne.edu/Academics/Our-Faculty/Religious-Studies/George-Coyne** (accessed May 2019).

126. **Harvard and the National Science Foundation:** Dr. George V. Coyne, S.J., Biography Index, Faith and Reason, PBS.org. Retrieved from: **www.pbs.org/faithandreason/bio/coyne-body.html** (accessed May 2019).

131. **"the noble descendants":** Pope John Paul II, "Apostolic Journey to the United States of America and Canada: Meeting with the Native Peoples of the Americas" (Phoenix: Memorial Coliseum, September 14, 1987).

131. **"The early encounter":** Ibid.

131. **fifteenth-century papal bulls:** Pope Nicholas V, "Dum Diversas" (June 18, 1452), and Pope Alexander VI, "Inter Caetera" (May 4, 1493).

131. **"I encourage you":** Pope John Paul II, Memorial Coliseum, September 14, 1987.

132. **"your project threatens our cultural survival":** Letter from Raleigh J. Thomson (interim chairman, San Carlos Apache Tribe) to Pope John Paul II (February 8, 1992).

132. **at the last minute, canceled:** "Apache Delegation Denied Audience with Pope," *Apache Moccasin* (May 26, 1992).

132. **embezzling funds from the tribe:** "Kitcheyan Pleads Guilty; Sentencing Sept. 19 in Tucson," *Apache Moccasin* (July 12, 1994).

132. **Following his arrest and conviction:** Chad Unrein, "Former Apache Chairman to Be Jailed," *Indian Country Today* (December 8, 1994).

132. **failed to appear . . . prohibited him from leaving Arizona:** Mark Genrich, "Mt. Graham: Holy War for the Arizona Mountaintop," *Phoenix Gazette* (June 17, 1992).

132. **private tour . . . posed for photos:** Dennis Wagner, "Pope Can't See Apaches for the Telescopes," *Phoenix Gazette* (July 7, 1992).

　　See also: "Apaches Supporting Telescope Project See John Paul II," *Apache Moccasin* (July 14, 1992); Tara Meyer, "Meeting with Pope Angers Tribal Group," *Arizona Summer Wildcat* (June 23, 1992); Tara Meyer, "Apaches Leave for Europe Leaderless," *Arizona Summer Wildcat* (June 16, 1992).

132. **Harvard . . . dropped out:** Harry James Wilson, "Telescope Site Set for Hawaii: Mt. Graham Location Rejected After Years of Controversy," *Harvard Crimson* (May 10, 1991).

132. **city council of Rome passed a motion:** "Mount Graham," Business of the Day or Motion, City Council of Rome (April 28, 1992).

133. **"We are not convinced. . . . If they could show us Apaches buried:"** Jim Erickson, "Astronomer-Priest Contends Science, Religion Don't Clash," *Arizona Daily Star* (November 22, 1992).

133. **"Dził Nchaa Si An is sacred. . . . If I have to go to jail":** Greg Clark, "San Carlos Apache man faces fines for trespassing, *Arizona Daily Wildcat* (September 16, 1997).

133. **entered a written plea of "not guilty":** Sandra Rambler, "Former Councilmember Cited by UA Officers for Praying on Sacred Apache Mountain," San Carlos Apache Tribe (San Carlos: September 9, 1997).

134. **"This is judicial code":** Walter R. Echo-Hawk, *In the Courts of the Conqueror: The 10 Worst Indian Law Cases Ever Decided* (Golden, CO: Fulcrum Publishing, 2010), 72.

134. **Congress passed the American Indian Religious Freedom Act (AIRFA):** The American Indian Religious Freedom Act of 1978 (AIRFA) (42 U.S.C. § 1996).

135. **"would cause serious and irreparable damage":** Dorothea J. Theodoratus et al., "*Cultural Resources of the Chimney Rock Section, Gasquet-Orleans Road, Six Rivers National Forest,*" (Fair Oaks, CA: Theodoratus Cultural Research, 1979). The Theodoratus Report was commissioned by the U.S. Forest Service.

135. **"an interstate through the Vatican":** Reuters, "Tribes Say Road Hurts a Holy Site," *The New York Times* (December 26, 1987).

135. **"astonishing":** William J. Brennan Jr., Dissenting Opinion, *Lyng v. Northwest Indian Cemetery*, 485 U.S. 439 (1988). Brennan wrote, "Religious freedom is threatened no less by governmental programs that make the practice of one's chosen faith impossible than by governmental programs that pressure one to engage in conduct inconsistent with religious beliefs." In the end, the G-O road was left incomplete, but not because Native concerns prevailed. Road construction was abandoned following the passage of the 1984 California Wilderness Act. The 1990 creation of the Smith River National Recreation Area established further protections. But the Supreme Court's *Lyng* decision not to protect indigenous sacred land stands as legal precedent.

135. **"People often feel guilty":** Vine Deloria Jr., *Custer Died for Your Sins: An Indian Manifesto* (New York: MacMillan, 1969), 54.

136. **"experienced something similar to Adam and Eve":** Bruce Johnston, "Vatican Evangelical Sets Sights on Outer Space," *London Daily Telegraph* (October 28, 1992).

136. **"The Church would be obliged":** Ibid.

137. **"We would be open to that sort of thing":** Ibid.

137. **"This does not conflict with our faith"**: Francesco M. Valiante, "The Extraterrestrial Is My Brother," *L'Osservatore Romano* (May 14, 2008).

See also: "Vatican Astronomer Cites Possibility of Extraterrestrial 'Brothers,'" *The New York Times* (May 14, 2008).

138. **hired Washington lobbyists Patton, Boggs**: Colman McCarthy, "Politics, the Pope, and Red Squirrels," *The Washington Post* (March 3, 1990).

138. **one of D.C.'s most powerful law firms**: Neil A. Lewis, "The Lawyer as Lobbyist; Lobbying Lures Fresh Faces as Lucrative Legal Specialty," *The New York Times* (December 29, 1989).

138. **client list included**: Raymond Bonner, "Nuclear Rivals Marshal Armies of Lobbyists in Washington," *The New York Times* (February 13, 2000).

See also: Adam Bernstein, "Lobbyist, Lawyer Thomas Boggs Dead at 73," *The Washington Post* (September 15, 2014).

140. **Wendsler Nosie was acquitted**: "Apache Cleared of Trespassing on Mt. Graham," *Arizona Daily Star* (January 22, 1998).

See also: S. J. Wilson, "Nosie Acquitted of Trespassing," *Navajo Hopi Observer* (February 4, 1998).

145. **"champagne flowed"**: Jim Erickson, "Mount Graham Scope Operational with 'First Light,'" *Arizona Daily Star* (September 17, 1993).

Chapter 9

146. **"crafty, bloodthirsty, [and] incredibly cruel"**: "Geronimo," *The New York Times* (February 18, 1909).

146. **"We have a visual on Geronimo"**: Mark Mazzetti, Helene Cooper, Peter Baker, "Behind the Hunt for Bin Laden," *The New York Times* (May 2, 2011).

See also: Nicholas Schmidle, "Getting Bin Laden," *The New Yorker* (August 8, 2011); Peter Bergen, "Did Robert O'Neill Really Kill Bin Laden?" CNN (November 4, 2014).

146. **"'Geronimo' . . . was code for Bin Laden"**: President Barack Obama interviewed by Steve Kroft, *60 Minutes,* CBS News (May 4, 2011).

There is mixed information on what exactly "Geronimo" referred to in the context of the Bin Laden operation. According to Schmidle's reporting in *The New Yorker,* "Crankshaft" was the military's codename for Osama Bin Laden, and "Geronimo" referred to the act of finding Bin Laden. ABC News's Jake Tapper reported that "Cakebread" was code for Bin Laden. (Jake Tapper, "Chapter Six: The President Takes Aim," ABC News, June 9, 2011). However, it appears from Leon Panetta's comment ("We have a visual on Geronimo") and from President Obama's *60 Minutes* interview, as well as the account of Matt Bissonnette, one of the Navy SEALs who participated in the raid, that regardless of how the coded nomenclature was originally conceived or intended, the name Geronimo was indeed used to refer to Osama Bin Laden himself.

For more on the U.S. government's framing of the "hunt" for Bin Laden in terms that evoked Wild West mythology, including George Bush's announcement that Bin Laden was wanted "Dead or Alive," see: Kathryn Westcott, "Osama Bin Laden: Why Geronimo?" BBC News (May 3, 2011).

146. **In an upstairs bedroom:** There is some dispute over the precise details of Bin Laden's killing (which SEAL shot him first, in what part of the body, etc.). As Peter Bergen writes, "By all accounts, it was a confusing situation the night of the raid. One of the SEAL team's helicopters had crashed, and there was a firefight with one of Bin Laden's bodyguards. All the electricity in the compound and the surrounding neighborhood was off on a moonless night and the SEALs were wearing night vision goggles, which only allowed them limited vision. . . . What is certain is that it was a team effort." (Peter Bergen, "Did Robert O'Neill Really Kill Bin Laden?" CNN, November 4, 2014.)

147. *Enemy killed in action*: Mazzetti, Cooper, Baker.

147. **Natives were angry:** Neely Tucker, "American Indians Object to 'Geronimo' as Code Name for Bin Laden Raid," *The Washington Post* (May 3, 2011).

147. **"an outrageous insult":** "Native Americans Object to Linking Geronimo to Bin Laden," Wire Staff, CNN (May 6, 2011).

147. **"how deeply embedded the [idea of] 'Indian as enemy' is":** Tucker.

147. **"The mountain . . . was named":** University of Arizona website, "Mount Graham International Observatory: An Astrophysical Research Site." Retrieved from **mgio. arizona.edu/history-mount-graham** (accessed June 2019).

148. **"each and every place that bears an Apache name":** Keith H. Basso, *Wisdom Sits in Places: Landscape and Language Among the Western Apache* (Albuquerque: University of New Mexico Press, 1996), 9.

148. ***"They spoke it first, a long time ago"***: Emphasis in original. Ibid, 10.

In their introduction to Grenville Goodwin's *Myths and Tales of the White Mountain Apache* (Tucson: University of Arizona Press, 1994), Elizabeth Brandt, Bonnie Lavender-Lewis, and Philip Greenfield write that Apache stories are used "to provide a continuous link between the Apache and their land by telling the events that happened and the places where they happened. Apache place names are often complete sentences that describe a place so perfectly that it can be recognized from the name alone."

148. **"the land makes the people live right":** Basso, 28.

149. **"The names . . . show what is different":** Ibid, 14.

149. **Ed Schieffelin was warned:** Bryd Howell Granger, *Arizona Place Names: X Marks the Spot* (Tucson: Treasure Chest, 1983), 417.

149. **Tombstone:** Today, the town of Tombstone, Arizona, is a tourist attraction. Visitors can ride in a stagecoach and visit a restored brothel. Wyatt Earp and Doc Holliday's infamous 1881 gunfight at the O.K. Corral is reenacted four times daily.

149. **Swillings was the first name:** Barnes, 327.

150. **"universal nose-bridge":** Retrieved from **www.thecuresafety.com/Apache_Safety _Glasses_p/sd110.htm** (accessed May 2019).

150. **"Hang on to your scalps":** Michelangelo Matos, "All Roads Lead to Apache," *Listen Again: A Momentary History of Pop Music* (edited by Eric Weisbard) (Durham: Duke University Press, 2007), 200.

150. **Dozens of cover versions . . . countless hip-hop songs:** Matos, 200–09.

150. **"Be kind of aggressive and kick some ass":** Robert McMillan, "Apache Power," *Linux Magazine* (April 15, 2000). See also a video interview with Brian Behlendorf **www. youtube.com/watch?v=6kRMlfIBMCY** (accessed May 2019).

150. sued Urban Outfitters: *Navajo Nation, Corp. v. Urban Outfitters, Inc.*, CIV No. 12-195 LH/LAM (D.N.M. Sep. 19, 2014).

150. "Navajo hipster panties": Ibid, 22.

150. "generic name for a type of style": Ibid, 15.

151. Amazon . . . and so on: Ibid, 7.

151. settled out of court: Nikki Woolf, "Urban Outfitters Settles with Navajo Nation after Illegally Using Tribe's Name," *The Guardian* (November 18, 2016).

151. Zuni word meaning "our enemies": There are other theories as to the origin of the name "Apache." For instance, some suggest that "apache" may be a Yavapai word, or that it may derive from "mapachin," an Aztec word for raccoon.

151. "She will introduce herself": Amanda Blackhorse, "Native American? American Indian? Nope. Refer to Us By Our Tribe, Nation," *Indian Country Today* (August 14, 2017).

152. other members of the San Carlos Apache: For instance, Naelyn Pike sometimes refers to the Apaches' mass suicide in public speeches.

153. avoid being enslaved in Spanish gold mines: "What Do You Want to Know? Apache Tears," *The Philadelphia Inquirer* (June 9, 1967).

153. "The group of blue-uniformed men": "Imbedded Apache Tears Lure Tourists," *Arizona Republic* (December 25, 1978).

155. a pendant on a gold chain: Antonio d'Ambrosio, *A Heartbeat and a Guitar: Johnny Cash and the Making of Bitter Tears* (New York: Nation Books, 2009), 165–66.

155. "Hoof prints and foot prints": "Apache Tears," Words and Music by Johnny Cash, Copyright 1964 (Renewed), Chappell & Co. Inc. All Rights Reserved, used by permission of Alfred Music.

155. "Whoever has one never has to cry again": Pelham-Grayson, Inc., *Unique Wholesale Gift & Collectibles*. Retrieved from **www.pelhamgrayson.com/Apache-Tears-Natural ---1lb-12-1-inch-siz-13022.html** (May 2019).

158. Apache Leap is 1,500 feet: According to the 2015 National Defense Authorization Act, "The term 'Apache Leap' means the approximately 807 acres of land depicted on the map entitled 'Southeast Arizona Land Exchange and Conservation Act of 2011–Apache Leap' and dated March 2011."

158. "fully protected in perpetuity": Andrew Lye, "United States Forest Service Finalizes Plan to Protect Apache Leap," (Superior: January 5, 2018).

158. Special Management Area: "Apache Leap Special Management Area Management Plan," Tonto National Forest, U.S. Forest Service (December 2017).

158. "effects are under analysis": Email exchange with John Scaggs, U.S. Forest Service, Tonto National Forest, Supervisor's Office (March 2018.)

158. "He was always going around": Albo Guzman's quotations are from telephone interviews conducted in 2017.

162. "When the squaws came": "What Do You Want to Know? Apache Tears," *The Philadelphia Inquirer* (June 9, 1967).

162. "Crowds of Arizonans": Thelma Heatwole, "Easy Picking Attract Rock Hounds to Pinal 'Mine,'" *Arizona Republic* (February 12, 1977).

162. "Recently . . . a group of fathers and sons": Ibid.

Chapter 10

164. **"We did what we had to do"**: Blake Nicholson, "Tribal Head Who Led Dakota Access Pipeline Fight Voted Out," Associated Press (September 28, 2017).

164. **Communities and Social Performance team**: In late 2017, Michael Betom's role at Resolution Copper changed, removing him from the communications department.

166. **"How would it have looked"**: Michael Betom's quotations are from his tour of Resolution Copper sites in September 2017.

166. **"On Site with Mike"**: Video gallery, **www.resolutioncopper.com**. Retrieved from: **resolutioncopper.com/media/video-gallery/** and **www.youtube.com/watch?v=SBu 0Uhc-S84** (accessed June 2019).

166. **"12 tribes that have historical ties"**: According to the "Alternatives Evaluation Report" for the Resolution Copper project's Environmental Impact Statement, these twelve tribes include: "The San Carlos Apache Tribe, White Mountain Apache Tribe, Yavapai-Apache Nation, Tonto Apache Tribe, Mescalero Apache Tribe, Fort McDowell Yavapai Nation, Yavapai Prescott Indian Tribe, Hopi Tribe, Gila River Indian Community, Salt River Pima-Maricopa Community, Ak-Chin Indian Community, and Pueblo of Zuni" ("Alternatives Evaluation Report," 2017).

171. **Duke of York, who visited**: Max Jarman, Lynh Bui, Jane Larson, "Prince Andrew Visits Arizona to Promote UK Relations," *Arizona Republic* (February 13, 2008).

171. **series of scandals**: "Prince Andrew: Envoy Career Plagued with Controversy," BBC (July 21, 2011).

Chapter 12

188. **"Where once man reigned supreme"**: "The Silver King Which Proclaimed the District" *Arizona Republican* (November 23, 1916).

188. **"Thus the world may witness"**: Ibid.

188. **opening of the Magma Copper mine**: There was some overlap in Superior's silver production and the early years of copper development. See David F. Briggs, "Superior, Arizona: An Old Mining Camp with Many Lives," *Economic Geologist,* Arizona Geological Survey (December 2015).

188. **"We can't send our children to school with no shoes"**: Bernie Roth, "Mining Town Crippled: Back-to-Work Move Started at Superior," *Arizona Daily Star* (November 6, 1959).

188. **Magma mine shut down**: A. V. Gullette, "Magma to Close Superior Mine Due to Low Demand, Slack Prices," *Arizona Republic* (August 10, 1982).

189. **produced an "Economic and Fiscal Impact Report"**: Elliott D. Pollack & Company, "Resolution Copper Company Economic and Fiscal Impact Report; Prepared for: Resolution Copper Company" (Scottsdale, AZ: September 2011).

   Though the late Senator John McCain and others have referred to the report as "independent," the report itself states on its cover "Prepared for Resolution Copper Company."

189. **The report's conjectures were treated as facts**: Later, in their public statements, Resolution Copper revised down the number of new jobs that they claimed the mine would create. Nevertheless, the Pollack Report's figures continue to be repeated in news

articles and in Congress. The Pollack Report figures also remain in company materials online: **resolutioncopper.com/wp-content/uploads/2016/03/Economic-and-Fiscal-Impact-Survey2.pdf** (accessed June 2019).

189. **"It is unusual"**: Power Consulting, Inc., "Volume II: A Review of Resolution Copper's Projected Beneficial Impacts of Its Proposed Mine, A Report Prepared for the San Carlos Apache Tribe" (Missoula, MO: August 2017), 2.

190. **1.6 billion tons . . . approximately 1.5 percent copper:** Resolution Copper, "General Plan of Operations" (May 2016), 125.

190. **1.5 billion tons of waste:** Ibid.

190. **arsenic, lead, mercury, and other hazardous materials:** Ivan ancucheo, D. Barrie Johnson, "Significance of Microbial Communities and Interactions in Safeguarding Reactive Mine Tailings by Ecological Engineering," *Applied and Environmental Microbiology,* American Society for Microbiology (2011).

See also: "Alternatives Evaluation Report" (2017); Tony Davis, "Toxic Releases by Arizona Mines Increasing," *Arizona Daily Star* (February 10, 2013).

190. **The Forest Service has explored:** "Alternatives Evaluation Report" (2017).

190. **embankment 10 miles long and 520 feet high:** U.S. Forest Service, "Resolution Copper Project – Tailings Alternatives: #2: Near West Proposed Action " (June 2019).

190. **8,600 acres:** U.S. Forest Service, "Resolution Copper Project – Tailings Alternatives: #6: Skunk Camp," (June 2019).

190. **Samarco Mineração SA . . . a subsidiary of BHP:** The company was called "BHP Billiton LTD" at the time of the Fundão Dam disaster. It has since renamed itself simply "BHP."

190. **"it left a reddish-brown plume visible from space":** Dom Phillips, "Samarco Dam Collapse: One Year on from Brazil's Worst Environmental Disaster," *The Guardian* (October 15, 2016).

190. **charged . . . with homicide:** Kirstin Ridley, Barbara Lewis, "BHP Prepares for UK Legal Battle over 2015 Brazil Dam Failure," Reuters (November 22, 2018).

191. **more than 230 people:** "Polícia Civil Registra 237 Mortos Identificados Após Tragédia Em Brumadinho," *Jornal Estado de Minas* (Belo Horizonte, Brazil: May 7, 2019).

191. **15 million cubic yards:** Dom Philips, " 'That's Going to Burst': Brazilian Dam Workers Say They Warned of Disaster," *The Guardian* (February 6, 2019).

191. **"among the highest-risk structures on Earth":** Paul Kiernan, "Mining Dams Grow to Colossal Heights, and So Do the Risks," *The Wall Street Journal* (April 5, 2016). Kiernan writes, "As tall as a 30-story building and holding enough refuse to fill 19 Dallas Cowboys stadiums, the dam was the largest structure of its kind ever to give way."

See also: Matthew Brown and Dan Elliot, "What Are Dangers of Mining Waste in Brazil?" (January 28, 2019). The article quotes David Chambers of the Center for Science in Public Participation: "We can't tell you where a failure is going to occur, but statistically we can tell you they are going to happen."

191. **"to the extent possible" . . . "Resolution Copper will take reasonable precautions":** General Plan of Operations (May 2016), 124–205.

191. **exposing workers to radiation in its uranium mine in Namibia:** John Vidal, "Uranium Workers Dying After Time at Namibia Mine, Report Warns," *The Guardian* (April 15, 2014).

191. **role in the civil war in Papua New Guinea:** Daniel Flitton, "Rio Tinto's Billion-Dollar Mess: 'Unprincipled, Shameful and Evil,'" *Sydney Morning Herald* (August 19, 2016).

   See also: "Blood and Treasure," Special Broadcasting Service (Australia), *Dateline* documentary, 2011.

191. **Norway said it would divest:** "The Government Pension Fund Divests Its Holdings in Mining Company," Ministry of Finance, Government of Norway (Olso, Norway: September 9, 2008).

191. **U.S. Securities and Exchange Commission charged Rio Tinto:** "Rio Tinto, Former Top Executives Charged With Fraud: Worldwide Mining Company Alleged to Have Inflated Asset Values," United States Securities and Exchange Commission (Washington: October 17, 2017).

   See also: Neil Hume, "Rio Tinto and Two Former Execs Must Face Fraud Charges Says SEC," *Financial Times* (January 24, 2018).

192. **two of its employees died on the job:** Zandi Shabalala, "Rio Tinto Defends Executive Bonus Structure," Reuters (April 11, 2018).

192. **"poster child for corporate malfeasance":** Danny Kennedy, "Rio Tinto: Global Compact Violations," Project Underground (July 13, 2001).

192. **40 productive years:** The 40-year figure refers to the period when the mine would be producing copper. This period would be bracketed by a few years on either side, for development and mine closure (demolition, rehabilitation of disturbed land, environmental monitoring, etc.).

192. **"how 'ghost towns' are generated":** Power Consulting, page iv. According to Power Consulting, "It is puzzling . . . to look across history and geography for signs of ongoing prosperity that has always been projected to follow mining. Whether one looks closely at Arizona or other mining regions across the United States or around the world, it usually difficult to find evidence that the projected sustained prosperity was actually realized." (Power Consulting, 5.)

192. **"It's a fantasy world that they're in":** Telephone interview with Thomas Power, March 2018.

Chapter 13

204–227. **the four days of the Sunrise Dance:** For the account of a Sunrise Dance relayed in this chapter, I am indebted to Theresa Nosie, Vanessa Nosie, Naelyn Pike, Nizhoni Pike, Baasé-O Pike, Sandra Rambler, and Wendsler Nosie. I relied on my own experience attending Sunrise Dances in San Carlos to add descriptive details of various moments.

205. **Apache creation myth:** There are various versions of the Apache creation story. To read a selection, see Greenville Goodwin's *Myths and Tales of the White Mountain Apache* (Tucson: University of Arizona Press, 1994) and Morris E. Opler's An Apache Life-Way: The Economic, Social, and Religious Institutions of the Chiricahua Indians (Lincoln: University of Nebraska Press, 1996).

220. **"white sand mixed with water and pollen":** *Glesh* can also be an ochre color, from yellow pollen.

224. **1883 Code of Indian Offenses:** Code of Indian Offenses (1883), Department of the Interior, Office of Indian Affairs (Washington: 1882).

224. **to "Christianize and civilize the Indian":** Ulysses S. Grant, State of the Union Address, Washington (December 5, 1870).

224. "an entire race . . . was proselytized": Echohawk, *In the Courts of the Conqueror* (Golden, CO: Fulcrum Publishing, 2012), 303.

225. "A small green hummingbird stared right at us": Naelyn Pike, "Attachments to Testimony of Terry Rambler," Senate Subcommittee on Public Lands, Forests, and Mining, Washington (November 20, 2013).

Chapter 14

229. "Save Oak Flat" repeal: See H.R. 666 Save Oak Flat and S. 173 Save Oak Flat Act, both introduced January 1, 2019.

229. "Oak Flat sets a precedent for all sacred sites": Naelyn Pike, Forum on Protecting Native American Sacred Sites, Rayburn House Office Building, Washington (November 4, 2015).

246. added to the National Register of Historic Places: Jessica Swarner, "Oak Flat Historic Designation a Win for Mine Opponents, but Fight Continues," *Tucson Sentinel* (March 14, 2016).

246. "Shame on the Park Service and Forest Service": Paul Gosar, "Rep. Gosar Leads Effort to Discourage 1.7 Million Acre Land Grab in Arizona," (Washington: February 18, 2016).

   Roxanne Dunbar-Ortiz and Dino Gilio-Whitaker discuss the Oak Flat land exchange, Gosar's comments, and federal Indian law in chapter 12 of their book *All the Real Indians Died Off: And 20 Other Myths about Native Americans* (Boston: Beacon Press, 2016).

246. "If Hollywood wanted to capture the emotional center": Limerick, 55.

   Before Anglo-European encroachment, this swath of the Southwest was indisputably indigenous homelands. The long U.S. military campaign to remove Apaches from the area is voluminously documented. But, today, in a bewildering disconnect, the Apache are forced to prove the validity of their attachment to this same land.

248. "the ability to do seemingly impossible things": James Kaywaykla's oral history in Eve Ball, *In the Days of Victorio: Recollections of a Warm Springs Apache* (Tucson: University of Arizona Press, 1970), 11.

248. "hands tingled and her palms changed color": Ibid, 11.

248. "There was a commotion": Ibid, 9–10.

Chapter 15

253. During one storm, he recorded: Mila Besich-Lira, "Massive Windstorm Causes Damage in Superior," *Copper Area News* (December 18, 2017).

256. black wind, black water, black thunder: Grenville Goodwin, *Myths and Tales of the White Mountain Apache* (Tucson: University of Arizona Press, 1939), 2–20.

256. the Sun is said to sink underground: Ibid, 5, 6, 19.

ACKNOWLEDGMENTS

I could not have written this book without the support of many people and a number of institutions.

My deepest gratitude to the Nosie and Gorham families. Thank you, Wendsler Nosie, Theresa Nosie, Vanessa Nosie, Naelyn Pike, Nizhoni Pike, and Baasé-O Pike. Thank you, Patricia Brown, Jackie Gorham, Evelyn Gorham, Mike McKee, and Deb McKee.

Many thanks also to Sandra Rambler for her help with my many questions about Apache language and traditions. Thank you to Mila Besich-Lira and the Lira family, especially Cheryl Lira-Castro and David Lira, who spoke with me about copper mining, the Magma mine, and life in Superior over the past century.

I am exceedingly grateful to my literary agent, Elyse Cheney, for guidance, for friendship, and for championing this project.

The support of the MacArthur Foundation, New America, and the Center for the Future of Arizona gave me the time and freedom to work on this book. Thank you to Peter Bergen, Lattie Coor, Sybil Francis, Awista Ayub, Konstantin Kakaes, and my fellow fellows.

Enormous thanks to everyone at Random House, especially Thomas Perry, Andy Ward, Hilary Redmon, Richard Elman, Benjamin Dreyer, Clio Seraphim, Matthew Martin, Maria Braeckel, Carrie Neill, Loren Noveck, Katie Tull, Kaley Baron, Jennifer Lynes Fernandez, Pam Feinstein, and Alice Gribbin. At Cheney Literary, I was fortunate to work with Adam Eaglin, Claire Gillespie, Isabel Mendia, and Alex Jacobs.

I relied on Derrick Alderman's meticulousness and sharp eye with design and production. Thank you to Natalie Meade for fact-checking the book. Any mistakes that remain are, of course, my own.

Joel Helfrich's work on the struggle over Mount Graham was crucial to my research. Janet Witzeman sent me a box full of primary source documents about the controversy over the telescopes that her husband, Bob Witzeman, had collected over many years. John Welch and Tom Wright spoke with me about the archaeological and natural history of Oak Flat. Many thanks also to Robin Silver.

Geologist Denton Ebel spoke with me about copper formation in stars. Dr. James Webster shared his expertise on metallic ore deposit formation.

I am grateful to my colleagues at the Parsons School of Design, in particular Anne Gaines and Joel Towers, who have made it possible for me to pursue my work.

Thank you to family and friends who have helped me with this project in various ways: Seth Redniss, Charlotte Herscher, Richard McGuire, Malcolm Gladwell, Jean Strouse, Gillian Kane, Whitney Chandler, Stewart Thorndike, Davie Lerner, Marc Rosen, Susan Grant Rosen, and Annie Novak.

Thank you to my parents, Rick and Robin Redniss, for many things, but especially for superlative grandparenting.

To Jody Rosen, Sasha, and Theo, I love you beyond measure.

For nearly a decade, Susan Kamil was a dream editor. I treasured her keen insights and trust. Susan died just as we were wrapping up this project. I am so grateful to have known her warmth, her generosity, and her joie de vivre.

This book is dedicated to Susan Kamil.

Published in the United States by Random House, an imprint and division of Penguin Random House LLC, New York.

Random House and the House colophon are registered trademarks of Penguin Random House LLC.

Author photo by Whitney Chandler.

Hardback ISBN 978-0-3995-8972-0
Ebook ISBN 978-0-3995-8974-4

Printed in China on acid-free paper

randomhousebooks.com

9 8 7 6 5 4 3 2 1

First Edition

Lauren Redniss is the author of several works of visual nonfiction and the recipient of a MacArthur Foundation "genius grant." Her book *Thunder & Lightning: Weather Past, Present, Future* won the 2016 PEN/E. O. Wilson Literary Science Writing Award. *Radioactive: Marie & Pierre Curie, A Tale of Love and Fallout* was a finalist for the 2011 National Book Award. She has been a Guggenheim fellow, a fellow at the New America Foundation and the Center for the Future of Arizona, and Artist-in-Residence at the American Museum of Natural History. She teaches at the Parsons School of Design in New York City.

To inquire about booking Lauren Redniss for a speaking engagement, please contact the Penguin Random House Speakers Bureau at speakers@penguinrandomhouse.com.

BY LAUREN REDNISS

Oak Flat: A Fight for Sacred Land in the American West

Thunder & Lightning: Weather Past, Present, Future

Radioactive: Marie & Pierre Curie, A Tale of Love and Fallout

Century Girl: 100 Years in the Life of Doris Eaton Travis,
Last Living Star of the Ziegfeld Follies

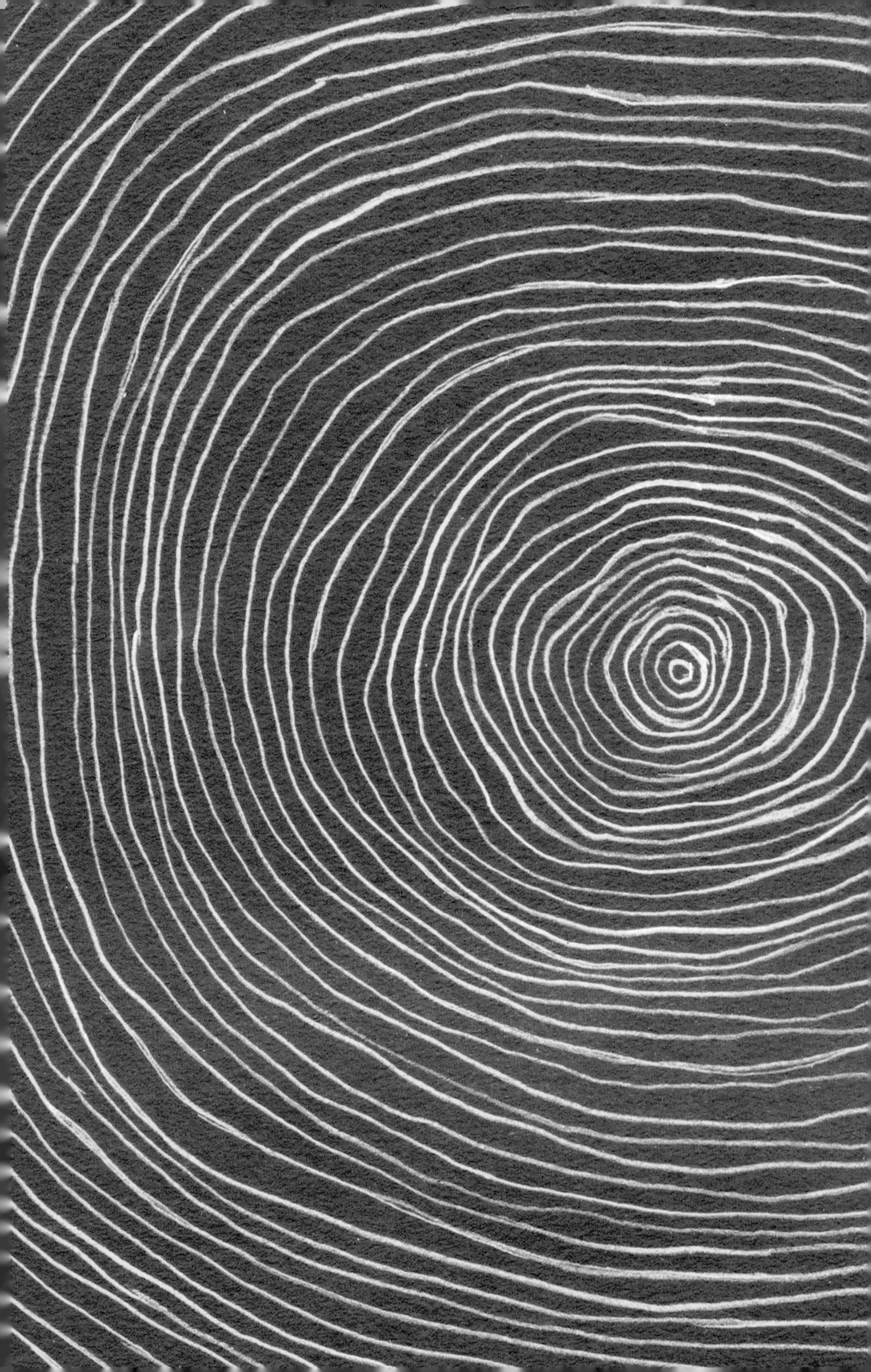